The Intelligent Layman's Book of

British Furniture

1600-2000

An epitaph for Sir Christopher Wren, suggests
that when you go to St Paul's you should simply
look around you. It is somewhat the same when
you look at furniture.

This book shows you what you are looking at,
who designed it, when and for whom. It is a
good start to feeding your interest.

Dr Clive Edwards
Research Director,
Fine Arts Department,
Loughborough University

Dr Peter Brewer
South Chilterns University

Treve Rosoman
Curator, English Heritage

Jonathan Meyer F.R.I.C.S.
Director of Furniture, Sotheby's

Michael Barrington
Chief Executive, BAFRA

Christopher Claxton Stevens
Director, Norman Adams Ltd

ISBN 947798 60 9

© The Intelligent Layman Publishers Ltd
Thornton House, Thorton Road
London SW19 4NG

Dr Clive Edwards, Treve Rosoman,
Jonathan Meyer, Michael Barrington,
Christopher Claxton Stevens assert
their moral rights to be identified as
the authors of this book.

Designed by 442 Design, Edinburgh
www.442design.com

Printed in Slovenia
by MKT PRINT on behalf of Compass Press

ISBN 947798 60 9

June 2005

Contents

The following pages show who was
commissioning furniture, who was
being commissioned, where and when

Scotland

North of England

East Midlands

Wales & West Midlands

South West

Greater London

South East

Scotland

Abbotsford, Roxburghshire
Home of Sir Walter Scott, furnished in an antiquarian taste by George Bullock.

Aberdeen, Provost Skene's House
Sixteenth and seventeenth century town house furnished with largely Georgian room settings.

Arniston, Midlothian
Early eighteenth century William Adam house, furniture of the Georgian period including items supplied by Thomas Chippendale.

Blair Castle, Perthshire
Home of the Earls and Dukes of Athol. Important furniture collection including items by John Gordon (1756), Robert Chipcase (1783) of seating furniture, gilt torcheres by Thomas Chippendale, cabinets by George Bullock and bookcases and other items by Sandeman of Perth.

Culzean Castle, Ayrshire
Extensive alterations by Robert Adam from 1777 for 10th Earl of Cassillis with contemporary furniture.

Drumlanrig Castle, Dumfriesshire
Late seventeenth century house of the Duke of Buccleuch with furniture by the Edinburgh makers John Thomson and William Trotter.

Dumfries House, Ayrshire
Eighteenth century house by William and Robert Adam containing furniture by Thomas Chippendale and the Edinburgh makers Francis Brodie, Alexander Peter and William Mathie.

Edinburgh
Lauriston Castle – Large Edwardian additions to a sixteenth century tower house with early twentieth furniture by Morrison & Co. of Edinburgh.
Gladstone's Land – Largely seventeenth century townhouse of an Edinburgh merchant with contemporary furnishings.
The Georgian House, Charlotte Square – Robert Adam town house in the New Town with appropriate room furnishing.
Palace of Holyroodhouse – Royal palace of the Scottish kings

enlarged by William Bruce after the accession of Charles II. Furniture by William Trotter for the exiled Comte d'Artois (1796).

Glasgow
Burrell Collection – Furniture from the sixteenth to the early eighteenth century displayed in reconstructed room settings from Sir William Burrell's house, Hutton Castle.
The Hunterian Art Gallery – Rooms from the house of Charles Rennie Mackintosh at 120 Mains St. (to 1906) with Mackintosh furniture.
Pollock House – William Adam house containing the eighteenth century furniture collection of Glasgow Museum & Art Gallery.

Haddo House, Aberdeenshire
William Adam Palladian house of the 1730s redecorated in 1880 by Wright & Mansfield of London and containing furniture by them and Miles & Edwards.

Hill House, Argyll
Designed by Charles Rennie Mackintosh for Walter Blackie, the Glasgow publisher with furniture to Rennie's design.

Hopetoun House, Midlothian
A William Bruce house greatly added to by William Adam in the first half of the eighteenth century. Furniture by James Cullen (1766-68), John Linnel (c1760) and Mathias Lock (1768). Upholstered suite by Thomas Welsh, estate wright.

House of Dun, Angus
William Adam Palladian house (1730) with furniture supplied by Richard Clerk (1807) and Trotter & Hamilton (1828) both of Edinburgh.

Inveraray, Argyll
Home of the Dukes of Argyll built 1745-90 to the designs of Roger Morris. Seating furniture by John Linnel c1775 for the 5th Earl of Argyll. Other furniture by Edinburgh makers.

Kellie Castle, Fife
Sixteenth and seventeenth century house restored by Robert Lorimer in the late nineteenth century with furniture to his design made by Whytock & Reid of Edinburgh.

Mount Stewart, Isle of Bute
Home of the Marquess of Bute built in the High Victorian gothic style. Tables and seating furniture for Lord Mount Stewart supplied in 1788 by Young & Trotter of Edinburgh.

Paxton House, Berwickshire
Built by John Adam 1758-62 for Patrick Home. Furniture by Thomas Chippendale (1774) and Thomas Chippendale Jr. (1788-91). Later commissions by William Trotter of Edinburgh 1814/15 and c1822.

Scone Palace, Perthshire
Home of the Earls of Mansfield. Present gothic house largely early nineteenth century. Furniture of many periods, some from Kenwood, London. Commissions undertaken by George Bullock c1803-12.

Stirling, Argyll's Lodging
A seventeenth century town house furnished as it would have been c1680 when it was occupied by the 9th Earl of Argyll.

Traquair House, Peebleshire
Largely seventeenth and eighteenth century in date though of earlier origin. Chairs supplied 1732 by Francis Brodie of Edinburgh for the Earl of Traquair.

North of England

1 Alnwick Castle, Northumberland (HHA)
Stronghold of the Percys, Earls of Northumberland containing furniture supplied 1823 by Morel & Hughes for Northumberland House, London. Castle extensively altered in 1850's and 60's and furniture sourced locally and from London.

2 Cragside, Northumberland (NT)
Country home of William Armstrong (Baron Armstrong), the Newcastle engineering and armaments entrepreneur (1880's). Furniture by Gillow of Lancaster, Holland & Sons and Howard & Sons of London.

3 Hutton-in-the-Forest, Cumbria (HHA)
Furniture by Gillow of Lancaster, late eighteenth century.

4 Raby Castle, Co. Durham (HHA)
Furniture in the Octagonal Drawing Room by George Morant, London 1848. Gilt suite of 1806 in Baron's Hall by Gillow for Cleveland House, London.

5 Blackwell, Cumbria
Built 1898-1900 to designs by M.H. Baillie Scott. Contains Arts & Crafts furniture by Morris & Co. and Simpsons of Kendal.

6 Abbot Hall, Kendal, Cumbria
A mid-eighteenth century Palladian house containing an extensive assembled collection of furniture by Gillow of Lancaster.

7 Leighton Hall, Lancs. (HHA)
An early nineteenth century Gothic Revival house, the home of the Gillow family from 1822. Contains much furniture by Gillow of Lancaster.

8 Judges' Lodgings, Lancaster
Now a museum with galleries illustrating the history of Gillow with furniture produced by them.

9 Newby Hall, Yorks. (HHA)
Robert Adam interiors with furniture to his designs by Thomas Chippendale, (1772-76).

10 Castle Howard, Yorks. (HHA)
Baroque house designed by John Vanbrugh (1699-1726). Furniture includes examples of the work of John Linnell.

11 Beningborough Hall, Yorks. (NT)
Early eighteenth century house with contemporary furniture. State bed in the style of Daniel Marot possibly by Francis Lapiere, chairs in the style of Giles Grendey and gilt tables and glasses in that of Gumley & Moore.

12 Fairfax House, York
A mid-eighteenth century town house furnished with the Noel Terry Collection of early to mid-eighteenth century furniture.

13 Harewood House, Yorks. (NT)
Robert Adam interiors with extensive ranges of furniture ordered from and installed by Thomas Chippendale. Library bookcases designed by Charles Barry c1845.

14 Lotherton Hall, Yorks.
Late Victorian house now maintained by Leeds City Council. Contains Gillow furniture supplied 1810-11 for Parlington Hall and by Marsh & Jones of Leeds to the designs of Charles Bevan for Titus Salt.

15 Temple Newsam, Leeds, Yorks.
Main furniture collections of Leeds City Council with extensive ranges from the seventeenth century and an emphasis on the work of Thomas Chippendale.

16 Gawthorpe Hall, Lancs. (NT)
Early seventeenth century house much altered by Charles Barry 1850-52. Furniture designed by A.W.N. Pugin and made by Crace. Also Gillow furniture of the 1850's and 80's.

17 Burton Constable, Yorks. (HHA)
Giltwood seat furniture and mirrors by Thomas Chippendale. Much additional furniture by York and Hull furniture makers of the late eighteenth and early nineteenth centuries.

18 Nostell Priory, Yorks. (NT)
Robert Adam interiors furnished by Thomas Chippendale for Sir Rowland Winn.

19 Normanby Hall, Lincs.
Regency house containing contemporary furniture including some by Gillow.

20 Brodsworth Hall, Yorks. (EH)
Early Victorian house furnished 1863 by Lapworth Brothers of Bond St., London at a cost of £7,282. Earlier pieces by T. & G. Seddon of London.

21 Cannon Hall, Yorks.
Mid-eighteenth century house containing furniture collections of Barnsley Borough Council. Examples of the work of Elwick of Wakefield, John Marshall of London and later items by Liberty.

22 Heaton Hall, Lancs.
Designed by James Wyatt and furnished with Wyatt-designed furniture, especially that from Heveningham Hall, Suffolk. Gillow bookcases of 1823 original to the house and a Gillow stamped table.

Wales & West Midlands

Lady Lever Art Gallery, Port Sunlight, Merseyside
In model village created by Lord Lever for his employees at the soap manufactory. Fine collection of largely eighteenth century furniture assembled by 1st Viscount Leverhulme.

Speke Hall, Merseyside (NT)
Tudor house, the great hall restored by George Bullock 1811-12, who also supplied furniture for his patron Richard Watt.

Penrhyn Castle, Gwynedd (NT)
Neo-Norman castle designed by Thomas Hopper (1820) for 1st Lord Penrhyn. Furniture designed by Hopper in the 'Norman' style. Slate bedstead in principal bedroom indicative of the source of Lord Penrhyn's wealth.

Chirk Castle, Clwyd (NT)
Medieval border fortress adapted from the late seventeenth century into an extensive house. The Saloon contains gilded pier tables and glasses by Mayhew & Ince (1782).

Erddig, Clwyd (NT)
Late seventeenth century house with lavish furnishings of 1720-26. Furniture from London by John Belchier, John Miller and Thomas Fenthram. Later furniture from John Cobb (1770) and dining table and chairs from Gillow, Lancaster (1827).

Powis Castle, Powys (NT)
Border castle extensively adapted from the late seventeenth century with fine state bed and upholstered furniture of this date. Later furniture sourced from London or locally. Collection of Indian objects brought here by Clive.

Castel Coch, Glamorgan
Romantic castle restored 1875-81 with lavish interiors and furniture by William Burgess for the 3rd Marquess of Bute.

Cardiff Castle, Glamorgan
Lavish pseudo-medieval house of the 3rd Marquess of Bute designed 1865-81 by William Burgess with High Victorian Gothic furniture of his design.

Attingham Park, Shropshire (NT)
Large eighteenth century house with fine contemporary furniture, some Continental but much English. Gillow supplied furniture, also Thomas Donaldson of Shrewsbury.

Croft Castle, Herefordshire (NT)
Border fortress with fine mid-eighteenth century interiors. Important English furniture including a combined writing table and filing cabinet known as a 'Croft', manufactured by Seddon c1780 for Sir Herbert Croft.

Hagley Hall, West Midlands (HHA)
Palladian house with fine mid-eighteenth century furniture including pier glasses in the Drawing Room carved by Samuel Norman & James Whittle.

Birmingham, Aston Hall
Jacobean mansion containing much seventeenth century oak furniture, also items specially designed by George Bullock and Richard Bridgens for James Watt Jnr.

Soho House
Designed for Matthew Boulton 1796-1809 and containing furniture by Gillow of Lancaster and James Newton.

Shugborough, Staffs. (NT)
Much added to in the mid to late Georgian period. Contains furniture by Gillow of Lancaster (late eighteenth century), Charles Smith & Co. (1794) and Morant & Boyd (1853).

Wightwick Manor, West Midlands (NT)
Late nineteenth century house furnished in Arts & Crafts Movement taste. Morris & Co. furniture.

Tatton Park, Cheshire (NT)
Built 1780-1813 with original furniture by Gillow supplied 1795-1812.

Tabley House, Cheshire (NT)
Palladian house by John Carr of York, completed 1767. Contains furniture by Gillow of Lancaster, George Bullock and mirrors and console tables attributed to Thomas Chippendale.

Rode Hall, Cheshire (HHA)
Largely eighteenth century house with much of the furniture sourced from Gillow 1783 to 1818.

Lyme Park, Cheshire (NT)
Palatial Georgian mansion with diverse furniture including tables designed by A.W.N. Pugin for Abney Hall, Cheshire and large set of Chippendale chairs introduced early in the twentieth century when Joubert was used to decorate interiors.

Bristol, The Red Lodge
Elizabethan garden lodge with fine interiors housing the Bristol Museum collection of furniture to the mid-eighteenth century which includes an elaborate early eighteenth century bureau cabinet attributed to Peter Miller of London.

The Georgian House
Late Georgian town house with contemporary furniture. Contains Bristol-made items such as a bureau bookcase by M. Milward of Keynsham (1789) and one of a set of ten chairs by Thomas Andrews for the Mansion House (1785).

Corsham Court, Wilts. (HHA)
An Elizabethan house containing a fine inlaid commode and torcheres by John Cobb (1772), four pier tables from John Hicks (1755) and furniture attributed to Thomas Chippendale.

Dyrham Court, Glos. (NT)
Late seventeenth century house with much Queen Anne period furniture. Also items by John Linnell and Gillow of Lancaster.

Broadway, Worcs.
The home of Gordon Russell Ltd. The Gordon Russell Trust has recently been set up with the aim of displaying examples of Russell furniture and explaining the history of the firm, in a museum.

Eastnor Castle, Herefordshire (HHA)
Gothic Revival house by Sir Robert Smirke who also designed oak benches and chairs in the Hall and Dining Room (c1812). Alterations to the Drawing Room by Pugin (1849) and associated furniture by Crace.

Cheltenham Museum & Art Gallery, Glos.
Displays of Arts & Crafts furniture by Sidney Barnsley and Ernest Gimson (1905-30). Also a collection of Voysey furniture.

Rodmarton Manor, Glos.
An Arts & Crafts house designed by Ernest Barnsley 1909 containing furniture by Ernest, Sidney and Edward Barnsley and Peter Waals. Also a chest designed by C.R. Ashbee for Kenton & Co. (1891).

Owlpen Manor, Glos.
Tudor manor house furnished with Arts & Crafts furniture by Sidney Barnsley including a settle made for Ernest Gimson (c1895). In the Great Hall a Jupe patent mahogany expanding table.

Tyntesfield, Somerset (NT)
Victorian Gothic Revival house, remodelled c1864, with furniture by Crace to Pugin designs. Carved oak items by Collier & Plunknett of Warwick.

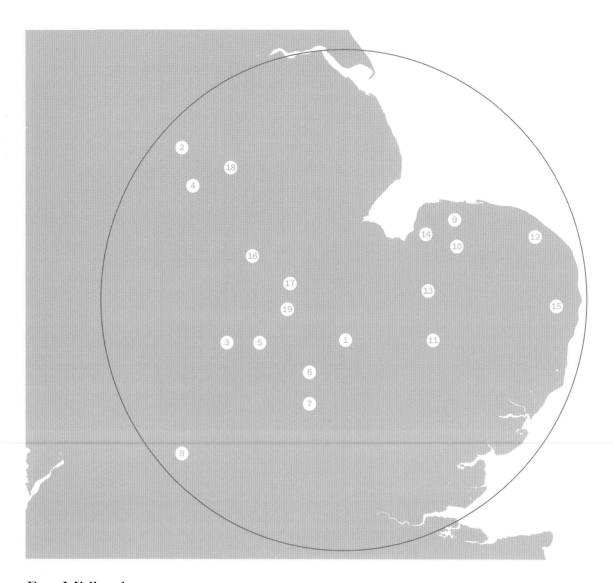

East Midlands

1. **Magdalene College, Cambridge**
Book presses (cases) made by Sympson, the joiner, for the diarist Samuel Pepys 1666.

2. **Chatsworth, Derbyshire**
Extensively rebuilt in a palatial manner in the two decades following 1691. Fine walnut furniture of this period, also items designed by William Kent from Chiswick and Wanstead.

3. **Althorp, Northants.**
Contains much furniture designed by John Vardy and James Stuart for Spencer House, St. James's, London. Also chairs in the Picture Gallery by William Vile and in the State Dining Room by George Seddon (1800).

4. **Kedleston Hall, Derbyshire** (NT)
Interiors designed by Robert Adam for the 1st Baron Scarsdale. Furniture sourced from John Linnell (1759-96) totalling nearly £3,000 and much still in the house.

5. **Northampton, 78 Derngate**
Red brick Victorian house decorated and furnished by Charles Rennie Mackintosh (1916-19) for W.J. Bassett-Lowke, with much surviving.

6. **Cecil Higgins Art Gallery, Bedford**
Noted for the Burgess Room containing furniture from Willam Burgess's own house, Tower House, Melbury Road, Kensington (1865). Other Victorian and Edwardian decorative art obtained after the dispersal of the Handley-Reed Collection in 1972.

7. **Woburn Abbey, Beds.** (HHA)
Largely eighteenth century house with furniture by Whittle & Norman and Pierre Langlois (1760) and later pieces designed by the architect Henry Holland and his associate William Tatham in the 1790's. Boulle caskets by Thomas Parker (1812).

8. **Charlecote Park, Warwickshire** (NT)
An Elizabethan house of 1558 extensively altered from 1828. Important Victorian furnishings including a massive carved sideboard in the Dining Room by J.M. Wilcox of Warwick (1858) who was also responsible for the bookcases and woodwork in the Library.

9. **Holkham Hall, Norfolk** (HHA)
William Kent Palladian house (1734-66) with much original furniture to his designs. Furniture supplied by William Hallett (1737) and by James Whittle, Benjamin Goodison, Thomas Chippendale and Paul Saunders (1757-58).

10. **Houghton Hall, Norfolk** (HHA)
A Palladian house with exteriors by James Gibbs and Colen Campbell. Interiors by William Kent who designed much of the furniture. Also a pair of thrones from the House of Lords designed by A.W.N. Pugin.

11. **Ickworth, Suffolk** (NT)
State rooms in central rotunda furnished in the 1820's for the 1st Marquess of Bristol by Banting, France & Co. Much of the furniture still in the house.

12. **Felbrigg Hall, Norfolk** (NT)
A largely seventeenth century house with much furniture by John Bladwell upholsterer of Bow Street, Covent Garden, London who was paid £1,000 in 1756. Additional items by Freeman & Co. of Norwich (c1825), George Church (1753) and Henry Clay (early nineteenth century).

13. **Oxburgh Hall, Norfolk** (NT)
Moated brick manor house dating from 1482. Furnishings of many periods including those of an antiquarian taste introduced in the Victorian period. Massive oak buffet from Alscot Park, Warwickshire by William Cookes of Warwick (1851).

14. **Sandringham, Norfolk**
Bought by the Prince & Princess of Wales and furnished by Holland & Sons from the 1860's with much of the original furniture remaining.

15. **Somerleyton Hall, Suffolk** (HHA)
An Elizabethan house altered and enlarged by Sir Morton Peto, the Victorian railway contractor. Interiors largely Victorian with oak library bookcases by J.M. Wilcox of Warwick.

16. **Burghley House, Cambs.** (HHA)
House completed 1587 but lavish Baroque painted interiors of the late seventeenth century. Furniture by Gerrit Jensen, also Mayhew & Ince (1767-79).

17. **Elton Hall, Cambs.** (HHA)
Gothic house, parts dating back to the seventeenth century. Interesting furniture acquired from the William Beckford Collection including a pair of cabinets in the Yellow Drawing Room designed by Vulliamy (1803).

18. **Hardwick Hall, Derbyshire** (NT)
Elizabethan house built by Bess of Hardwick. Original furniture can be identified from the 1601 inventory including the 'Sea Dog' table to designs by du Cerceau and the 'Eglantine' table, carved and inlaid in the Great High Chamber. Bed tester in the Long Gallery by Francois Lapierre (1697).

19. **Boughton House, Northants.** (HHA)
Baroque house with much late seventeenth century furniture. Jean Pelletier and his two sons, Thomas and Rene supplied much gilded furniture to Ralph Montague in the 1690's.

South West

Montacute House, Somerset (NT)
Elizabethan mansion with much seventeenth and eighteenth century furniture including chairs in the Drawing Room by William Linnell (1753) and a centre table in the Parlour by Thomas Chippendale Jnr. (c1800).

Saltram, Devon (NT)
Fine Adam interiors and furniture supplied for these by Thomas Chippendale (1770-72). Additional labelled furniture by Robert Campbell, Henry Kettle and J. McLean & Son.

Tapeley Park, Devon
Altered Queen Anne house. William Morris secretaire and bookcase in the Sea Room.

Stourhead, Wilts. (NT)
Palladian house (1741-80). Giles Grendey paid £200 for chairs in 1746. Much furniture in the Picture Gallery, Library and Cabinet Room by Thomas Chippendale Jnr. (1795-1820).

Knightshayes Court, Devon (NT)
House designed by William Burgess but he designed no furniture for it. However now contains a bookcase by Burgess from his Kensington house, a centre table probably designed by A.W.N. Pugin, a Gillow library table and cabinets in the Dining Room designed H.W. Batley and made by Henry Ogden & Son of Manchester.

Castle Drogo, Devon (NT)
By Sir Edwin Lutyens, started 1911. He also designed the fixed woodwork including the Library bookcases. Work undertaken by Dart & Francis of Crediton.

Kingston Lacey, Dorset (NT)
Late seventeenth century house extensively altered by Charles Barry (1836-40). Dining Room sideboard by Mayhew & Ince (1786) and much other Georgian furniture. Exotic and antiquarian items bought in London in connection with Barry's alterations from Emanuel Brothers of Bishopgate and Nixon & Son of Great Portland St.

Sherborne Castle, Dorset (HHA)
Late Elizabethan house containing furniture supplied by Mayhew & Ince (1763-85) including inlaid commodes, and Pierre Langlois (1762-64) including console tables.

Powderham Castle, Devon (HHA)
Pair of brass-inlaid bookcases in the Ante-room signed J. Channon 1740. Bookcases in the First Library by Avants of Dawlish (1820's) and gilt seat furniture in the Music Room and Second Library by Elward, Marsh & Tatham.

South East

1 Arundel Castle, West Sussex
Romantic castle rebuilt from the late eighteenth century. Bedroom furniture supplied by George Morant for the visit by Queen Victoria (1846) and items from Norfolk House, London (c1760) designed by G.B. Bora and carved by J.A. Cuenot. Chairs by Joseph Metcalfe (1752).

2 Brighton, East Sussex
The Royal Pavilion
Early nineteenth century fantasy with Chinese interiors for the Prince Regent. Chairs and commodes in imitation of bamboo by Elward, Marsh & Tatham (1802). Other furniture by James Newton, Louis le Gaigneur and Crace. Items from Thomas Hope's house in Duchess St., London, the Greenwich Hospital suite (1815) and elbow chairs by Tatham & Bailey from Carlton House (1807).

Preston Manor
Eighteenth century house enlarged early in the twentieth century. Contains the Macquoid Collection of sixteenth and seventeenth century furniture. Furniture original to the house includes items by Howard & Sons, Wright & Mansfield and Fox of Ship St., Brighton.

Museum & Art Gallery
Late nineteenth and twentieth-century gallery containing furniture by Shoolbred

& Co., C.F.A Voysey, Charles Rennie Mackintosh, Frank Brangwyn, Serge Chermayeff (for Waring & Gillow), Ernest Race and Robin Day.

3 Highclere Castle, Hants. (HHA)
House in the Elizabethan style designed by Charles Barry dating from the 1830's containing furniture by George Bullock and Pierre Langlois.

4 Knole, Kent (NT)
Vast mansion dating from medieval to Jacobean times. Outstanding seventeenth century upholstered furniture including beds and chairs obtained by the 6th Earl of Dorset as perquisites when he was Lord Chamberlain to William III. Late Stuart silver furniture.

5 Windsor Castle, Berkshire
Medieval castle with Royal Apartments of the time of Charles II and George IV. Furniture by Gerrit Jensen, Louis le Gaigneur and Thomas Parker. George IV's State Apartments furnished by Morel & Seddon (1826-30) with the young A.W.N. Pugin providing designs.

6 Uppark, West Sussex (NT)
Late seventeenth century house with fine eighteenth century furniture. William Hallett was paid £43 5s 6d by Sir Matthew Fetherstonhaugh in 1754, probably for the elaborate pagoda cabinet in the house.

7 Standen, West Sussex (NT)
Designed by Philip Webb and furnished by Morris & Co. Other furniture by T.H. Kendell of Warwick, Collinson & Lock, Heal, C.R. Ashbee, Liberty and S & H Jewell.

8 Petworth House, West Sussex (NT)
Baroque house with furniture supplied by Gerrit Jensen (1690). Fine carving in the state rooms by Grinling Gibbons and John Selden.

9 Firle Place, East Sussex (HHA)
Tudor house remodelled in the eighteenth century. In the Upper Drawing Room are a pair of satinwood marquetry cabinets attributed to Thomas Chippendale.

10 The Vyne, Hants. (NT)
Sixteenth century brick house altered in the seventeenth and eighteenth centuries. William Vile supplied a stand for a Florentine pietra dura cabinet in 1752 and chairs in 1753. France & Bradburn bills exist (1765-68) for settees and upholstered chairs in the house.

11 Claydon House, Bucks. (NT)
Mid-eighteenth century house part-demolished noted for its elaborate wood carving in the rococo Chinese and gothic manner by Luke Lightfoot (1757-69). Has a fine inlaid wooden staircase.

12 West Wycombe Park, Bucks. (NT)
Mid-eighteenth century house with furniture of the same period including a pair of commodes attributed to Pierre Langlois.

13 Basildon Park, Berks. (NT)
Palladian mansion by John Carr of York with much fine eighteenth-century furniture including gilded console tables and pier glasses of 1773 by Alexander Murray and eight armchairs designed by William Porden for Eaton Hall (c1810).

14 Kelmscott Manor, Oxfordshire
Tudor manor house, the home of William Morris from 1871 and furnished by Morris & Co. Furniture designed by Philip Webb and George Jack including an ebonised armchair shown at the 1862 International Exhibition.

15 Osborne House, Isle of Wight (EH)
Designed by Prince Albert and Thomas Cubitt in the Italianate style as a retreat for the Royal Family. Furnished from the mid-1840's by Holland & Dowbiggin with rooms little altered since Queen Victoria's residence here.

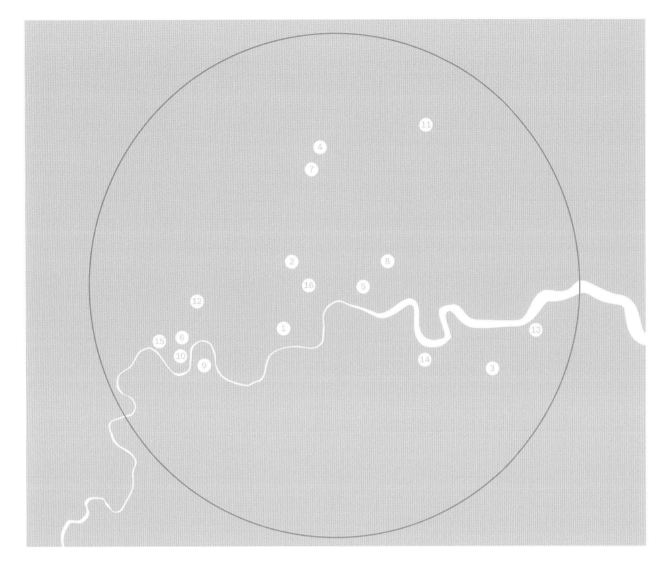

Greater London

Chiswick House (EH)
Palladian villa designed by Lord Burlington with interiors by William Kent. Baroque furniture original to the house by or attributed to G.B. Guelfi, Stephen Langley and Benjamin Goodison (c1730-40).

Kensington Palace
Late seventeenth century house commenced by William III and Mary II with State Apartments added by George I and II. Late seventeenth century furniture by Gerrit Jensen and mirror frames by Grinling Gibbons. Eighteenth century cabinet by Benjamin Goodison altered by William Vile 1763, Victorian furniture in rooms occupied by Princess Victoria and her mother.

Eltham Palace (EH)
The 1930's house of the Coutaulds added to the original medieval hall of the Palace. Art Deco interiors have been restored with original or replica furniture. Entrance hall designed by Rolf Engstromer, other rooms by Peter Malacrida.

Kenwood House, Hampstead (EH)
Largely eighteenth century with interiors by Robert Adam who designed some of the furniture. Furniture by James Lawson (c1764), Fell & Turton (c1767-70) for

Moor Park, Herts., and by William France & John Bradburn for Croome Court, Worcs. (1765). Furniture original to the house by William France and Thomas Chippendale supplied mirror glass.

Spencer House, St James's
London house of the Earls Spencer designed by John Vardy and James Stuart (1756-66), who also designed furniture. Items original to the house by William & John Gordon (c1760), Mayhew & Ince (c1770) and early nineteenth century Dining Room chairs of Gillow manufacture.

Syon House, Brentford
Interiors by Robert Adam from 1761 and John Linnell was paid over £1,000 for their furnishing between 1763 and 1772. Additional furniture from the demolished Northumberland House, Strand, London, by Mayhew & Ince and Morel & Hughes.

Fenton House, Hampstead (NT)
Late seventeenth century merchant's house containing the Benton Fletcher collection of early keyboard musical instruments and the bequest of largely Georgian furniture of Lady Binning.

Geffrye Museum, Shoreditch
Devoted to English furniture and housed in the former Ironmonger's Company almshouses of c1715. An arrangement of room settlings from c1600 to Victorian

times with a modern extension devoted to the twentieth century.

Ham House, Richmond (NT)
A seventeenth century house with lavish schemes of interior decoration 1637-39 by Franz Cleyn and of 1673-75, with much original furniture. Later items by George Nix of Covent Garden (1729-43).

Marble Hill House, Twickenham (EH)
Palladian villa 1724-29 for the Countess of Suffolk and furnished in the style of her period of occupation. Mirror frames and a console table in the Great Room probably carved by James Richards (1726). Also the Lazenby Bequest of Chinoiserie, rich in painted mirrors.

William Morris Gallery, Walthemstow
Established to display Morris furniture and furnishings and also those of his contemporaries such as A.H. Mackmurdo and the Century Guild. William Morris was born at Walthamstow.

Osterley Park, Isleworth (NT)
Fine interiors by Robert Adam from 1763. He also designed some of the furniture which was largely supplied by John Linnell (1760-84). Other furniture by Thomas Chippendale and Henry Clay.

Red House, Bexleyheath (NT)
Built for William Morris after his wedding in 1859 and designed by Philip Webb. Contains Webb furniture designed for the house and items brought by Morris from his lodgings in Red Lion Square, London. Morris also painted a settle-cum-cupboard designed by Webb in the Entrance Hall.

Ranger's House, Blackheath (EH)
Red-brick villa 1700-20 with mid-century additions. Collector's cabinet by George Bullock (c1814) original to the house. Gilded pier tables attributed to Henry Flitcroft (c1745) and Mayhew & Ince (c1770). Contains the Wernher Collection of Decorative Arts.

Hampton Court Palace
Much fine late seventeenth and early eighteenth century furniture in the State Apartments including gilded tables by John Moore, mirrors by Gumley & Moore, a writing table by Gerrit Jensen and several fine state beds.

Victoria & Albert Museum, South Kensington
The National Collection of the decorative arts. Furniture from c1500 to 1900 is displayed in the English Primary Galleries with many examples by major designers and makers. The display is continued in the twentieth century Gallery.

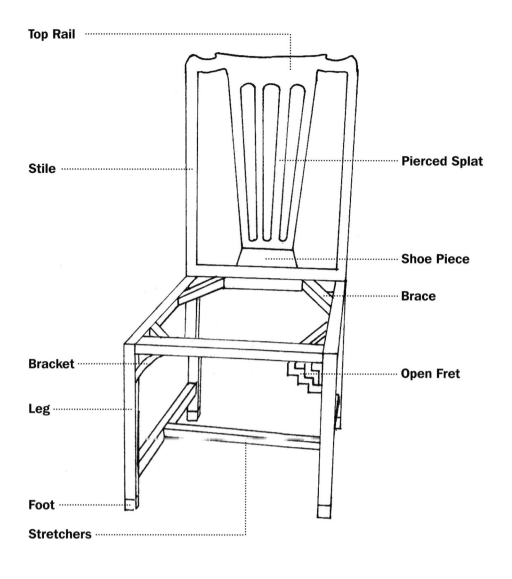

Top Rail

Stile

Pierced Splat

Shoe Piece

Brace

Bracket

Open Fret

Leg

Foot

Stretchers

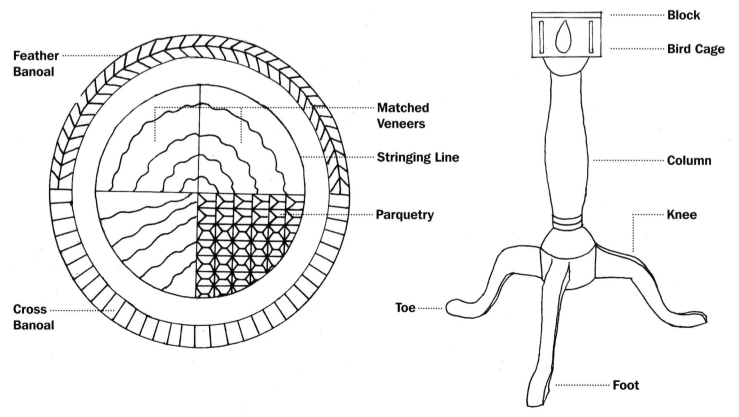

Feather
Banoal

Matched
Veneers

Stringing Line

Parquetry

Cross
Banoal

Block

Bird Cage

Column

Knee

Toe

Foot

Prospect — Pigeon Holes

Fall Front — Lopers

Beading

Escutcheon

Marquetry Panels — Oyster Veneer

Moulding — Bracket Foot

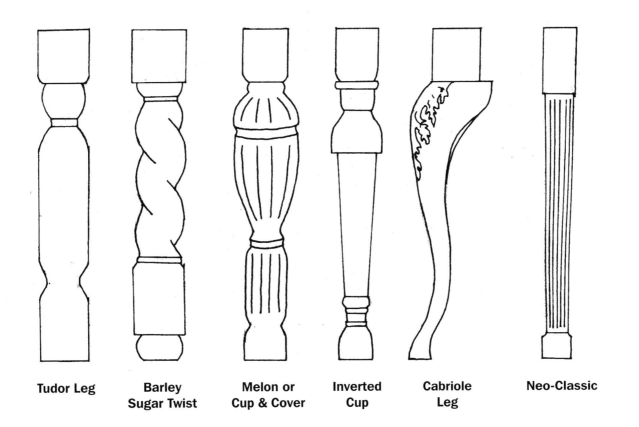

Tudor Leg   **Barley Sugar Twist**   **Melon or Cup & Cover**   **Inverted Cup**   **Cabriole Leg**   **Neo-Classic**

I
The Beginning of the Present

Clive Edwards

Clive Edwards is Senior Lecturer in the History of Art and Design at Loughborough University. After a career in the retailing of furniture and interiors he took an MA in the History of Design at the Royal College of Art/Victoria and Albert Museum and subsequently completed a PhD on Victorian furniture technology. His works include monographs on aspects of furniture technology, materials and trades, furnishing textiles and the retailing of domestic furnishings, as well as contributions to multi-authored works on interiors, architecture and home furnishings. His interest in cross-disciplinary study is evident in his work, which includes research on design, materials and technology, consumption, business and retailing. Examples of books published include Eighteenth Century Furniture, Victorian Furniture, Technology and Design, Twentieth Century Furniture materials, manufacture and markets all in the Manchester University Press series Studies in Material Culture and Design. More recently he has completed an Encyclopaedia of Furniture Materials Trades and Techniques and a work on retailing an consumption entitled Turning Houses into Homes for Ashgate

Clive Edwards has contributed articles to: Journal of Design History, Furniture History, Textile History, History of Technology,Studies in the Decorative Arts, Comparative Technology Transfer and Society

He has also contributed essays to the following works: Encyclopaedia of Interior Design, Oxford Encyclopaedia of Economic History, Furnishing Textiles in Western Europe,1600-1900, Conservation of Furniture and Related Wooden Objects, Cultures of Selling and Twentieth Century Architecture.

Currently working on a range of projects including Second-hand furniture and its place in society, an historical Encyclopaedia of Furnishing Fabric and Soft Furnishings and contributions to a work on Conservation of Twentieth Century Furniture , Clive Edwards continues to develop cross disciplinary interests in design, technology, retailing and consumption of domestic furnishings and issues surrounding the home.

I

The Beginning of the Present

Stability and Professionalism

Dr Clive Edwards

Romayne carvings showing typical small profile heads in medallions, early 16th Century

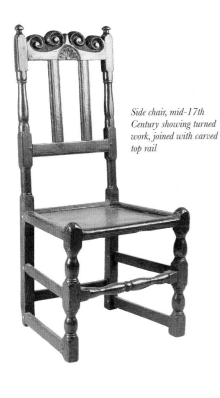

Side chair, mid-17th Century showing turned work, joined with carved top rail

Mid-17th Century armchair with boarded seat and floridly carved top crest rail

Oak joined chair, second quarter of the 16th Century. "Linenfold" motif is found on the four panels and the top panel is decorated with renaissance designs (V&A)

In England, from the 15th Century there had been a gradual change towards a more secure and ordered life and this in turn had created a demand for more comfortable and decorative furniture. The beginning of a growth in demand for furniture, from a wider populace, due in part to a settling of the population and a increase in prosperity, put greater demands on furniture makers. The supremacy of the Renaissance, although delayed in England, eventually increased the influence of Classical architecture on the form and ornament of furniture. Furniture makers were able to develop new styles for their own work from the designs of the buildings and interiors that were being developed around them and for which they were to make objects.

The powerful Tudor dynasty destroyed the old feudal system and encouraged the growth of an economically powerful middle class society. The new wealth encouraged a spate of house building, and a subsequent demand for new and improved furniture. The furniture was designed not only to equip these houses for personal use, but also to create a favourable impression upon others, hence a need and desire for furniture that was up to date and fashionable.

With little direct contact with the artisans of Italy, furniture makers in Northern Europe, who needed detailed information on styles, had to rely on the published pattern books that began to appear in the middle of the 16th Century. These books ensured that new ideas, fashionable patterns, and designs, would be available to a wider marketplace for both buyer and maker. Therefore it is at this moment in furniture history that we begin to see some of the first *"named designers"*, whom we are able to identify as a source of particular compositions, rather than the unsung and anonymous makers of previous times. It is important to recognize that these were designers and not makers, but their names often are attached to furniture that is based on their drawings.

One of the earliest of these appears to have been Sebastianio Serlio, whose architectural pattern books were available in England by the middle of the 16th Century. These patterns were very important in distributing details of the classical orders. Serlio (1475-1554) works are a milestone in the progress of engraved design. An Italian painter, born in Bologna, who later moved to Venice, he was the first to bring out a widely illustrated book on architecture. The work entitled *L'Architettura* was published in six non-consecutive parts between 1537 and 1551. Their wide influence was soon apparent. The engraved work which represented the architectural orders as well as examples of the grotesque were reprinted with translations into Flemish in 1539, German in 1542, French in 1545, Spanish in 1563, and English in 1611. This clearly demonstrates the spread of Italianate Renaissance and Mannerist styles in Northern Europe. Serlio's illustrations were used widely by furniture carvers and for panelling work, whilst his ceiling designs were particularly

Inlaid chest in the "Nonsuch" style of architectural designs, c.1600 (V&A)

recommended for transfer to furniture. Serlio's Books IV and VII include designs for chimney pieces that can be found in Burghley House and Hardwick Hall.

The furniture designs of Jacques Androuet DuCerceau, which were based on classical proportions, overlaid with geometric patterns and representational carving, date from around 1560, and comprise the earliest large group of furniture designs. From his *Grotesques* (1550) to *Les plus excellents batiments de France* (1576 and 1579) with a number of influential works in between, DuCerceau's role, as a disseminator of Mannerist and grotesque ornament cannot be underestimated. DuCerceau appears to have been somewhat of a plagiarist, but his importance remains as a disseminator of an exuberant Renaissance style. The "Sea-dog" table that survives in Hardwick Hall is based on one of his designs. In conjunction with DuCerceau, the published works of Hughes Sambin, an architect, and furniture maker from Dijon, were also highly influential in the development of a taste for carving in both low and high relief.

Hans Vredeman de Vries's (1526-1604) work *Variae Architecturae Formae* published in Antwerp during 1560 which was soon followed by the same designer's works on ornament, had an influence that spread far beyond his native country as his designs were usually practical rather than inventive, making them accessible to a whole range of craftsmen. . Its series of drawings of realistic contemporary furniture design therefore provide significant examples of this period. These design books, and others, had the effect of introducing the classical orders, as well as other decorative features such as grotesques, strap work and perspective into the repertoire of English furniture design. The complex relationships between the various designers can be exemplified in de Vries's borrowings from du Cerceau, and Crispin de Passe's borrowings from de Vries. Perhaps these interconnections helped in the construction or development of a codified style

German skills in engraving included the work of Peter Flötner (1493-1546) of Nuremburg who used woodcuts to illustrate designs that incorporated classical motifs, grotesques, arabesques etc. He is remembered for his *Kunstbuch* published three years after his death. It has Moresque designs that were to be very influential throughout Germany. The Master HS also produced woodcuts for furniture and wall panels around 1530-40 and although derived from Flötner, are of a "crude" artisanal quality. His importance therefore lies in the demonstration of a craftsman producing his own interpretation of high-style models. On the other hand, the influence of Crispin de Passe's *Oficina Arcularia* (1621) with its depictions of the orders followed by furniture designs, was to set the tone for many subsequent publications up to the end of the eighteenth century.

Below:
Detail of 'Romayne' Panel Showing Profile Head Motif. These Panels were used in Chests, Bed and Wall Panelling, 16th Century

Apart from the stylistic developments, there were major advances in furniture making in this period that were the responsibility of the artisans rather than the designers. The refinement of the change from carpenter's to joiner's work by the development of the framed panel system was the major improvement. Horizontal and vertical members known as rails and muntins, using a mortise and tenon joint, framed thin rectangular panels. This method had been introduced from Flanders in the latter part of the 15th Century. The frame and panelling technique could be either left open for chairs, stools, or tables, or enclosed with the panels for use in wall coverings, boxes, chests, and settles. The system's advantages were, that it combined lightness with strength and obviated the risk of warping, splitting, and shrinking. In addition, they were lighter and much better looking. During the 16th Century, the development of the true constructional mitre allowed the mouldings to be pre-cut on the stiles and posts before assembly, rather than being cut like masons' mouldings over the true joint. The mouldings could be simply decorated by the use of a scratch tool. Thus, these newer techniques of making were established and would serve the joiner well, until the advent of the cabinetmaker in the later 17th Century.

The conversion of timbers to useful sizes for joinery has always been of prime concern to woodworkers, and this period was no exception. In the early part of the century, oak logs were converted by splitting with a beetle and wedge, or a riving iron, or by being hand sawn in a sawpit. The first method was quite successful as the split timber followed its natural grain and did not waste anything in sawdust.

It was also less labour-intensive than the two-man sawpit. It did not however, give such a level surface and this unevenness may have suggested the well known linenfold motif that was a favourite device for chair backs, wall, and chest panels.

Apart from mouldings and inlays supplied by the joiner, the merits of turning were being fully appreciated by the 1560's. Although the process had been used for making rudimentary chairs, it was in the middle of the century that turning became an essential part of furniture decoration. Turning created some of the more elaborate forms of chair during the 16th and early 17th Century. The descriptive term "turned all over" gives an indication of the design. These chairs, the work of turners, were different from traditional chair construction in that their joints were dowelled and pegged rather than mortised and tenoned.

During the 16th Century, carving was a highly prized method of decoration, often comprising mixed Gothic and Renaissance motifs, which resulted in a highly eclectic style. In the early part of the century, these motifs included the so-called "Romayne panels" (which were carved profile heads set in medallions), Gothic curved rib panels, tracery designs, and "grotesque" ornament. These were mostly achieved by shallow chip carving using a chisel and gouge. Later in the century the Mannerist strapwork, an intricate arabesque or geometric ornament, carved in low relief, was used on flat panels.

Inlays of woods such as holly, box, and Irish bog oak were chosen to produce polychrome effects which were particularly used on chair backs and the so-called, "Nonesuch" chests. These pieces, with their perspective pictures, which were once thought to represent Henry Vlll's palace at Nonesuch, are often fine examples of the inlayer's technique. These perhaps originated in the trompe l'oeil perspective techniques of intarsia, found particularly in Italy, which are good examples of the Mannerist decoration of interiors that influenced

furniture decoration. Many of these were probably made in the Southwark district of London by immigrant cabinetmakers.

Although there were examples of painted and gilded finishes, the fashion for inlays and carvings resulted in the development of finishing methods to protect the surfaces. Oil polishing with linseed and nut oils was the first method to be used, followed by a combination of beeswax and turpentine towards the end of the 16th Century.

The range of furniture types was influenced by the decline of the hall as the most important room, and the rise of a variety of other rooms for private use. The distinction between furniture and fittings was also more marked as a greater variety of moveable furniture was made to accommodate the demands of the new and more stable society. The trestle table was now longer, and made with a fixed top using a panelled construction, and a fixed underframe. The most important innovation however, was the development of the extending table mechanism, which allowed the leaves to be drawn out upon tapered bearers (lopers) so virtually doubling the size of the tabletop. The large bulbous melon-like turnings sometimes referred to as cup

Above:
Turned Chair with Solid Seat. Produced by Furness using a range of spindle sizes, these chairs were made in a wide range of styles and local variants. This example is "Turned all over"

and cover, which became a popular feature on table legs and bedposts. Constructionally unnecessary, and often built up from smaller sections of timber, their development illustrates the changing fashion of furniture decoration during this time. These bulbous shapes were often carved with Renaissance motifs such as the gadroon, scrolled acanthus leaf-work, and capitals drawn from the available pattern books.

Chairs, developed from a box-panelled shape, possibly based on the chest with a built-on back, gradually began to be less heavy; more open and were usually fitted with arms. They were given a slight rake to the back, as an intimation of comfort, whilst the legs remained straight for strength. Chairs, often with prestigious ornament inlaid into the backs, continued to be made by joiners. These chairs were usually referred to as "joyned", to distinguish them from the products of the turner.

The bed was usually the most expensive piece of furniture and was considered an heirloom. Four-poster beds were enlarged and fitted with highly carved canopies and testers, often with the frame separate from the end posts. The Great Bed of Ware is an example that was famous even in its own time.

Storage of household items became more important. Originally, the "cup-board" had been literally that: i.e. a board for storing cups and plate. During the period, the single board developed into a series of shelves or boards that were eventually enclosed by doors making the transition from "a cupboard with things on, to one with things in". The term cupboard has now become a generic name for all receptacles fitted with doors whether fixed or moveable. The raised chest on tall legs became the first sideboard or table, whilst the original cupboard gradually developed into the court cupboard and buffet.

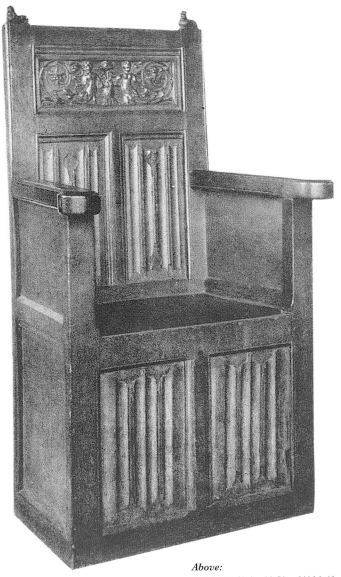

Above:
Oak Joined Chair with Linenfold Motifs. Second Quarter of 16th Century. This joined chair shows a link with the wall panelling of the period. (V&A)

Above:
Inlaid oak chest with mother-of-pearl decoration and applied mouldings and split balusters. (V&A)

II
The Seventeenth Century

Clive Edwards

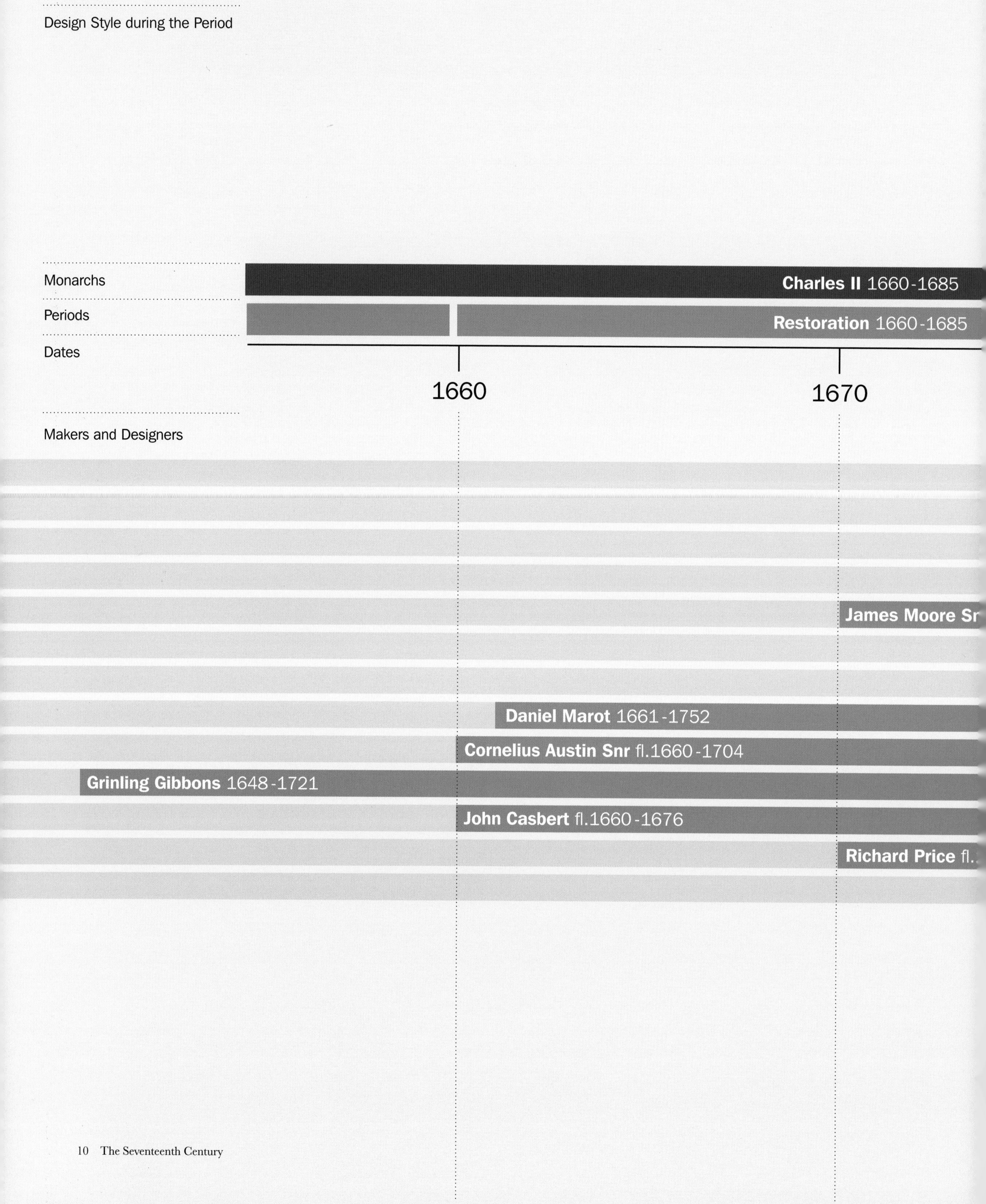

Design Style during the Period

Monarchs		**Charles II** 1660-1685
Periods		**Restoration** 1660-1685
Dates	1660	1670

Makers and Designers

James Moore Sr

Daniel Marot 1661-1752

Cornelius Austin Snr fl.1660-1704

Grinling Gibbons 1648-1721

John Casbert fl.1660-1676

Richard Price fl.

A William & Mary ivory-inlaid walnut and marquetry cabinet on stand

From a set of four William & Mary red and gilt japanmed open armchairs

James II 1685-1688　　　　　**William III & Mary II** 1688-1702

Baroque 1685-1725

1680　　　　　　　　1690　　　　　　　　1700

Philip Guibert fl.1692-1739

lizabeth Gumley 1674-1751

Gerrit Jensen fl.1680-1715

Francis Lapierre fl.1688-1717

-1726

John Pelletier fl.1690-1710

Thomas Roberts fl.1685-1714

33

John Coxed fl.1696-1718

II

The Seventeenth Century

Architects and Activists

Dr Clive Edwards

Cabinet on stand, c.1680, showing
"oyster" veneer and interior drawers.
The cabinet is on a wallnut stand with
"barley-sugar" turned legs. (Mallett)

Late 17th Century lacquer cabinet on
stand. The English lacquer work is
contrasted with a silver carved base
and top cresting (V&A)

A detail of "oyster" veneering which uses slices of branch wood
veneers to build up a pattern of circles. In this case combined
with floral marquetry

A highly decorated metal/marquetry
bureau by Gerrit Jenson, c.1700.
Jenson enjoyed Royal patronage for
his work. By kind permission of Her
Majesty Queen Elizabeth II

Opposite: Late 17th Century Cabinet Makers Workshop. Note the Customer being Shown Work in Progress

The Seventeenth Century   13

The period between 1600-1700 is marked by a number of significant changes; economic, political and religious. Economically the period was one of relative prosperity and growth, with the 'mercantile system' being established in which a favourable trading balance was to be maintained. Politically it was a time of upheaval, culminating in the 1642-49 Civil War, the Commonwealth, and the reduction of the powers of the Monarchy. With the 1660 Restoration of the Monarchy, Charles II introduced exciting new manners and ideas from European courts. Newly fashionable furniture and craftsmen were imported into Britain, and trading links further encouraged an interchange of ideas and designs with Holland, Portugal and the Far East. This flow of continental talent was enhanced after 1685, when Louis XIV revoked the Edict of Nantes that resulted in Huguenot craftsmen coming to Britain. One such was Daniel Marot, born in Paris c. 1662; he left France and worked for the Prince of Orange before arriving in England in 1694. His designed engravings were used by many cabinetmakers as a source for furniture of various sorts. Queen Mary used Marot as her dessinateur-en-chef and he was probably one of the first designers to produce a co-ordinated interior. Marot's interpretation of the seventeenth century French style with elements of Baroque and Chinoiserie was influential in the English Dutch and French court circles.

Above:
State bed at Knole, c.1680. Note the elaborate upholstery, feather plumes and matching accessories, all supplied by the upholsterer

Below:
Table of veneered "oysters" and barley-sugar twist legs with an "X" shaped stretche. c.1680 (Mallett)

Right:
Cabinet on stand c.1680. Walnut finish showing cross overs of design features: compare table on left (Mallett)

It was the bed that Huguenot upholsterers such as Francis Lapierre, Jean Casbert and Jean Poitevin developed into such magnificent objects, often based on the designs of Marot. It is important to distinguish between the designers of pattern books and prints that may have given inspiration for a piece of furniture and the workshops that made them. Particular makers associated with actual objects ran the latter.

This period was also the beginning of architect-builders. Under the patronage of Charles I and his court, Inigo Jones for example, developed the ideas of Palladio and the Baroque. The extensive building programme with luxurious interiors was not limited to London: many fine country houses were built at this time that incorporated classical planning and detail. Although having emphasised the fashionable bases for changes in furniture design and making, it must be pointed out that there was also a development of regional styles based on local centres of production which contrasted with the internationalism of the capital cities of Europe. In addition, the colonisation of North America brought existing European traditions to that area which could exploit the vast tracts of timber including oaks, maple, and pine. Although some American furniture of the period reflects the dour and simple Pilgrim style, many surviving examples demonstrate a healthy delight in the use of paint, carving, mouldings and turnings to decorate surfaces. Apart from the English traditions, the influence of Dutch work was also important at this time. The Dutch immigrants of the seventeenth century who settled in isolated areas in New Jersey, Long Island and the Hudson river valley brought the kas, for storage, which remained a staple (either plain oak, painted, or inlaid) piece of

furniture. Other design features such as elaborate turnings, complex curves on cupboards as well as sensible multi-purpose furniture resulted from Dutch originals.

The early part of the century was still dominated by the use of oak, and all the time that wood was seen as a constructional material, rather than a decorative one in its own right, this would remain the case. However by the reign of Charles II, oak was becoming displaced by walnut, beech, cherry, cedar, olive, yew and laburnum, as well as burrs of various woods. These woods worked well in veneer form thus encouraging the replacement of oak for carcases, with the more stable yellow pine. The use of veneers opened up the decorative possibilities of parquetry, marquetry and oyster veneering (see below). The use of ebony in some cabinets in the first half of the seventeenth century, combined with bright, contrasting inlays of ivory, tortoiseshell, pietre dure etc., showed how the architecturally influenced form was becoming subservient to the cabinet-made surface effect.

Between 1600 and 1640, the demand for fashionable furnishings and the desire to keep up with the court, continued to encourage the growth of the trade, as furniture became more common and began to be regarded as a necessity rather than a luxury. Although comfort became a major consideration, furniture was now as important for show, as for practical use. There was a move to develop furniture types for special purposes, especially to increase comfort. The farthingale chair is one of the best known, made to accommodate the fashionably wide skirts of the period, but at other end of the century also, the tea-table is a response to the social habit of tea drinking.

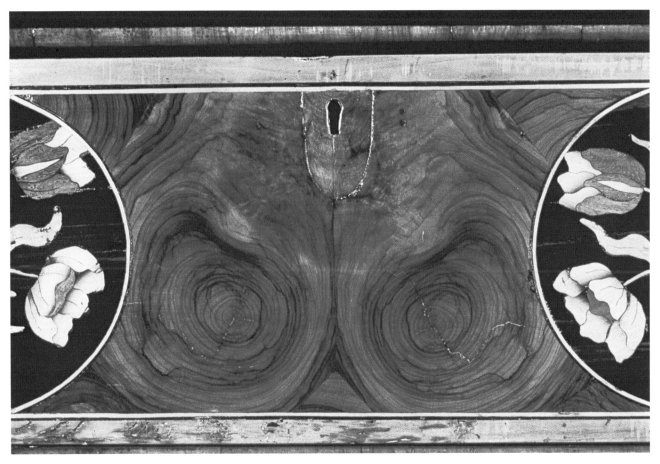

Above:

A Late 17th Century marquetry drawer front showing "oyster" veneering, stringing and banding

Chairs continued to be made in massive and solid forms, but there was a demand for comfort and luxury such as was found abroad. The result of this was the beginning of upholstery. The earliest examples were simply based on stretched coverings over a frame. This developed into the X-frame chair that was supplied with loose cushions. The farthingale chair mentioned above was often covered in Turkey work, a canvas with a knotted pile, introduced to imitate Turkish carpets. The settle was sometimes further developed into a combination piece, with the back turning into a table. In America, the chairs characterised by turned spindles have been known as Brewster or Carver chairs based on their possible original owners, but many chairs still relied on English models as the basis of their design.

Elizabethan table styles continued into the new century but with a tendency to reduce the amount of carving and the thickness of legs. Initially made from built-up sections, they were later made just from the thickness of the leg timber. Gate-leg tables, with circular, rectangular or oval tops were developed to suit smaller family living quarters. This form of table demanded some improvement to the hinge so that the leaves could be dropped more carefully.

The development of the court cupboard and the buffet was the major feature of the Jacobean period. Both forms originated in the previous century but the later versions were noticeably less decorated and were not made with a canted upper stage. By the 1650s they were a shadow of their former glory and gradually disappeared from fashion. The development of the chest into its final form with drawers began with the introduction of the mule chest that had a single drawer in the base. It was not then a big step to introduce the drawers into the whole carcase. During the period the range of chests, cupboards and boxes expanded and examples relate to regional styles as much as any other furniture type. In America they range from simple six-boarded variety to more decorated panelled and carved versions. The famous Hadley and Hartford types attest to this local tradition. These sometimes have a drawer underneath the chest proper, a harbinger of a new form of the chest of drawers. The forms of court cupboards and presses in America again followed English traditions.

The Commonwealth period (1649-1660) is often seen as a severe style with little emphasis on comfort or convenience with few new initiatives in design or production. Fashion was in abeyance during this Puritan period that was clearly one of little ornament. However, turned work became more elaborate as exemplified by bobbin and ball turning. During the 1640s the *"Yorkshire and Derbyshire"* chairs were produced with their distinctive knob-turned front legs, and back consisting of two wide carved crescent-shaped rails. In this period leather was no longer slung as a seat but instead used as a close covering, fitted by brass studs.

The exuberant epoch that occurred during the reign of Charles II was followed by a restrained period under William and Mary (1689-1702). Nevertheless, the whole period was one of change in form, construction and decoration. There was a rise in taste for oriental objects, and a further increase in the desire for comfort. Pieces were scaled to fit the smaller rooms in the newer townhouses and there was generally a lighter touch to furniture designs. The period was one of success in economic and political terms and this was reflected in a demand for more and better furniture. To satisfy this demand a number of new or improved items of furniture came into the repertoire of the furnisher. These included clocks with long cases; easy chairs with high backs and wings (at the end of the period); chests of drawers; chests on stands; cabinets on stands; bureaux; scrutoires;

card tables; daybeds; chandeliers and sconces; girandoles; looking glasses; hanging corner-cupboards, and dressers.

Without a doubt the most momentous change in the latter part of the seventeenth century was the need to introduce new methods of construction. These were required so that English makers could supply new fashions from the Continent. The introduction of veneering, using walnut, hastened the transition from oak panelled and joined construction to bring the true cabinetmaker to the forefront of the trade.

Joined chairs remained important and back-stools or armless chairs were an innovation. By the Restoration, twist turning had become a typical feature of the period, and the tall-backed walnut chairs with caned seats and back panels are easily recognisable. Constructionally they were not always sound, since in many cases, seat-rails were simply placed on top of the legs and dowelled instead of being tenoned in between. However, the introduction of the splayed back leg does show some consideration for the possibility of overbalancing. The double-scroll Flemish leg changed to a Dutch bandy-leg that gradually led to the cabriole shape. By the 1690's the inverted cup

and trumpet were used for legs on tables, tallboys and cabinets. Castors, using leather or wood rollers, were introduced around 1690. An interesting chair type apparently designed by Franz Cleyn with carved shell back and Italianate features was an example of the style that he used probably in conjunction with Inigo Jones, Daybeds or couches, with six legs, had cane and carved or turned-wood decoration to match the chairs. Settee-backs were divided to resemble chairs joined together, and in dining chairs drop-in seats and the stuff-over method were both used.

Tudor forms in storage furniture continued with some modification until the Restoration when the court cupboard was abandoned in favour of the cabinet-on-stand, with either a twist-turned or scroll-legged base. Chests became the dominant furniture item in many rooms but dressers, cupboards, china cabinets, writing desks and bureaux, and bookcases were all made to meet the particular requirements of the time. The Mannerist engravings of DuCerceau, Wendel Ditterlin or Martin de Vos sometimes inspired these. Bookcases, some with hooded pediments and most with nailed shelf-bearers, became popular: the first one recorded, was made for Samuel Pepys.

With the increase in business, letter writing, and the spread of literature, the need for specialist furniture again became evident. Bureaux were first made in two halves and later the sides were of one piece. The panelled doors that were sometimes fitted with mirrors distinguish them. Writing tables were often designed with recesses for knees and were usually made with cabriole legs and apron pieces. The secretaire is made so that the whole of the front drops down to form a writing top, with the interior invariably fitted out with various pigeonholes and cupboards. The decoration was often in the form of marquetry but in some of the bigger items the veneers were not large enough to cover in one piece, so the quartering technique was devised which turned a necessity into a decorative practice.

China cabinets were another example of objects designed to meet specific needs. The collecting of Oriental chinaware and "curiosities" was very popular in the later seventeenth century and it was a matter of course that a display case was required which included glazed doors. The subdivision of doors by small glazing bars appears to have been necessary, due to the size of the glass panes but it was so successful, decoratively, that it remained popular even when the glass was big enough to fill the space in one piece.

Right:
Writing desk by Gerrit Jensen 1695. Finished in rare woods and a range of metals including pewter and brass. By kind permission of Her Majesty Queen Elizabeth II

Beds became very tall and exuberant, surmounted by testers with all the woodwork covered with fabric. Beds are good examples of changing taste, for whilst at the beginning of the century, they would have been proudly carved, they were now hung with expensive fabrics, being demonstrations of the upholsterers' art rather than the carvers'

Mirrors and picture frames were considered essential to a stylish interior, but mirror glass was still expensive and only made in small panes. Nevertheless, freestanding and wall-mounted mirrors were extremely popular by the end of the century. Lime-wood carving in naturalistic forms is associated with the last part of the century and particularly with Grinling Gibbons. Yet again Gibbons was inspired by Dutch examples of carving. Canework, originally of Chinese origin, found instant success in the 1660s, and by the end of the century cane-workers had established themselves as part of the furniture-making fraternity. Cane never usurped the position of textiles, but its use as a flexible and decorative material for chair seats and backs ensured its popularity. It was most commonly used in this period in conjunction with carved and perforated splats for chair backs and seats.

During the second half of the century, brass began to displace iron, and began its monopoly in the manufacture of cabinet mounts. This was due to the fact that brass was a good colour, easy to work, and, by casting, could be reproduced accurately. The results were ideal for use on the lighter forms of furniture that were characteristic of the later seventeenth century. In the seventeenth century, "tortoiseshell" (actually turtle shell) was widely used both in Italy and the Low Countries. As it was malleable when heated, it could be used as a veneer. Laid in conjunction with metals such as brass and pewter on coloured grounds, it represented a high point in marquetry work. This process is usually associated with André-Charles Boulle.

The use of metal in furniture decoration in the period was not common but did occur. Furniture covered in sheet silver or made from solid cast silver was made in the Restoration though little now survives. During the last quarter of the seventeenth century, Boulle work was introduced which used brass or pewter inlays in a tortoiseshell base, sometimes framed by an ebony veneer. The boulle process is considered similar to marquetry in that both sheet materials, metal and shell, were cut simultaneously. Recent research seems to show that early boulle work was not necessarily cut in this way, but individually from the same pattern. It was only in the eighteenth century that multiple cutting (of several pattern repeats at one time) was adopted. André-Charles Boulle worked in Paris as ébéniste du Roi from 1672 and Gerrit Jensen adopted his distinctive process for his work in London.

Gerrit Jensen was a Fleming who worked in England at the time of William and Mary who was highly regarded for marquetry in the style of Boulle. From 1689, he was a major supplier to the Royal Wardrobe as well as a range of private patrons. His products included writing desks, pier glasses, tables and stands. His work was varied, and included "seaweed" marquetry, walnut veneers inlaid with pewter, as well as the better-known brass and tortoiseshell Boulle techniques. His designs have been traced to the influence of Berain but with a tendency to emphasise the geometric basis of the patterns and excluded the more overt imagery. He was also influenced by the patterns of Daniel Marot who was working for the Queen at the same time. Jensen supplied the Queen Mary with; "one ebbbine cabbonette plated with silver and look glass ..., and stands of ebboinne plated with silver and looking glass." He made furniture for use in Kensington Palace as well as for other Royal residences. Interestingly he supplied William and Mary on one occasion with two models of a desk and table for £6.00, presumably as samples before the project was undertaken fully. Apart from marquetry he had an interest in japanning as seen in the description of a room in Chatsworth (now lost), where the panels were "richly beautiful with Indian paint, where there are figures of Birds as drawn by the Native Indians."

Jensen was patronised by John Hervey, later to become first Earl of Bristol. In1696 Hervey paid "Mr Gerrit Johnson, ye cabinet maker in full of his bill for ye black sett of glass table and stands and for ye glasses etc., over the chimneys and elsewhere in my dear wife's apartment: £70." It appears that he closed business in 1715 as an advertisement for a sale in The Daily Courant of May 2nd 1715 read:

"On Thursday the 12th inst, the goods of Mr Johnson, cabinet maker to her late Majesty Queen Anne, having left off trade, at his house in St. Martin's Lane, upon Pavements, near Long Acre; consisting of several very large looking glasses in frames... and all sorts of cabinet makers ware."

Drawer construction is a reference point for the skill of cabinetmakers, and drawer development is related to the rise of the cabinetmaker. The frames were invariably of oak, possibly due to wear-ability on sliding surfaces, whereas oak and pine were used for drawer fronts. Drawers sliding on the dust board, improved the fixing of drawers by hanging them on runners and grooves. Drawer baseboards were fixed in rebates on the sides. The grain of drawer bottoms at first ran from front to back but was later changed to run from side to side. Drawers with dovetailed fronts replaced nailed and rebated ones. After 1670, the crude through dovetailing of the fronts of drawers, used in the early part of the century, was replaced with lapped or stopped dovetailing which gave a better ground for veneering.

Early panelled work used mouldings that were run on oak and used as a framing surround. By the seventeenth century, mouldings for cornices, plinths, friezes, edges of tables, drawers and so on were important for decorative effect and were usually finished with cross-grained veneer. The cavetto (hollow) shape was used on tall chests and the half-round on carcase fronts; the double half-round was used between 1700-1715. On drawers after 1710, an ovolo moulding was set so that the join between the opening and the drawer was hidden when closed.

The name of Austin, a father and son business of joiners working out of Cambridge was important in the field of joinery. Cornelius Austin senior (c.1660-1704) was best known for his joinery work made while he was employed by some of the Colleges. Kings chapel, Emmanuel chapel and the Wren library at Trinity all have examples of his work. He supplied furniture for some of the rooms that he worked on as in the case of the Emmanuel library where he supplied not only wall panelling, but also bookcases, tables and stools. He had a good relationship with St. Johns College, which his son continued. The son, Cornelius junior (c.1698-1729) followed his father by working on commissions for Cambridge colleges. In 1704, he supplied "28 stools for the scholars to kneel on" in chapel which were upholstered by a Thomas Moulder. The details of his other commissions are scrappy although it is known that he altered earlier furniture and fittings.

Until the early seventeenth century turnings were produced on dead-centre lathes, driven by treadle or wheel or on the pole-lathe. For much of the century, knop and ring turning and bobbin turning were repeated, but towards the end of the century there were some contrivances introduced that allowed a twist or spiral to be put in on the lathe rather than by using hand-rasping to achieve the effect.

In the first half of the century, cabinetwork was often decorated with split turnings and raised faceted mouldings that were applied to

Above:
Late 17th Century Lacquered Cabinet
on Carved, Silvered Stand, with Silvered
Pediment. English. An example of the
taste for "oriental" styles. (V&A)

surfaces and sometimes painted black and inlaid with bone or mother-of-pearl. Carving was generally flatter, (than previously) with acanthus scrolls, guilloche, lunettes, and gadrooning. The Commonwealth period encouraged simpler decoration. From the Restoration, decorative processes became very important again due to the practice of veneering cabinets.

The techniques associated with the use of veneer include cross banding, marquetry, parquetry and oyster veneering. All these practices involved applying veneers of decorative wood to a suitable substrate, sometimes separately, or at other times in conjunction with each other. In most cases banding was part of the scheme as it provided a finished edge treatment. Parquetry and oyster work used woods to create a geometric effect, whilst "seaweed" marquetry used arabesque designs to great advantage. Although seaweed marquetry appears to be the height of the marquetry cutter's skill, it was relatively straightforward in that only two woods were used, box or holly for the pattern, and walnut for the ground. The skill in seaweed marquetry was in using a very fine saw to keep to the design lines and at the same time cut at an angle, to ensure as close a fit as possible between the pieces. These methods were often the only way certain woods could be used satisfactorily.

There was a great demand for floral marquetry in the last part of the century, perhaps because it depicted the popular Dutch flower painters' scenes; at any rate it certainly showed the skills of the cabinetmaker. By the end of the century, marquetry was toned down to two shades of brown. Veneers were also carefully matched to form geometric patterns by book-matching or quartering.

Interest in oriental products, particularly imported lacquer wares, encouraged European makers to attempt to copy them. Oriental lacquer imported into Europe were of two distinct types. One type had the ornament in relief; the other, sometimes known as Bantam work, had the ornament incised or cut into the surface. Japanners, who cut out a pattern in a gesso ground then coloured and gilded the result, imitated the process. In 1688 John Stalker and George Parker published their *Treatise of Japanning and Varnishing*. This publication identified three elements, essential to the art of japanning. These were gums, metals, and colours. The gums were used to prepare varnishes; metals were used in powder or dust form and were worked into the varnish, and colours were put down to make backgrounds.

Around 1660, varnishing was introduced as an alternative wood finish. Stalker and Parker also gave recipes for shellac spirit-varnish that was used for coating all sorts of wood products. After the application of each coat, the spirits evaporated leaving a thin film of shellac on the surface. After this had been built up to ten or twelve coats, it was given a high polish with a mineral called Tripoli. This high quality finish was favoured for walnut and later for mahogany and satinwood. In other cases oil was used hot, to rub into walnut to give it a "black and sleek" appearance.

Japanned cabinets were often made to fit onto gilded or silvered stands. These stands were roughly posted and then gesso was applied in thin coats. Once it had hardened, it was re-carved, sanded and gilded. After the Restoration, the fashion for gilding required both water gilding and oil gilding processes to be used. Water gilding required a wet clay base, which was sometimes double gilded and usually burnished. Although this was the finer finish, oil gilding was the more durable method and hence more popular.

Around 1680 the earliest Tunbridge ware was recorded. Originally produced in Tunbridge Wells, the process flourished for the next one hundred and fifty years. The process was initially one of tiny cuts of veneers built into a mosaic pattern, often with a cubic or elongated rectangular theme.

An important business that spanned the end of the seventeenth and early eighteenth was that of the Gumley family. Elizabeth Gumley (1674-1751) and John Gumley (1691-1727) ran a flourishing cabinet making business. It was established by mother and son who traded together until John's death in 1727. John Gumley was also a well-known glass dealer. He established a glass factory in 1705 and a later a retail business at the New Exchange on the south side of the Strand, London in 1714. In the same year, he made a partnership with James Moore that lasted until Moore died in 1726.

Although gilt gesso furniture was a speciality that replaced the marquetry furniture of Jensen and his like, Gumley was particularly well known for his mirror work. The announcement for the new shop in 1714 noted that it had:

"the largest and finest looking glasses in frames, and out of frames... likewise all sorts of coach -glasses, union suits. Dressing boxes, swinging glasses, glass chandeleres, lanthorns, gilt brockets desks and book cases, India chests and cabinets, screens, tea tables, card tables of all kinds... "

From c.1691 to 1725, the business supplied the Royal palaces with various furnishings. It is not surprising that many of the objects were mirrors. One example from 1715 is for "a large glass in a glass frame and festoon finely done with carved and gilt work, £149.00". The firm were eventually removed from favour by the Comptroller of the Great Wardrobe "on account of their notorious impositions". This situation was based on the fact that they had apparently done very little of the work they charged for, so the bill was abated. Nevertheless, the Gumleys had a number of important patrons including the Duke of Bedford, the Duke of Devonshire and the Duke of Montrose. When John Gumley died he bequeathed to his mother Elizabeth Gumley the "use and benefit during her life" of the "goods and stock in trade at his glass warehouse at the New Exchange in the Strand", and she continued the business in partnership with a William Turing.

The seventeenth century had seen a commercial, political and technical revolution in England that set the scene for the exciting developments in furniture design and making that occurred in the eighteenth century.

Further Reading

Beard, G. Upholsterers and Interior Furnishing in England 1530-1840, New Haven and London: Yale, 1997.

Bowett, A. English Furniture 1660-1714, Woodbridge: Antique Collectors Club 2002.

Chinnery, V. Oak Furniture The British Tradition, Woodbridge: Antique Collectors Club, 1979.

Edwards C. Encyclopaedia of Furniture Materials Trades and Techniques, Aldershot: Ashgate, 2000

Edwards, R. The Shorter dictionary of English furniture from the Middle Ages to the Late Georgian Period, London: Country Life, 1964.

Forman, Benno. American Seating Furniture 1630-1730, Norton: New York, 1988

Jervis, S. Printed Furniture Designs before 1650, Furniture History: London, 1974.

Jourdain, M. English Decoration and Furniture of the Early Renaissance, 1500-1650, London: T. Batsford, 1924.

Mercer, E. Furniture 700-1700, London: Weidenfeld and Nicolson, 1969.

Symonds, R.W. Furniture Making in Seventeenth and Eighteenth Century England, London: Connoisseur, 1950

Thornton, Peter. Seventeenth Century Interior Decoration in England, France and Holland, New Haven and London: Yale, 1978.

Wolsey S.W. and Luff, R. W. P. Furniture in England - The Age of the Joiner, London 1968.

Upholstery

Dr Peter J. Brewer

Upholstery is an important part of house furnishing, providing comfort, warmth and privacy, and the decorative effect created says much about us. The bed and the chair have been status symbols and their textile coverings were often a crucial part. The upholsterer or upholsteress, as there have been many of the latter, was the person who assembled the parts to form a coherent whole. There is no physical evidence from the early years of upholstering, but records demonstrate that considerable sums were spent on upholstery, and the splendour can still be seen in paintings. Upholsterers' status has varied over the years but at its height in the 18th & 19th centuries they were the lynch-pins of household furnishings, the interior decorators of their time, with control over all aspects: wall-papering, carpeting, curtaining, furniture, lighting, mirrors, etc.

The extensive use of textiles was their forte and this included funeral work. One of the most important and expensive parts of early upholstering was the state bed and we are fortunate enough to have examples spread

A black-painted and gilded sofa covered in Genoa velvet, c.1700. ex. Duke of Leeds, Hornby Castle, Yorkshire.

throughout the realm. The cost of a bed made for Queen Elizabeth I in 1582 was: £16 for the carved wooden frame, £20 for painting and gilding it, and £86 for the soft furnishings. When one considers that labour at that time was cheap, the cost of making the hangings, black velvet – embroidered, fringed with silk and apparently with gold and silver threads embedded, at today's value of around £12, 000 (just for the textiles) seems quite reasonable.

The upholsterer's art has come down to the majority of us through seating. The development of edge workings for it are crucial to its visual effect and comfort.

Clearly upholstery developed from the times when people simply draped cloths or animal skins over benches, boxes, and chests. Cushions consisting of bags of hay, wool or feathers added to the comfort. Pictures from the period show that during the 16th Century chairs also had some fixed upholstery. A loose cushion provides a superb seat. However the contents settle with use, compact and move towards the back and sides. Restoration of comfort is achieved by removing the cushion and shaking it to re-distribute the contents. As smaller, lighter chairs were introduced there came a need for fixed upholstery and different materials and techniques emerged. The upholsterer developed, or adapted from the saddle-maker, techniques to control the stuffing materials, especially at the front edge where wear and stresses are concentrated.

Not only does the method chosen determine the performance of the upholstery, but it also has an impact on the visual effect of the chair. It is important to match the contours of upholstery to the frame and intended textile cover. This dictates the whole look of the furniture and the way it fits within the room.

When approaching a restoration project the treatment of the frame is usually set within narrow limits, but the upholstery can have many options. An informed choice about the most appropriate style will add to the enjoyment of your own furniture, as well as providing a means of appreciating furniture in its context within historic houses and museums, the Antiques Roadshow and other TV programmes.

Front edge work predominated in most furniture seats. The simplest upholstery form was to put stuffing on the platform and pull a cover over it. However this had limited durability, as the action of the sitter tended to push the stuffing back and the cover quickly wore through. Various preventative systems were explored from the late 17th Century, accelerating from the second quarter of the 18th Century.

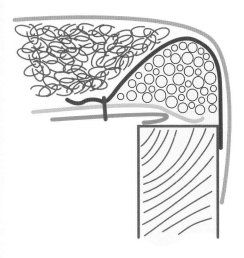

Figure1. Sketch outlining a roll edge without any stitching. This was the system used before the advent of the stitched edge and was used well into the 19th Century, especially on lower status pieces.

Tough edge rolls were introduced early in the 18th Century, initially with a bundle of straw. Then the English developed a stitched support of hair using linen or webs now called a 'welted edge'. The French introduced another system using scrim and the 'French edge' became an important part of the visual effect of upholstery design, as well as serving as edge control.

Edge rolls take various forms and appear to have developed from tacking bags of stuffing to the rails. The common form illustrated below is a strip of hessian sewn to the base cloth, which was pulled over the filling material and tacked onto the face of the rail. The most popular stuffing materials for the rolls were stout stems from wheat straw, rushes, and tow, which would not compress and lose their strength, but more resilient hair was also an alternative.

Where there was hair stuffing, stitches were often used; however with the stiffer materials there was no need for them. The basic technique continued in the second half of the 19th Century to achieve a gentle roll around the edge of seats and backs.

The illustrations of fashionable designers by the start of the 19th Century showed crisp edges and vertical edges to the seat. In addition, the back pads and arms frequently displayed facets with highlights of rope or braid.

A stitched edge is where the upholsterer has added stitches through the front edge of the stuffing cover (or web) to pull some of the stuffing to it. The purpose of the stitched edge was twofold: firstly, to facilitate the design objectives of people such as Chippendale, Sheraton, Hope and Smith; secondly to help maintain the shape and profile of upholstery edges in use.

Mid-18th Century examples used relatively shallow upholstery and generated a crisp edge. The earlier edge rolls often gave good support

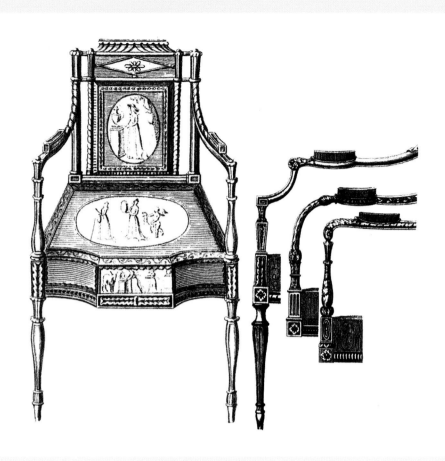

*Two Sheraton designs of 1792 and 1794 from **The Cabinet-making and Upholsterer's Drawing-Book**; The Drawing Room chair has a structured seat requiring greater control of the stitched work to incorporate the vertical panel and to provide the crisp edges and this would almost certainly require a "French edge".*

The details also show the upright seats and the rather severe stitched arm-pads; many examples of these still exist in pristine condition, even though the seats have worn out and been replaced.

The back of the armchair illustrates a tablet back requiring a feather edge to give the desired facets.

but were only able to produce limited height and in most cases they are finished in a rounded profile.

The major transition between the roll edge and the stitched edge appears to be just before the end of the 18th Century. The early years of the 19th Century saw the consolidation of the new system, though the softer profiles continued to be used.

Having produced a roll around the seat edge, the next step was to try and hold the bulk of it forward. A roll was formed as before, but using hair. Then stitches were made through the roll and they were also taken round tacks on the seat-rail. Once any adjustment had been made the tacks could be driven home to support the edge. These tack stitches have been recorded in several late 18th Century examples.

This system is still used by restorers to support 'failing' stitched edges. In cases where the fabric used on a stitched edge is breaking down, a new line of tacked stitches can relieve the strain and give added life to the existing edge.

A welted edge has a web or linen upstand around the seat-rail and once some of the stuffing has been stitched to it, the rest of the seat is filled and the stuffing cover is sewn to the top. The French edge has the stuffing cover in one piece, but once mastered is quicker and has become the standard method of traditional edge work.

The final type of edge treatment is a feather edge, using a blanket stitch that produces a sharp edge. When used on the top of a stitched edge it enabled a right-angle to be formed, such as on upright seat edges and tablet profiles shown on the chairs in the Sheraton illustrations and below.

Small edges needed few rows of stitches, whereas the taller profiles, such as the Sheraton ones, could only be satisfactorily maintained using many rows of stitching. As this was highly skilled and time, consuming work, it became a target area for cost reduction.

The methods of edgework were the standard systems used in medium and better quality work. At the lower end of the scale, cost reduction brought the replacement of the stitched edge with wood and one form was patented in1887. In the UK the approach adopted was to make a soft upholstered top over this, either by preparing a shallow roll, just using a top stitch, or adding a dug roll, which was a pre-formed roll of stuffing material within a textile wrap tacked on to the wood. The name was derived from the term to describe a cow's teat and it is generally of standard size (one inch or 25mm diameter). In many instances the dug

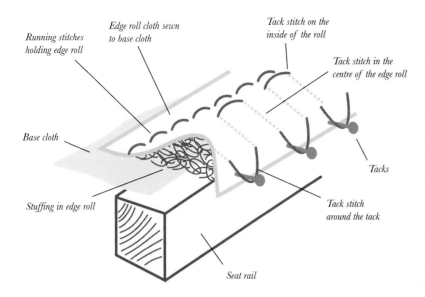

Running stitches
holding edge roll

Edge roll cloth sewn
to base cloth

Tack stitch on the
inside of the roll

Tack stitch in the
centre of the edge roll

Base cloth

Tacks

Stuffing in edge roll

Tack stitch
around the tack

Seat rail

Sketch showing the tack stitch; this represents a transition from the earlier form of edge roll by replacing the harder rushes etc. with softer stuffing, such as hair which could then be consolidated and held nearer the edge.

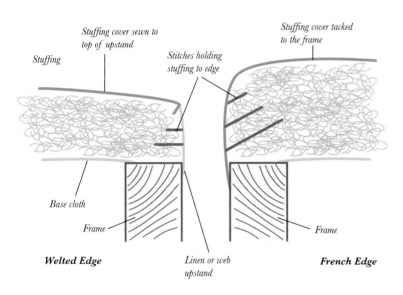

Stuffing cover sewn to
top of upstand

Stuffing cover tacked
to the frame

Stuffing

Stitches holding
stuffing to edge

Base cloth

Frame

Frame

Welted Edge

Linen or web
upstand

French Edge

Comparison between a welted edge (left) and a French edge (right). The welted edge has a shallow upstand and once some of the stuffing has been stitched to it, the rest of the seat is filled and the stuffing cover is sewn to the top. The French edge has the stuffing cover in one piece but, once mastered, is quicker and has become the standard method of traditional edge work.

The profile shown here is relatively rounded but can be altered to suit, for example by bringing the stitches out on to the top of the stuffing cover, a squarer shape can be made. The feather edge illustrated in figure 5 is made by adding tight stitches to the top corners.

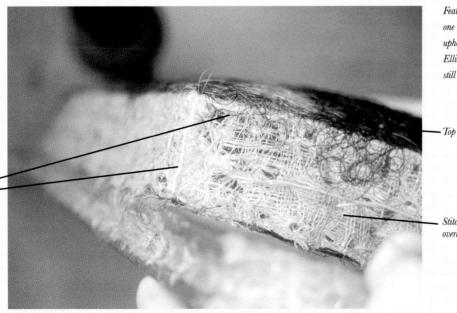

Feather edges worked on to the top and corners of the back of one of the Windsor Castle Garter Throne Room armchairs. The upholsteress Joan Curtis signed it when she was working for Charles Elliott in 1807; the top covers have been changed but her upholstery is still in mint condition.

Top stuffing

...dge to
...orner

Stitches
overlapping

roll was made using off-cuts of the top cover. Leather substitute materials were especially popular. The dug roll was tacked to the top of the wood so that it would project out to the side to make a neat edge. It was clearly a cheap substitute for the stitched edge but did provide a durable support and many examples survive to demonstrate its effectiveness. Modern equivalents are still widely used.

When the coil spring was introduced in the 1820's there was no change to the seat profiles. However later in the century there were novel developments when systems for sprung edges were perfected. The top edge often had a neat roll and below it a deep panel with either buttons or ruched fabric. Near to the end of the 19th Century a spring wire above the platform allowed the upholsterer to give the seat a mock pillow effect.

Upholsterers learnt the art of edge work and its effect on the changing forms of desired profiles. The 18th Century types were rounded and fairly shallow, but as expertise developed they were able to cope with the late 19th Century excesses and maintain tall and well-defined edges with facets.

The stuffing materials used also changed as the most expensive and preferred choice, hair, was replaced by coconut fibre (coir), shredded leaves and grasses, wood shavings (excelsior), seaweed (alva marina), and a few bizarre things such as: moss, cork, and even asbestos! These were the legitimate types however. Restoration workshops abound with stories of the rubbish that had been used by "upholsterers": fabric offcuts, shredded whale-bone, odd leaves and grasses, and "sweepings" (from workshop floors)! In fact some upholsterers' fraudulent claims about their stuffing materials led to the introduction of the Merchandise Marks Act in 1897 which prohibited them from using any "alva…flock…alva marina…and sweepings" as part of their "all hair".

Most original upholstery has disappeared but occasionally chairs come to light with at least part surviving. Unlike cabinet furniture, whose surfaces acquire valuable patination, upholstery deteriorates. The covers become worn and soiled and the under-upholstery looses resilience and can harbour all sorts of odours and pests. Anything over 100 years old was used in houses with open fires, subject to damp, and without cleaning aids like vacuum cleaners.

Upholstery was designed to be re-coverable and the sub-structure could often survive a couple of top covers. The miraculous thing is that some remain relatively intact and can still perform their function and be reused.

Few people realise or can be bothered to know that hair can be washed and used again. In fact much old hair is of far better quality than that available today and it makes no sense to buy expensive new hair that is inferior. Period upholstery is little understood and is often summarily discarded, to be replaced by inferior work and materials.

There is now so little left that unless we start, by conservation and restoration, to value those fragments that do exist, we shall loose the upholsterer's art. What is needed are clients with enough understanding and vision to instruct their upholsterers to retain as much original material as possible and to adapt their techniques to replicate the honest work of their predecessors.

This armchair was made towards the end of Queen Victoria's reign and has many of the features developed by upholsterers. They were able to make supremely comfortable chairs and had the fashionable details of deep buttoning, ruched edges and braids with the latest feature of a spring edge. The whole back was hinged and sprung to allow the sitter to recline. The quality of the upholsterer's art is evidenced as when it was sold at auction recently it was still complete with its original materials.

*A Pair of George III
Armchairs c.1760*

*The backs, seats and
arms are upholstered in
contemporary needlework
depicting birds, flowers
and animals surrounding
vignettes of pastoral
scenes. Image below shows
a detail of the arm*

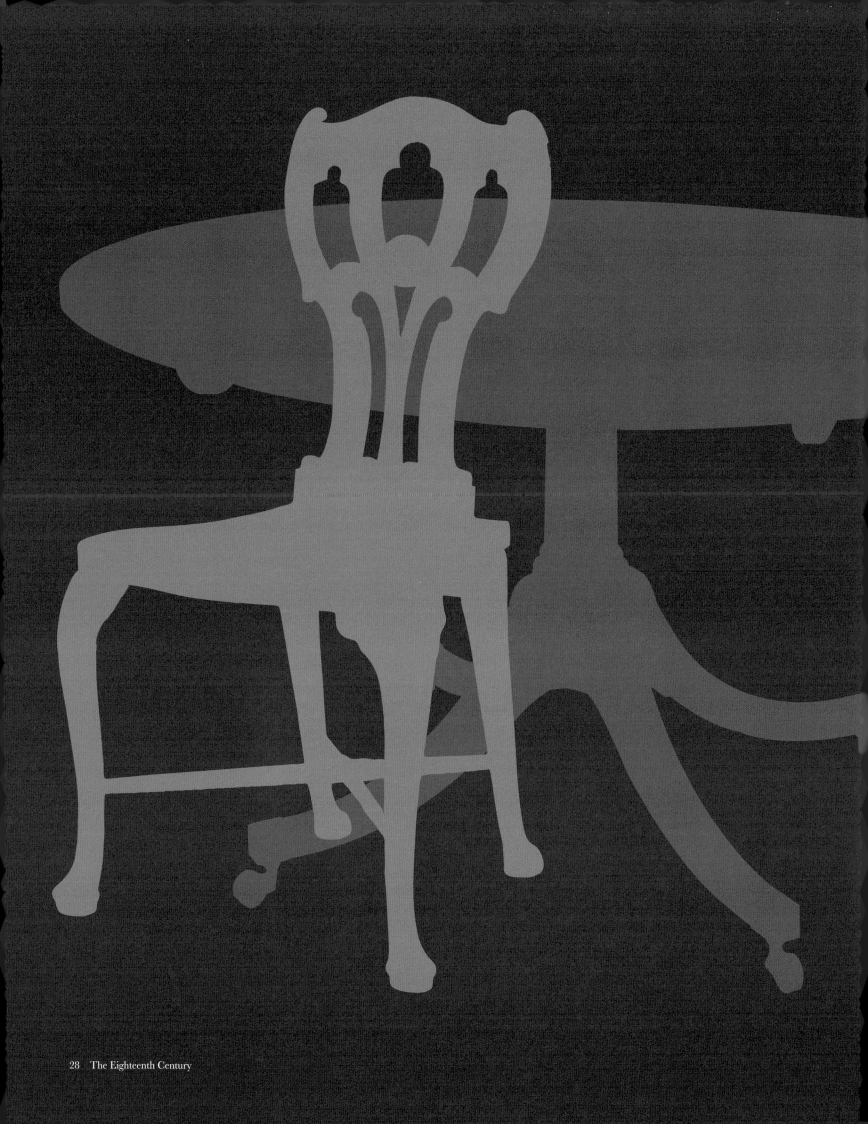

III
Furniture of the Eighteenth Century

Treve Rosoman

Treve Rosoman has had a passionate interest in 'old things' since childhood. As a boy he collected militaria and was given a military campaign chest-of-drawers for his 12th birthday. Predictably, after school he became an antique dealer and worked for a number of firms in the London area before starting his own business. This hands-on approach has been invaluable.

Deciding that the furniture itself was of a great deal more interest than dealing he changed direction. Following university he worked as a volunteer at the Victoria & Albert Museum's Department of Furniture and Woodwork under Peter Thornton, discovering a fascination not only for furniture but for the history of interior decoration.

On graduation he was asked to research the interior furnishings of Chiswick House. He worked with the Greater London Council's Historic Buildings Division looking after their collection of architectural fragments. He moved to English Heritage in 1986, where he became one of the curators responsible for looking after the Houses and collections, especially in the London region. In 1995 Treve was part of the team working on the opening to the public of Eltham Palace. As Project Curator he was responsible for re-creating the interiors as they were when the Art Deco house finished for the Courtaulds in 1936; that is having furniture made, carpets rewoven, sourcing suitable fabric for curtains and upholstery etc. he has recently finished the restoration of the mid-eighteenth century Danson House, in south east London which involved the making and hanging of hand-blocked wallpaper.

He has published widely; in 1985 his research on Chiswick House was published in The Burlington. 1992 saw the publication, and exhibition, of a history of London Wallpapers. Treve has written for Country Life and other magazines; he has also lectured in England, the USA and Turkey.

Treve lives with his family in West London.

Design Style during the Period

George I pewter inlaid, stained maple & walnut bureau cabinet c.1715

Monarchs	**Anne** 1702-1714	**George I** 1714-1727	**George**
Periods	**Baroque** 1685-1725		**Palladian** 1725-1745
Dates			
Makers and Designers	1700	1720	1740

John Belchier fl.1717-1753

Richard Roberts fl.1714-1729

John Cannon fl.1711-1783

Thomas Chippendale Snr 1718-1779

John Cobb c.1715-1778

William France

Robert Gillow 1704-1772

Benjamin Goodison c.1700-1767

William Hallett 1707-1781

George Hepplewhite c.172

William Kent 1685-1748

William Linnell c.1703-1763

John Linnell 1729-1796

John Mayhe

Robert Adam 1728-1792

John Boson c.1705-1743

George II carved and giltwood armchair designed by William Kent, c.1735

George II mahogany side chair c.1755

George III mahogany china table c.1780

George III rosewood, birch & marquetry bombé commode c.1780

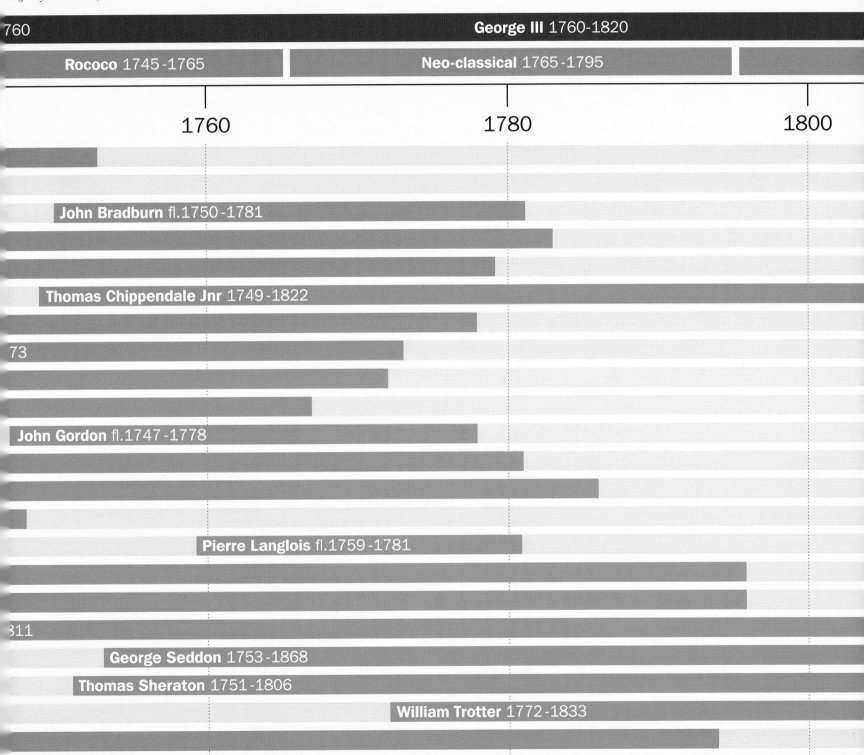

760

George III 1760-1820

Rococo 1745-1765

Neo-classical 1765-1795

1760

1780

1800

John Bradburn fl.1750-1781

Thomas Chippendale Jnr 1749-1822

73

John Gordon fl.1747-1778

Pierre Langlois fl.1759-1781

311

George Seddon 1753-1868

Thomas Sheraton 1751-1806

William Trotter 1772-1833

III

The Eighteenth Century

Inspiration and Individualism

Treve Rosoman

It is quite arguable that the 18th Century was the era which produced the most enduring, and best loved, designs for English furniture. It was both a period which consciously looked to the past for inspiration, and forward in terms of subtle changing social patterns. The architectural surroundings created by men like William Kent and, to a greater extent, the furniture by Thomas Chippendale are with us in the 21st Century and viewed regularly on TV screens. The sheer beauty of furniture, and the exceptionally high quality shewn in their manufacture, are displayed at many great houses open to the public through the National Trust, English Heritage, private owners and the many independent galleries and museums up and down the country.

There are two main strands in the development of English furniture during the 18th Century: firstly the influences of Classical Greece and, especially, Rome; secondly there were practical changes, particularly in two areas: the decline in the use of walnut and its substitution by mahogany and the huge increase in the urban population of Britain, especially in London. This inexorable growth engendered great social changes and was against a background of the late 18th Century's advances of the agricultural and industrial revolutions.

One arm and a single chair from a fine set of dining chairs in the Chippendale manner, c.1765. They are made from mahogany with shallow carved relief decoration on the backs. The legs are chamfered along the inside and reeded vertically on the outer edge which makes them look lighter. The seats are of the drop-in type and were probably covered in leather if used originally in a dining room. Courtesy of Norman Adams.

Opposite: *Detail of the Dolphin sofas in Kedlestone, Derbyshire. Designed by Robert Adam for Lord Scarsdale and made by John Linnell in 1765.*

During the 17th Century, Inigo Jones (1573-1652) had introduced the basic concepts of Classical Palladian design to England, having made two trips to Italy in c.1601 and c.1613-14. What Jones saw in Italy resulted directly in the Banqueting House, Whitehall, built in 1622. However his ideas temporarily sank from view during the political upheavals of the Civil War and later 17th Century. It remained for Lord Burlington in the 1720's, nearly a hundred years after Jones, to re-establish the architectural ideas of Palladio and Serlio. Although the grammar of ornament – egg-&-dart moulding, Vitruvian scrolls, running guilloche etc. – had never really gone out of use, even in the medieval period, their correct usage in a scheme of proportional architecture had become debased and their pattern often stylised.

The 18th Century was a time of relative peace and great prosperity for Britain and an increasing number of wealthy young men were sent on the Grand Tour to Italy. Richard Boyle, 3rd Earl of Burlington (1694-1753) first travelled to Rome during 1714-15 at the relatively late age of 20. He returned to Italy again in 1719, specifically to look at architecture and to try to acquire as many original drawings by Palladio as he could. He met, and returned to England with, William Kent to whom he became principal patron.

Kent was a brilliant decorator and had a flamboyant style of using Classical ornament. He had sketched in the ruins of ancient Rome while dealing in antique sculpture to the English milord on the Tour, so he had a sound basis of understanding how the ancients used decoration on temples, arches etc. Kent became one of the first British architects who not only designed the building, but much of what went into it as well; for example at Holkham, Norfolk, for

the Earl of Leicester and Chiswick House, now in West London, for and in collaboration with Lord Burlington.

By the middle of the century other less aristocratic men were going to Italy to look and learn. One such was Robert Adam (1728-1792). The son of a Scottish architect, his less robust version of classical, or neo-classical as it is called, ornament has passed into the English language, Adam's name being synonymous with late 18th Century design. Certainly Adam designed furniture, but he made none. His designs were carried out by a number of great cabinet-makers, for example Thomas Chippendale, John Linnell, and others such as James Lawson who is today virtually unknown. It is Chippendale, though, whose products seem to absolutely define Georgian elegance.

A Yorkshireman of humble origins, Chippendale rose to own a considerable business in St. Martin's Lane, London. Not only did his men make all types of furniture, but he hired out "rout chairs" for balls and dances (like the gilt chairs one sees at functions today) and supplied all the apparel needed for funerals and much else. Chippendale though is best known today for his book of designs, *The Gentleman & Cabinet Maker's Director*, published in various editions from 1754 to 1762.

Once they had finished their training, English cabinet-makers such as Chippendale rarely made furniture themselves. As is often the case a foreigner's, or an outsider's, view is usually the most enlightening. In 1767 Justus Moser, a German specialist in commercial matters, gave a pen-portrait of the typical English cabinet-maker – who in this case may well have been Chippendale:

"The trading craftsman in England first learns his trade, then he studies commerce. The journeyman of a trading cabinet-maker must be as qualified an accountant as any merchant. The master himself no longer touches a tool. Instead he oversees the work of his forty journeymen, evaluates what they have produced, corrects their mistakes, and shows them ways and methods by which they can better their work or improve their technique. He may invent new tools and will observe what is going on in the development of fashion. He keeps in touch with people of taste and visits artists who might be of assistance to him."

This mid-18th Century view really reflects the whole century. A young man would be apprenticed when aged about 14, or earlier, for a period of seven years. Then at 21 he became a journeyman and could begin to earn money, while still learning about the business side of his trade. Most never really made it past this stage, however good they may have been at making fine furniture. To progress, one needed a good business sense, a source of capital, a fair amount of luck and an ability to get on with rich clients. One of the most common steps up this ladder was to marry one's master's daughter.

Above:
An exceptional inlaid lyre-back chair designed by Robert Adam for Francis Child's library at Osterley Park, Middlesex. Unknown origin.

Above:
A fine mahogany tripod with what is sometimes called a 'pie-crust' top. The top is fitted onto a cage that not only allows to top to tilt but also to revolve. Such tables were for occasional use and would have been kept in the corner of a room hence the usefulness of the tilting top so that the table took up less room. c.1770. Marble Hill, Richmond, Middlesex. Courtesy of English Heritage.

Above:
A walnut bureau-cabinet. In two sections the upper part has an elaborate interior with vertical pigeon holes for papers, drawers for assorted writing paraphernalia while in the lower section secret drawers are always to e found somewhere around the writing compartment in furniture of this period; sometimes the cabinet-maker has been extremely cunning in devising hidden drawers. c.1730. 89" H; 40" W; 22¼" D. Courtesy of Christie's. Lot No 135 Sale No 6648

The outward appearance of furniture changed during the century. The dominant timber used in the early 18th Century was walnut: both in the solid and as a highly decorative veneer. The curvilinear form of early 18th Century walnut chairs and cabinet-work have their roots in 17th Century Dutch and French fashion. All design, of course, is subject to evolution and change and so the flowing lines of walnut chairs and ornate burr-walnut veneered chests of drawers gave way to the straighter, more hard-edged Italianate shapes of William Kent's later architectural style. The fact was that walnut trees in Europe became diseased. For this new work cabinet-makers started to use mahogany, imported from the West Indian colonies: Mahogany was a dark wood that took a high polish and gave a crisp, sharp finish when carved.

Like design, society also evolves. During the 18th Century life became less formal and the way that people arranged their domestic surroundings changed. For example, until the end of the century furniture, especially dining chairs, were put against the walls when not in use, so that there was no decoration on the back. A client would no more pay for things one cannot see than they would today. In the later 1780's householders began to arrange furniture in permanently small groups in the drawing room, and tables and chairs would then be viewed from all angles. A consequence was that the hitherto plain backs started to become carved or inlaid. This trend became much more prominent during the next century. Thus looking at any antique, not just as a piece of furniture, can reveal much of how it was first used and compare its use with other periods.

Above:
Pair of walnut side chairs with cabriole legs with scrolled feet. The aprons to the chair rails have shallow relief carving that looks forward to the rococo style. The upholstery is modern. Courtesy of Norman Adams.

Left:
A George I open armchair with the seat upholstered in petit point floral needlework that may be original. The shaped back, bookend veneered in figured walnut. Note the shepherd's crook-like arms. c.1720. Courtesy of Christie's. Lot No 56 Sale No 6648

Left:
A pair of George III side chairs which are transitional in design. The pierced vase-shaped back-splats are in essence Chippendale and thus forward looking while the cabriole front legs and the stretchers are earlier in style. c.1750. Courtesy of Christie's. Lot No 369 Sale No 6019

So all the light and elegant decorative elements which Robert Adam saw on his travels in Italy became translated into chairs, sofas, tables, cabinets and carpets. The latter may, or may not, have mirrored the ceiling design of their intended room. Adam not only created the architecture and furniture but the fittings as well – door handles, door-cases, curtain pelmet-boxes etc. – in fact everything. He was the "architect-designer". The often waspish Horace Walpole wrote in a letter of 1776 that "from Kent's mahogany we are dwindled to Adam's filigree; grandeur and simplicity are not in fashion." Certainly Adam's work is far lighter and more delicate, and it set the fashion from c.1760 to 1800 as society became more refined and genteel. Furthermore, it can be said that his taste, or a slightly debased form of it, carried on into the last half of the 19th Century and early 20th Century, usually being labelled "Adams". When one thinks of the great British country houses and their contents, there will be far more by Adam than any other: Syon House, Osterley Park and Kenwood on the outskirts of London, Harewood House, Nostell Priory and Newby Hall in Yorkshire, Saltram House in Devon, Audley End in Essex, Culzean and Mellerstain in Scotland, to name a few, and this does not even start on the London town houses for which he was both architect and developer. Adam's output and influence were prodigious.

William Kent published little under his own name, but illustrations of his work were quite widespread. Robert Adam however, set out his ideas, with his brother James, in their *Works in Architecture* of 1773. Adam designed for a very wealthy clientele but simplified forms of the style filtered well down the social scale.

London underwent considerable expansion in the 18th Century and all the new houses needed to be furnished. New occupants wanted new furniture in the latest fashion. Thus one can find oval-backed mahogany chairs which are covered in crisp, shallow relief carving, with a stuff-over upholstered seat finished with decorative brass nailing, but also find the same basic design stripped of all of its carved embellishment, a drop-in horse-hair seat and made from an indifferent quality of mahogany. Both satisfied the fashionable aspirations of clients with unequal incomes.

Right:
A scroll-ended sofa of mahogany with carved neo-classical enrichment, c.1765. Made for the Gallery at Lord Coventry's Croome Court, Worcestershire, by William France and John Bradburn to designs by Robert Adam; the carving was carried out by the Sefferin Alken, another of Adam's specialist tradesmen. Such sofas are often called window seats as they were usually made to go in the window recess and therefore had no need of a back. Now at Kenwood House, Hampstead, London. Courtesy of English Heritage. J920204

Right:
A carved and painted mahogany hall stool probably made by John Linnell to designs by Robert Adam for Bowood House, Wiltshire. Stools very similar to this were designed by Adam for the entrance hall cum dining room at Kenwood but their present whereabouts is unknown. Courtesy of English Heritage. J880052

Once again like Kent, Adam had a favoured circle of tradesman whom he would recommend to his clients as craftsmen who were suitable to carry out his designs. Most are not well known today due to the reluctance of English cabinet-makers habitually to mark their pieces. In 18th Century France it was a guild requirement to mark furniture, in case there were any disputes, whereas in Britain, if a piece is marked, it is usually by a trade card stuck in one of the drawers or otherwise out of the way. The only real exception was the provincial firm of Gillows of Lancaster. It is through bills and receipts that most cabinet-makers are known today where these have survived in country house muniment or archive rooms. The problem then comes to relating the receipt to the piece, often no easy thing. So men like William France, William Vile or John Linnell are very little known.

Occasionally in published letters it is possible to come across accounts of visits to cabinet shops such as when Lady Shelburne, in the 1760's, visited the large workshop and home of John Linnell at 28 Berkeley Square, in the heart of London's West End. She was inspecting the items designed by Robert Adam and being made for her Wiltshire house, Bowood, and London home, Lansdowne House in Berkeley Square. Linnell also supplied furniture to Osterley and Syon, but possibly his most outstanding commission was that for Kedleston, Derbyshire, once again to designs by Adam.

However there is still one name that towers over the history of English furniture and stands out in the popular imagination, and that is Thomas Chippendale. To look at his business is to see the whole of 18th Century trade: what furniture was made, how it was made and to whom it was sold – even how it was dispatched to clients whose homes were many miles from London.

Above:
A side board set consisting of a central table with a mahogany top fixed to a painted frame above a mahogany wine-cooler, or cistern, flanked by two pedestals on bases. The left urn is a container for knives and forks while that on the right is for water to wipe the dirty plates before temporary storage in the base below; when the meal was finished the staff would come in and take away everything to be cleaned and stored. Designed by Robert Adam and illustrated in his book **The Works of Robert Adam**, *1774. Courtesy of English Heritage. J940247*

Above:
Plate VIII, **The Works in Architecture of Robert and James Adam**. *Vol. I. this plate from the Works shows Adams furniture designs for Kenwood. Note the sideboard and how it was displayed. 1778. Courtesy of English Heritage.*

A pair of gilt arm chairs upholstered in their original Genoese cut velvet. Probably made c.1715 by James Moore (1670-1726) for the Duke of Chandos' grand "palazzo" at Canons, near Edgeware, Hertfordshire. Acquired by Sir Robert Walpole for his new house, Houghton, Norfolk, when Canons was sold up and demolished. These chairs are perfect example of chair design in transition. The arm supports are quite French and late seventeenth century in style, while the hipped front legs clearly look forward the elegant early eighteenth century cabriole leg. Although the chairs are plainly not by William Kent, they certainly anticipate his designs; however they still sit a little oddly within the real Kentian Marble Dining Room at Houghton. Originally from Houghton Norfolk. Courtesy of Christie's FRE081294135

Side view of one of the Houghton chairs from the Marble Dining Room and probably made by James Moore. Originally from Houghton Norfolk. Courtesy of Christie's FRE081294135A

View of the back of one of the chairs. The back is most unusual in that it is clipped in place by three brass turn-buckles. These allowed the upholstered back to be removed and so protect the valuable upholstery. The pale red material on the back is a plain wool textile, probably moreen. It is fixed in position by threading the cover onto the back via button holes; it was done this way to facilitate removal. The upholstered backs of chairs before c.1790 were always covered in a plainer, slightly cheaper material as they were not going to be seen by those using them. Originally from Houghton Norfolk. Courtesy of Christie's FRE081294135X

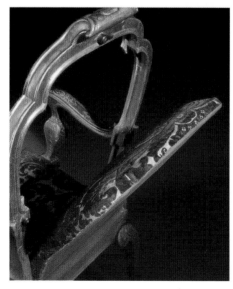

Detail showing the back partially removed. Courtesy of Christie's FRE081294135M

Detail of the top of the front leg. The punched, scale-like ground "behind" the carving is very noticeable here and its purpose was the same as that of sanding the surface. Also clear here is the way that the cut velvet upholstery is fixed over a hessian base. This top cover may be what was called in inventories of the time, a "false cover" and was a very tight, close fitting loose cover only put on for grand occasions. Originally from Houghton Norfolk. Courtesy of Christie's FRE081294135X

A pair of walnut side chairs by Thomas Roberts complete with original silk damask upholstery. The legs are strengthened by turned, hipped H-stretchers. Instead of brass nailing to give a decorative finish to the edges of the upholstery the tacks have been covered with a patterned braid carefully pleated to curve around the shell carving at the top of the legs. c.1725. Originally from Houghton, Norfolk Courtesy of Christie's FRE081294128 A & C

Side view of an exceptional George I side chair from Sir Robert Walpole's house Houghton, Norfolk. Made from burr-walnut the chair has parcel-gilt decoration and is upholstered in its original silk velvet. Probably made by one of the Roberts family, Thomas (1685-1714) or Richard (1714-1729) who were prominent chair makers, carvers and gilders during the period; Walpole owed the Roberts' firm £1,420-8s-7¹/₂ d "less £200 by cash" in 1729. Note the magnificent sweep of the back legs, the animal-like nature underlined by the hoof feet. Courtesy of Christie's FRE081294126A

One of a pair of gilt wood arm chairs, c1735. The upholstery is the original blue silk damask, close nailed at the edge to secure the fabric and enhance the shape of the chair. The cabriole front legs end in claw-&-ball feet, a feature used by early Chippendale designs and common on American furniture until at least the end of the eighteenth century. The flat ground of the gilded area is sanded, that is fine sand was sprinkled onto the gesso before applying the gold finish. It creates a pleasing difference in texture, tone and colour, giving a greater depth to the finished chair. It is a technique often used on mirrors and picture frames, but more rarely on fragile furniture. Originally from Houghton Norfolk. Courtesy of Christie's FRE081294130A

The Dining Room

An oval drop-leaf dining table. This simple, elegant table has a plain, moulded edge to the top, curving, cabriole legs ending in splendid hoof feet. Early eighteenth century dining tables were often plain and folding because they were not kept set out in the dining-room but folded up and put away in a side passage. When in use the table would have been set up, covered by a fine, worked table cloth and laid with silver forks and spoons - the steel knives may have had silver or porcelain handles - and a range of table decoration suitable to the occasion. c.1730. 29¹/₂" H; 66¹/₄" W; 54" D. Courtesy of Christie's. Lot No. 116 Sale No. 5543

Above:

A pair of walnut dining chairs raised on cabriole legs with pad feet. The drop in seats may originally have been "matted", that is upholstered with twisted reeds. c.1735. Courtesy of Norman Adams.

Left:

A bureau cabinet made from mahogany with brass and mother-of-pearl inlay. The cabinet maker was probably John Channon in 1745-50. Another possible maker was a German Moravian expatriate, Frederick Hintz, who was known to use mother-of-pearl inlay. Now at Kenwood House, Hampstead, London. Courtesy of English Heritage. J920226

A mahogany chair of rather a transitional nature. It dates to around 1745. Made from mahogany rather than walnut it has long favoured cabriole legs but finished with claw and ball feet, a design feature much used by Chippendale. The shallow carving on the knees point forward to the rococo while the pierced splat back and shaped top rail are again rather Chippendale. The chair displays the features current when Chippendale was starting in London, some ten years before he published the Director.
Courtesy of Norman Adams.   Detail of the above

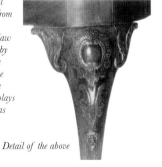

A late eighteenth century mahogany breakfast table with an oval, satinwood crossbanded tilt-top. Compared to [Lot No 153 Sale No 6019] this table may be slightly later in date. 28" H; 56" W; 45" D. Courtesy of Christie's. Courtesy of Christie's Lot No 66 Sale No 6077

A George III mahogany breakfast table on a central column support and four, sweeping, tapering legs on castors. The oval top is satinwood crossbanded with boxwood and ebony stringing. The whole top tilts upward so that the table can be rolled out of the way on its castors and set into a corner, thus taking up little space. Note the way the legs gracefully curve in a smooth line from the central pillar, a good sign of an eighteenth century table and early for this type of table; later tables tend to have kinks and large 'bumps' where the leg leaves the column. c.1970. 29" H, 54¼" W; 42" D. Courtesy of Christie's. Lot No 153 Sale No 6019

A late eighteenth century curved sideboard, veneered in mahogany, with boxwood and ebonised stringing. The long deep central drawer was often used for cutlery; of the two deep drawers either side the one on the right is lined out with metal to act as a wine cooler when filled with ice and bottles while more bottles would have been in the other drawer. Occasionally it is possible to find a small deep drawer on one side that was intended for a potty, so that gentleman could relieve themselves during a long dinner. c.1790. 37" H; 70" W; 29¾" D. Courtesy of Christie's. Lot No 64 Sale No 6648

A mahogany bottle carrier on stand. The square carrier, for six bottles, has shaped side and a central pierced handle. It is set into a stand raised on square tapered legs ending in brass caps and castors. Such a carrier would have been used by the butler, who alone of the staff would have a key to the wine cellar, to carry bottles up to the dining room. c.1780. 18" H; 15" sq. Courtesy of Christie's. Lot No 48 Sale No 6077

Below:
A plain D-end, mahogany dining table. It is made up by a central section drop-leaf table and two D-shaped ends that can double as free-standing side tables. The sections were fixed together with brass clips. Thus one could seat any number of people from two to ten depending on how much or how little of the table was used. 28" H; 45¹/₂" W; 94" extended. Courtesy of Christie's. Lot No 461 Sale No 6019

A mahogany D-end dining table. This is a variation on [Lot No 461 Sale No 6019] as the D-ends have attached drop-leaves supported by the D's back legs which pivot round to take the weight, and there is a separate, central loose leaf. 28ins H; 95" L extended; 53" W Courtesy of Christie's. Lot No 57 Sale No 6077

Burr-elm veneered chest of drawers. Raised on turned bun-feet, probably original; certainly one would expect to find feet of this shape during the first years of the eighteenth century. Note how the moulding of the top matches that of the bottom. The top is quartered in matched veneer and, like the drawers, banded by a relatively wide strip of inlay. The handles have bales held by one split-pin each. The timber is burr-elm, that is wood cut from a protrusion that grows out of elms, walnut and oak, and when cut reveals tightly curled and figured timber; they were, and still are, expensive veneers. This type of chest is more usually found veneered in walnut. c.1710. 35³/4" H; 38¹/4" W; 22³/4" D. Courtesy of Christie's. Lot No 107 Sale No 5879.

A walnut chest on chest. Made from well figured walnut, veneered onto softwood with oak lined drawers. It represents a fairly typical late piece of walnut furniture. The plain cavetto-moulded cornice, probably a removable separate section, does not conceal a shallow drawer, as in earlier years. Beneath the cornice is a row of three small drawers set above three graduated drawers. The top section is finished off by having canted, fluted corners. The bottom section has just three deep drawers, of which the lowest has a sunburst of inlaid ivory and ebony. It is raised on bracket feet into which have been set, probably at a later date, brass castors. When this chest on chest, or tallboy, was made the handles were secured by round nuts on hand-cut, course threaded bolts, into which the swan-neck bales fitted; the round nuts would have been tightened using pincers as spanners had not been widely introduced at this date. c.1740. 75¹/2" H; 43³/4" W; 23" D. Courtesy of Christie's. Lot No 159 Sale No 5879.

A mid-eighteenth century chest of drawers on bracket feet. It is the arrangement of the drawers that reveals that this is not quite a standard item; the slightly deeper top drawer is fitted as a secretaire for writing. When pulled out the front drops down to the horizontal to form a flat writing surface. It was common during the whole eighteenth century to have a bureau or secretaire in a bedroom. c.1755. 33" H; 31" W; 18" D. Courtesy of Christie's. Lot No 224 Sale No 6077

A simple stool with oak cabriole legs covered with its original silk upholstery. Note how thin the seat is in relation to the rest of the stool. Originally from Houghton, Norfolk. Courtesy of Christie's FRE081294106

A walnut stool on cabriole legs, with pad feet, joined by an elaborate curved stretcher. Note the shaped apron, thin top and the drop-in seat. The pattern of the gros point needlework fits the seat which may imply that it is the original, certainly it is of a similar date. Needlework designers in the eighteenth century specifically produced patterns that would exactly fit chairs and stools. c.1720. 18" H; 21" W; 16" D. Courtesy of Christie's. Lot No 47 Sale No 6648

A walnut-veneered lowboy raised on cabriole legs with pad feet. The top has a moulded edge with re-entrant corners and, like the drawers, has feather banding around the perimeter. Note the shaped apron and the original handles; the handles proper, called bales, were held in place by split-pins and not nuts and bolts. c.1720. 28¹/2" H; 31" W; 19¹/4" D. Courtesy of Christie's. Lot No 68 Sale No 5879.

Half-tester, or "angel" bed. This form of bed was very popular in the early eighteenth century, to judge from illustration on the trade cards of upholsterers and other contemporary pictures by artists like Hogarth. The tester is suspended from the ceiling by chains or rods, which can just be made out here in the musician George Frederick Handel's recreated bedroom. The bed is made from a simple wooden frame upon which wool fabric is stretched, glued and tacked into shape; the "ears" of the valences around the tester are stiffened with buckram. Note also the bare dry rubbed floor-boards and the painted softwood panelled walls of the second floor front room, overlooking fashionable, then as now, Upper Brook St, off Bond St.; it is a typical early eighteenth century London interior. A walnut "bachelor's" chest of drawers is on one side of the bed while rush-seat, or "matted" walnut chair is on the other. At the foot of the bed is a rare round, oak close-stool, the origin of the "thunder-box". These were not always left out in the room but put away into a small cupboard, or closet, from where the term water-closet or WC derived when plumbing became more common. c.1735. courtesy of the Handel House Museum.

A small mahogany four post bed in the manner of a field-bed. Shown here in its "naked" state it is possible to see how a late eighteenth century bed was constructed and without its "furniture" - that is the curtains, valances, coverlets, mattresses, feather bed, bolster and pillows (compare this bed with the Handel House bed Left). It is possible to see where the mattresses should come up to on the undecorated square section of the foot posts; the bolster and pillows would start where the shaping begins on the headboard. Across the softwood bed-frame narrow boards might have been laid to support the bedding. Otherwise a sheet of canvas laced to strips of canvas tacked to the frame would have provided a modicum of springing to the bed; the lacing could be tightened as the ropes stretched with use of the bed. Mattresses were made of a variety of materials from straw and hay stuffed into cotton-ticking cases to feather or coiled horse hair filling. Springs were a late nineteenth century improvement. A bed such as this one probably had a light chintz set of curtains and a heavier woollen set for winter. c.1800-1810. 85" H; 37 1/4" W; 76" L. Courtesy of Christie's. Lot No.33 Sale No. 5543

A mid-Georgian four post bed frame with a moulded frieze. The decorative parts are turned and carved from mahogany while the rest of the frame is of softwood, probably of Baltic origin - as it would have been covered with curtains etc and not seen there was no need to use expensive timber. It is possible to see here the sockets on the long sides of the bed which held the slats upon which the mattresses lay; also noticeable here is the rebated slot in the left head post, into which was fitted the headboard. The carved and moulded cornice is possibly not original to this bed but one like it would have held wrought-iron rods from which hung the curtains; it is just possible to see where the decoration stops on the foot posts below the cornice as these were hidden by the fabric. The great expense of all eighteenth century beds lay in their textile hangings, of furniture, as it was called. Such hangings displayed the height of the art and skill of the upholsterer as he would make the bed hangings, the room curtains and the chair upholstery from matching fabric. c.1770. 97 1/2" H; 64 1/4" W; 79 1/2" L. Courtesy of Christie's. Lot No. 190 Sale No. 5852.

A very fine pair of turned and carved mahogany foot posts, in the style called "Roman". The bun feet, surface carved with foliage, hide castors, or rollers, made from lignum vitae, a very hard tropical wood. Beds usually had castors of some sort to enable them to be moved for housekeeping. Above the feet are later nineteenth century reeded covers to hide the bed-bolts that secure the frame. Then come swirling fluted turned baluster vases below fluted Corinthian columns. The bed was probably supplied to Henry Spencer, Esq., a tobacco merchant from Dulwich village, now part of south London. c.1755. 98" H. Courtesy of Christie's. Lot No. 51 Sale No. 6648

A red, black and gilt japanned bureau-cabinet. Such highly decorative pieces like this were commonly bedroom or dressing room items; for example there is a very splendid example at Erdigg, near Wrexham, N. Wales. The taste for lacquering or japanning had started in the seventeenth century when the first pieces appeared in Europe from the Far East. The fashion was spread by the publication by Stalker & Parker of their **Treatise of Japanning and Varnishing**, 1688 filled with little vignettes for anyone to copy. The images were often wildly inaccurate but were considered exotic by people in Britain. Lacquered or japanned furniture was really only paint on a gesso ground. The favourite colour was red, but green, blue, occasionally yellow and very rarely white and possibly the most common item of japanned furniture was the longcase clock. c.1715-20. 92" H; 41" W; 23" D. Courtesy of Christie's. Lot No 230 Sale No 6077

A set of mahogany bed steps. The three treads are inlaid with green leather panels. Note how the legs are tapered and the risers chamfered, devises that appear to lighten the piece and reduce its bulk. An excellent example of plain English cabinet-work. At a time when four-post beds were quite high structures with several layers of mattresses the bed could be two and half feet from the ground, thus steps were often needed to get into bed. c.1800. 24¹/²" H, 18¹/²" D. Courtesy of Christie's. Lot No 187 Sale No 7013

A pair of mahogany pot cupboards with shaped aprons and pierced gallery. These were bedside items; the doors opened to a cupboard for a pot and the apron pulled forward to make a seat for another ceramic, or pewter, pot. These elegant pieces of Georgian furniture have long been popular, usually migrating from the bedroom to the sitting-room where they can be used as a drinks table. They are still sometimes called, euphemistically and descriptively, tray-top commodes. Courtesy of Christie's. Lot No 144 Sale No 7013

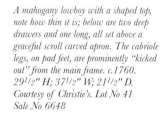

A mahogany lowboy with a shaped top, note how thin it is; below are two deep drawers and one long, all set above a graceful scroll carved apron. The cabriole legs, on pad feet, are prominently "kicked out" from the main frame. c.1760. 29¹/²" H; 37¹/²" W; 21¹/²" D. Courtesy of Christie's. Lot No 41 Sale No 6648

A fine mahogany serpentine fronted chest of drawers, with canted corners and set on ogee bracket feet. A cabinet-maker needed great skill to make the serpentine shape and not waste prodigious amounts of expensive timber. The top is crossbanded and has a moulded edge. c.1770. 33" H; 40" W; 24" D. Courtesy of Christie's. 33" H; 40" W; 24" D. Lot No 477 Sale No 6045

A mahogany chest of drawers of the type that was often described in the eighteenth century as "neat and plain". What appears as a common four drawer arrangement is not as it seems; in fact there are two long drawers, set beneath a brushing slide, and then one very deep drawer simulated on the exterior, to look like two standard drawers. Such an item must have been a special commission. c.1770. 34" H; 29" W; 18" D. Courtesy of Christie's. Lot No 475 Sale No 6045

A mahogany chest-on-chest raised on bracket feet. The cornice and canted corners have blind-fret gothick decoration. The bottom drawer of the top section is a secretaire. A brushing slide is set just above the top drawer of the lower section. c.1770. 75" H; 48" W; 23" D. Courtesy of Christie's. Lot No 179 Sale No 6077

A mahogany bow-front chest of drawers. Boxwood stringing outlines the drawer fronts and the ring-handles are original; the handles may imply a date of c.1800-1810. This graceful form of chest has the refined feature of swept, French feet; these are often prone to damage due to careless moving, especially if it has been dragged across a floor. Plate 76 of Hepplewhite's 1788 Guide shows a similar pattern. 41" H; 42" W; 23" D. Courtesy of Christie's. Lot No 180 Sale No 6077

A dressing table veneered in fustic. This piece is shewn both open and closed. When open the sections either side of the mirror consist of lidded well that would have held brushes, ointments, beauty-spots, scent etc. Fustic was an imported timber from tropical America and was usually used as the main ingredient for making yellow dye. It was also prized for inlay work. Sadly over time the original colour of the wood fades, as Sheraton noted in his Cabinet Dictionary, 1803. c.1780. 33³/4" H; 23¹/2" W; 19¹/2" D. Courtesy of Christie's. Lot No 127 Sale No 6648

A severe grained softwood chest of drawers. Furniture for "below stairs" was usually made from either oak or pine with painted graining to make it look better; if furniture was made from softwood it was rarely left unpainted, almost without exception it was "improved" with paint. This is typical staff quarters furniture; well made but devoid of expense, it even has wooden handles. Sadly today pieces like this are now rare thanks to the market for stripped pine. c.1790. 41¹/4" H, 42¹/4" W, 20¹/2" D. Courtesy of Christie's. Lot No 76 Sale No 7013

A large verre eglomisé pier glass. A mirror was always described as "a glass" in contemporary accounts and a "pier glass" was a tall narrow mirror that hung between two windows. In the late seventeenth and early eighteenth centuries they were usually associated with a matching table and two pedestals, or candlestands. This mirror is made in the Louis XIV's "antique" or Roman fashion, made popular by Daniel Marot (1662-1752)(qv). It was probably made by James Moore (1670-1726) or John Gumley (c.1674-1751) - they were in partnership from 1714 until 1726. A signed mirror by Gumley is in the State Apartments at Hampton Court. Verre eglomisé was method of painting and gilding underneath glass. c.1705-10. 72" H, 32¹/₂" W Courtesy of Christie's. Lot No 6 Sale No 6648

A walnut open arm chair but with an upholstered seat and back. The original covering may have been either leather or some of needlework. Compare to [Lot No 56 Sale No 6648]. Courtesy of Christie's. Lot No 49 Sale No 6648

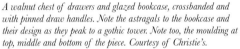

A walnut chest of drawers and glazed bookcase, crossbanded and with pinned draw handles. Note the astragals to the bookcase and their design as they peak to a gothic tower. Note too, the moulding at top, middle and bottom of the piece. Courtesy of Christie's.

A small walnut chest of drawers with a fold-out top, a so-called bachelor's chest. The top unfolded for writing and was supported on lofas located either side of the first drawer. The top and drawer fronts are feather-banded around the edges and the handles are of the drop type which were held in place by split-pins; both signs of early eighteenth century cabinet making. c.1720. 30" H; 31" W; 13" D. Courtesy of Christie's. Lot No 50 Sale No 6045

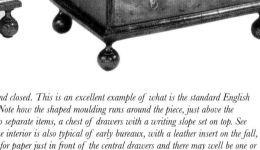

A burr walnut veneered bureau, c.1715, shewn open and closed. This is an excellent example of what is the standard English bureau, but it still exhibits traits of how they evolved. Note how the shaped moulding runs around the piece, just above the drawers; this is a remnant from when bureaux were two separate items, a chest of drawers with a writing slope set on top. See also the bun feet again reminiscent of earlier chests. The interior is also typical of early bureaux, with a leather insert on the fall, the small drawers coming forward on the side, the well for paper just in front of the central drawers and there may well be one or two secret document drawers hidden away. Courtesy of Norman Adams.

Pair of upholstered side chairs on plain mahogany cabriole legs with pad feet. The upholstery is original but may be slightly older than the chair, possibly late 17th Century. The backs are covered in a dark green moreen. Such chairs would have been set around the walls of a drawing room, only being moved for use. In Hogarth's Marriage A La Mode, Plate II a servant is shewn replacing such chairs back against the wall after a riotous evening. These chairs were probably made for Admiral George Delaval's Yorkshire house, Seaton Delaval in c.1720.
Courtesy of Christie's. Lot No 88 Sale No 6648

Pair of upholstered backstools probably by the Roberts' firm. Originally from Houghton, Norfolk. Courtesy of Christie's FRE081294126

A mahogany "easy chair". This chair has striking, bold proportions that may be related, in a sense, to Robert Adam's Moor Park Suite chairs. Made from mahogany with beech underframe, the chair has a vitruvian scroll seat rail with short cabriole legs which have carved masks of vestal virgins at the knees and claw and ball feet. The upholstery is of eighteenth century tapestry but perhaps does not fit the chair well enough to be original; certainly the chair would have been close-nailed, as it is. The chair came from Broome Park, Kent. c.1745. Courtesy of Christie's. Lot No 129 Sale No 5879

Gilt wood side chair, designed by William Kent for Lord Burlington's Chiswick House. This type of chair was often described in eighteenth century inventories as a "backstool", and was probably one of the chairs that were designed for the Red and Green Velvet Rooms at Chiswick. The chair is now covered in a modern reproduction of an early eighteenth century cut, Genoese, velvet that may still be seen at Houghton, Norfolk. Courtesy of English Heritage. K940796

William Kent
(1686-1748)

Carved and giltwood armchair, c.1735

Carved and giltwood armchair designed by William Kent, and made by Stephen Langley, c.1735

Allegory of Painting: ceiling painting by William Kent, c.1730

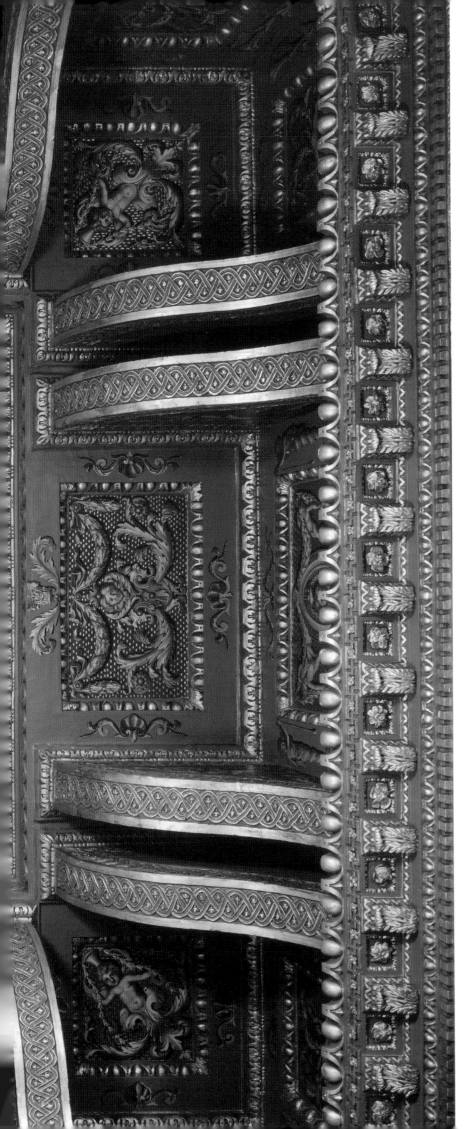

William Kent was born in Yorkshire and trained as a coachpainter and sign-writer. His promise was recognised by fellow Yorkshireman Burrell Masingberd, who became his patron and, with a group of friends, sent Kent to Italy to study in 1710. To supplement his allowance, Kent started to deal in works of art as well as studying and drawing the Classical ruins of ancient Rome. In 1715 he first met Lord Burlington who incidentally had a large estate in East Yorkshire. Again, on Burlington's return trip in 1719, they arranged to meet in Genoa. With the new patronage of the influential Lord Burlington, the two young men together set about changing the taste of a nation.

One of Kent's first major undertakings was to decorate the Cupola Room at Kensington Palace between 1721 and 1725. He was elevated to Master Carpenter at the Office of Works and also succeeded Charles Jervas as Principle Painter to the Crown in 1726. Such a rapid rise did not go without criticism. William Hogarth described him as "a contemptible dauber" and certainly his paintings were of variable quality. However, he was a superb "interior decorator", to use the modern term.

Furniture was a vital part of the unified conception of his decorative schemes, and it is still possible to see some of them now, most notably the Grand Saloon of Houghton, Norfolk, carried out 1726-30 for Robert Walpole. Kent's style was rich and Horace Walpole noted that it could be "audacious, splendid, sumptuous" but that it could also be "immeasurably ponderous".

Right:
William Kent, by William Kent, 1723-25. Kent is shown in this oil painting soon after his return from Italy with his patron, Lord Burlington, in 1719. This was before his real triumphs at Kensington Palace, Chiswick House, the gardens at Rousham, Oxfordshire etc. and when he was more of a painter than an architect. Kent is dressed in a banyan, or nightgown, fashionable wear for artistic people at leisure. On his head, instead of a wig, is a night-cap. Neither of these items was worn in bed, despite their names; they were items for informal wear at home. There is a portrait of Lord Burlington in similar clothes which stress his artistic pretensions, rather than his aristocratic standing. National Portrait Gallery.

Left: Ceiling of the Blue Velvet Room, Chiswick House, Middlesex. Designed and painted by William Kent for Lord Burlington, c.1730. The central panel is an allegory of Architecture. The Blue Velvet Room was Burlington's private closet, or study, where he kept some of his favourite paintings and books on architecture. Courtesy of English Heritage. J940518

The principle influence on Kent was that of a baroque interpretation of classical Rome, which is not too surprising considering that he had spent nearly ten years studying there. He was fond of using bold, sculptured, carved work of which the Italians were, and still are, the absolute masters. His style is in direct contrast with the next generation's master, Robert Adam, despite the fact that both men used the same patterns and shapes and had seen and drawn the same buildings.

An excellent example of Kent's early work may be seen in the pair of gilded, marble-topped tables made for Chiswick House in about 1720. The ornate inlaid marble tops, or "slabs", were a souvenir from Burlington's 1719 trip to Italy. The table frames were almost certainly carved by an Italian sculptor/carver Giovanni Guelphi, another Italian brought back by Burlington and part of his household for some years, as was the composer George Frederick Handel. The tables display many of Kent's favourite decorative ornaments: fish-scales, shells, putti and female heads. The frames were made from pine, probably imported from the Baltic, and built up by gluing together blocks of pine and then carving away excess timber. The surface was then covered using oil-gilding, a finish more robust than the water-gilt method. The tables were made for Chiswick House and may be seen today in the Gallery there, a place which they have occupied since at least 1730.

Kent lived in rooms within the great Burlington House, Piccadilly, the London home of his patron. In about 1735, Burlington and his wife left their central London house to live permanently at Chiswick, about 6 miles to the west. William Kent was a close family friend, called Kentino or Il Signor by Lord and Lady Burlington; he was certainly not just one of the servants and he was free to come and go as he pleased.

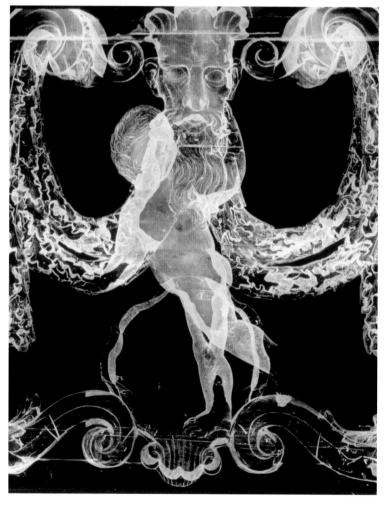

His output, other than pure architecture, included interior schemes, such as the truly astonishing staircase in 44 Berkeley Square, royal barges for ceremonial use on the Thames (and the oarsmen's uniforms as well), the Pelham Gold Cup for horse racing (a beautiful two handled solid gold cup about eight inches high, made by George Wickes), a "Chandelier for the King" and a tomb for the chief bricklayer of Chiswick House.

Kent was also an important, innovative garden designer (another of Burlington's passions) and he formed a vital link between the formal 17th Century style and the classic English landscape gardens of "Capability" Brown. Kent worked in a close world; he had his patron, Burlington, who not only found him his Court appointments, but Burlington's circle of friends used Kent to design houses and gardens for them. His patron's artistic friends, such as the poet Alexander Pope, were also Kent's friends, and they all discussed ideas together. Finally, Kent used a relatively small number of craftsmen to execute his designs: men such as John Boson and Benjamin Goodison. It is often said that 18th Century London was a series of connected villages, but one could also say that society was made up of close inter-dependent groups with their own allegiances.

William Kent died on 12 April 1748 and is buried in the parish church of Chiswick, in his patron's family vault.

Opposite Page:
View of the Gallery, Chiswick House, Middlesex, finished c.1730, and designed by William Kent both with, and for Lord and Lady Burlington. The Venetian, or Serlian, window on the left leads out into the garden, while straight ahead is the Octagonal Room through which one could gain access to the old Jacobean building that was once part of Chiswick House. The large red porphyry vases are, like the tables, original to the room and were also brought back from Burlington's travels in Italy. The gilt wood pedestals may have been made either by John Boson [qv] or Benjamin Goodison [qv] and are very similar to a pair made for Lady Burlington in 1735 by Boson and illustrated in the Gallery in a painting of 1822. The pediment-backed mahogany hall chair, one of a large set, is also original to the room. Courtesy of English Heritage. J010011

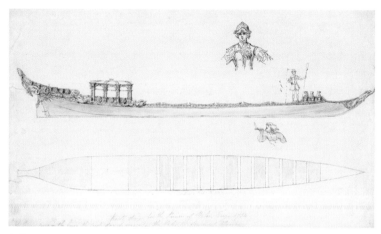

William Kent's design for Frederick, Prince of Wale's state barge, or shallop, 1732. This splendid royal barge was 63 feet long and seven feet wide and with a cabin that was also seven feet long, the boat must have been quite a handful to manoeuvre. Note how similar the cabin's design is to the owl decorated pier table, (see main image, John Boson). The bulwarks of the craft have a vitruvian scroll running the whole length and there are many more nautical motifs, such as dolphins and shells, which Kent liked to use in his designs of rather less seafaring furniture. The ornate carved taffrail of stern-board was executed by John Boson. Last used in 1846 the shallop may be seen today in the National Maritime Museum, Greenwich. The oarsmen's uniform is reminiscent of the decorative renaissance costume worn by the players of the Calcio Storico in Florence, whom Kent would have seen during his time there in c.1715. Courtesy of the RIBA.

A giltwood armchair. This rather grand chair is a pair to one in the Victoria & Albert Museum that is reputed to have belonged to the wife of the great eighteenth century actor David Garrick. The chair rails are decorated with a greek-key pattern filled with flowers, very similar to the Kent designed, Stephen Langley chairs made for Lady Burlington's Garden Room at Chiswick House, see below. It is a possibility that this chair may also be designed by Kent and made by Langley. Both this chair and the Victoria & Albert Museum example have been slightly cut down in size. c.1735.
Courtesy of Christie's. Lot No 14 Sale No 6648

One of a set of carved and gilded arm-chairs made by Stephen Langley in 1735 for Countess of Burlington and designed by William Kent. It is one of a set of ten arm-chairs and two sofas for which Langley charged the very high price of £198-2s-8d. There is a delightful pencil sketch of Lady Burlington sitting on one of the chairs while painting which goes to show that such very fine furniture was not always kept for special occasions. Chiswick House, Middlesex. Courtesy of English Heritage. M940549

Detail of an arm from one of the chairs made by Stephen Langley in 1734. Note the unusual Greek key pattern, carved in shallow relief, which is shot through with acorns and oak leaves. Courtesy of English Heritage. M940544

Pier glass and table. The complete set of furniture was made by John Boson for Lady Burlington's Garden Room at Chiswick House. The receipt is dated 11th September 1735 and was paid for by Lady Burlington and the carved and gilded owls on the tables and surmounting the mirrors represent the family crest of the Savile's, Lady Burlington's maiden name. The tables are made from mahogany with gilded enrichment; this is called parcel gilding in twentieth century terminology but was referred to as "party gilt" when they were made. The tops have inlaid panels of tooled leather. The whole suite was designed by William Kent and Lady Burlington refers to them in a letter of 17th April 1735 to her husband, writing "I hope the signor has remembered about my tables and glasses." Signor was a family nick-name for Kent. The date is also of interest as the receipt is only dated some six months later, a relatively short time for such a grand set of furniture. Glass: 71$^{1/2}$" H; 52ins W. Table: 35$^{3/4}$" H; 59$^{1/2}$" W; 31$^{1/2}$" D. Chatsworth, The Trustees of the Chatsworth Settlement.

Biography:

John Boson
(1705-1743)

Giltwood pier glass, attributed to John Boson, c.1735

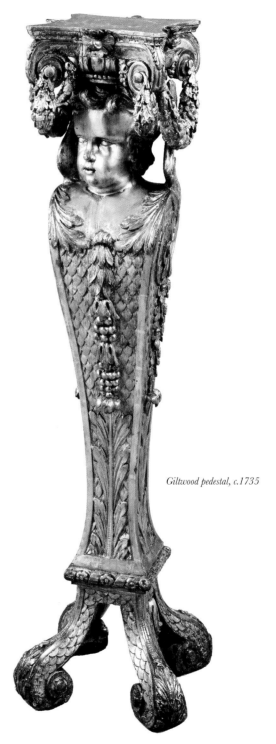

Giltwood pedestal, c.1735

John Boson, carver and gilder, was another important figure in the Burlington circle. The furniture-making trade in London was divided up into various specialisms: there were upholsterers, cabinet-makers, chair-makers, carvers and gilders, and many more. Upholsterers often ran businesses somewhat similar to modern interior decorators, in that they could organise everything to fit-out a house, from lighting to furniture via curtaining. They could also undertake to provide the complete funeral service or fit out temporary rooms for balls and soirees, supplying marquees, floor coverings and flowers.

John Boson may have learnt his trade as a carver and gilder by carving ships' ornament for the Royal Navy, for he was recorded in 1720 as having a yard at Deptford in south-east London, a major centre for Naval ship-building in the 18th Century. Much of his early recorded work was for church fittings but, as befitted an ambitious craftsman, he was a subscriber to books like Leoni's *Alberti*, 1726 – one of the seminal books on *Palladian* style design – and the English architect Isaac Ware's book, *Palladio*, in 1738. The possession of such books was important as they showed that the owner was interested in fashionable taste: subscribes established themselves as leaders of fashion. The engraver and commentator Vertue wrote of Boson that

he was "a man of great ingenuity and undertook great works in his way for the prime people of quality and made his fortune well in the world".

The years from 1730 until his early death in 1743 were highly productive for Boson. In 1734, he took a long lease from Lord Burlington for a plot in Savile Row and a house and workshop was built to a design by Kent. This also reveals how much he was part of the Burlington circle. Boson was a carver who produced picture and mirror frames, for which Kent produced very distinctive designs, chimney-pieces and related works. He could carve in both stone and wood. One of his clients was Frederick, Prince of Wales, and Boson was commissioned to carve the elaborate taffrail, or stern-board, for the Prince's State Barge, again to designs by Kent. The barge may be seen today in the National Maritime Museum, Greenwich.

One of the best documented products of Boson's workshop is a pair of pier tables and their matching pier glasses. These were made for, and paid for, by his patron's wife, Lady Dorothy Burlington, in 1735 and intended for her drawing room at Chiswick. The suite is unified by the use of an owl motif: a great dumpy owl sits, spread-winged, atop each of the mirrors while six more owls, with folded wings, make

Gilded softwood pedestal or torchères possibly made by either John Boson or Benjamin Goodison. Such pedestals were usually used to support candelabrum as part of a grand room's lighting. Courtesy of English Heritage. J920160

22 Savile Row. This was the home and workshop of John Boson until his death in 1743. Probably designed by William Kent the house stood on ground owned and developed by Lord Burlington in the period 1720-30; the street was also named after his wife, Dorothy's maiden name Savile. This picture was taken in 1922 and the building was demolished in 1938. Savile Row was always a fashionable street in a smart area; the façade of the house reveals changes in taste with the first floor central windows being lowed to an inserted balcony, c.1810, and the replacement of the glazing bars of the windows with plate glass c.1840. It is rare to see where a successful cabinet-maker/carver and gilder would live and work; John Linnell who worked for Adam later in the century lived and worked in nearby Berkeley Sq. Courtesy of the London Metropolitan Archive.

a set of vertical supports to the leather-topped tables. As the furniture was paid for by Lady Burlington, Kent incorporated her Savile family crest depicting an owl. The immensely rich tables are made from mahogany with gilded, carved ornament while the gilded mirrors are carved pine. They are superb examples of English cabinet work, in its widest sense, and whilst it was unusual for such tables to be made by a carver and gilder, the mirrors are typical of their work.

The use of Kentian ornament has often created much discussion and confusion concerning the attribution of furniture to individual makers. Benjamin Goodison, for example, was a Royal Cabinet-maker whose name is often associated with furniture to Kent's designs for houses with which he was closely involved, such as Holkham in Norfolk. With such a small group, the question of attribution is always going to arise in the absence of a signature or a bill which can be securely fixed to a particular item.

A pair of gilded wood pedestals attributed to either John Boson or Benjamin Goodison. The pedestals are in the form of classical Roman religious boundary markers, or terms, a pattern much favoured by Lord Burlington and William Kent; it is possible that the pedestals were actually designed by Kent. The pair is very similar to a pair at Chatsworth, Derbyshire that had come originally from Chiswick, having been made by John Boson for Lady Burlington. They are made from blocks of softwood glued together and then carved and then gilded using both oil and water-gilding – water gilding allowed a greater degree of bright burnishing but was more fragile, while the oil gilding created a different coloured surface. It is difficult to differentiate between Boson and Goodison's work but due to this pairs' similarity to the Lady Burlington set – which have their receipt signed by Boson and dated 11th September 1735 – it may be that this pair were also made by Boson. Note the total lack of decoration on the back and the reduced work on the sides. c.1735. 50" H; tops 11" sq. Courtesy of Christie's. Lot No 250 Sale No 1359

A giltwood pier glass. This is an excellent example of Kentian design; almost an archetype. The strongly architectural feel, the scrolled pediment and the use of classical ornament such as egg & dart, husks and serpentine foliage. The plate, as the mirror glass is called, is original and has an expensive bevelled edge; the plate's flattering dark colour is due to the original mercury "silvering". The frame has been attributed to the work of the carver John Boson and was almost certainly supplied to the 4th Earl of Shaftsbury's seat at St Giles House, Dorset. c.1735. 48$\frac{1}{2}$" H; 27$\frac{1}{2}$" W. Courtesy of Christie's. Lot No 12 Sale No 6462

The Picture Gallery, Longford Castle, Wiltshire. This view, looking east, was taken in 1930 and shows the Gallery as it was after a restoration of c.1870, but still largely unchanged from its original furnishing in c.1740. Benjamin Goodison made the furniture for this long gallery displaying paintings, while the upholsterer was William Kilpin. The suite consists of two large day beds 8ft 6" long two long six-legged stools, each 5ft 4" long and eight smaller four-legged stools. All were upholstered in green silk damask. The "quilted" nature of the shallow tufting of the cushions is very clear in this evocative photograph. Country Life Picture Library.

Benjamin Goodison
(1700-1767)

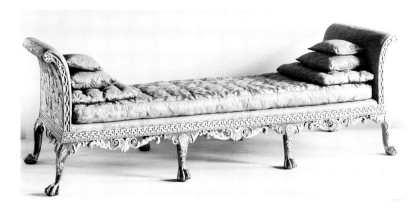

Carved and "party gilt" mahogany day-bed, upholstered in green silk damask, and made by Benjamin Goodison, 1740

Carved giltwood pier glass, attributed to Benjamin Goodison, c.1740

Fustic and padouk card table, attributed to Benjamin Goodison, c.1757

Benjamin Goodison was a cabinet-maker in Royal service from 1726 until his death in 1767. Thus he saw considerable changes in fashion and taste during the time of the first three Georges: from the French stimulus to design when Goodison was apprenticed to his master James Moore – also a Royal Cabinet-maker – through William Kent's Italianate style of the 1730's and 40's and back to a less strongly French-influenced and eclectic gothick and chinoiserie fashion, drawn in design books such as Chippendale's *Director* that appeared towards the end of Goodison's life.

Besides being a cabinet-maker, Benjamin Goodison also dealt in second-hand furniture; he made and supplied walnut, mahogany, carved and gilded furniture for Royal palaces and yachts; he could also provide light fittings such as the great brass lantern for the Queen's Staircase, Hampton Court, in 1729 at a cost of £138. It still hangs there today. All this came from his home and workshop in Long Acre, off Covent Garden, an area of 18th Century London noted for quality cabinet-makers, coach-builders and other luxury trades. Such large scale firms as Goodison's were often known as upholsterers or undertakers. The latter term was also used in the modern sense as they could arrange funerals as well. Indeed in 1751 Goodison provided 80 large black candle-sticks when he staged the funeral of Frederick, Prince of Wales, in the Henry VII Chapel of Westminster

Abbey. When Goodison died, his business was taken over by his nephew, who had also been one of his apprentices. He formed a partnership with Goodison's son in which the supply of funeral services was a prominent part. Goodison left £16,000, a large house in Mitcham, Surrey, as well as his central London workshop.

So Goodison was a successful businessman, but Royal contracts could be fickle and very slow in paying for work carried out; delays of years were not uncommon. Being in Royal service did, however, bring some benefits in that the firm's name became widely known, especially in aristocratic circles; not that they were any quicker in paying. Payment was always a problem for 18th Century cabinet-makers, as the slow settling of accounts led to cash-flow problems in the paying of suppliers and the workforce. Thus it was one of the main contributions to the numerous bankruptcies that plagued businesses. Even Thomas Chippendale went bust due to the death of his then business partner.

It was word of mouth that was the most significant aspect of many businesses – not unlike today. Thus it was that when Goodison took over from his master in 1726, he also acquired his list of customers, including the formidable Sarah, Duchess of Marlborough and then, via her, he was introduced to more clients. Most notable was the

A giltwood pier glass. Compared to [Lot No 12 Sale No 6462] this mirror is less obviously Kent inspired, although the plumed mask of Diana is rather Kentian. The glass has been attributed to the hand of Benjamin Goodison as it is related to a group of three mirrors at Goodwood, Sussex. The plate itself is a later replacement and the frame has been regilded. 48" H; 32¹/₂" W. Courtesy of Christie's. Lot No 289 Sale No 1359

Duchess's son-in-law John, Duke of Montague and his family. Montague not only had a house in Whitehall but also a grand French-style country seat, Boughton House, in Northamptonshire. Another of the Duchess of Marlborough's children, a daughter, lived at Althorp, also in Northamptonshire for which Goodison probably supplied furniture, as he drew up an inventory of the house contents – yet another aspect of the cabinet-making/upholstery trade.

Amongst Goodison's most famous items of firmly attributed furniture is a matching set of two large, scroll-ended day-beds, two large stools and eight smaller ones, made for the gallery of Longford Castle, Wiltshire, the seat of Viscount Folkestone, at a cost of £400. They are made of mahogany and raised on short, bold cabriole legs with hairy lion's paw feet. The set has carved gilt enrichment and had green silk damask upholstery with an applied Greek-key fret along the seat-rails, fixed over the damask. The large day-beds still have their original piled, graduated cushions. The cushions for the complete set have shallow tufting, giving them a quilted look. In 1740 when they were made, the silk damask cost 12/- (60p) per yard; this at a time when a curate would consider himself fortunate if he received £30 a year and a footman might be paid about £3 a year. This rich set of furniture displays design features reminiscent of William Kent, such as the gilded enrichment of the mahogany and the Greek-key pattern,

but they were certainly not designed by him. However Kent and Goodison came together at Holkham in Norfolk, for another of Lord Burlington's circle, Sir Thomas Coke, later Earl of Leicester.

Various items at Holkham, probably by Kent, are listed in the household accounts, starting with mahogany stools for "ye temple at Holkham" in 1739. At the same time Goodison was paid 12/- (60p) for repairing and fixing the water-closet seat in the London house. After Kent's death in 1748 Goodison carried on working for Lord Leicester, supplying in 1757 an elaborate carved gilded frame for a painting by the Italian Old Master, Pietro da Cortona. The frame cost £74!

Goodison was a top-class cabinet-maker, but the vast range of services that his firm offered and the versatility of the media in which he worked, have only served to make more difficult absolute attributions to him for individual items, despite the wealth of surviving bills and receipts.

A George II pedestal made from softwood and lime. Here it is possible to see what a gilded, or painted pedestal looked like before decoration. The main material used for the carcase is a softwood, almost certainly of Baltic origin; this is slow growing timber due to the cold climate and has close growth rings producing wood that is strong but easy to work. The carved decoration is made from lime, a hard, dense, grainless wood excellent for such work. No item of good furniture would have been left naked like this, such an inferior timber would always have been painted or gilded, or both. The pedestal was probably intended for a large sculpture or bust. It is related to a similar example at the Earl Spencer's seat, Althorp, Northamptonshire, and almost certainly supplied by Benjamin Goodison. c.1743. 56" H; 37" W; 22¹/₂" D. Courtesy of Christie's. Lot No 268 Sale No 1359

A pair of giltwood pedestals, or terms. These have been attributed to Benjamin Goodison and may be compared to [Lot No 250 Sale No 1359] to see the difficulties of attribution. The Ionic capitals are replacements and they do seem too large in proportion. c.1740. 51" H; tops 14sq. Courtesy of Christie's. Lot No 92 Sale No 9590

Biography:

Robert Adam
(1728-1792)

Moor Park Suite sofa, designed by Robert Adam for Sir Lawrence Dundas, 1764

Giltwood armchair designed by Robert Adam for Sir Lawrence Dundas and made by Thomas Chippendale for 19 Arlington St, London, 1764

Armchair from the Moor Park Suite, 1764

Opposite: *A view into the Library, Kenwood, Hampstead, north London. Designed by Robert Adam for Lord Mansfield, 1764-79. Courtesy of English Heritage. J900502*

Robert Adam was an architect and designer, and like Inigo Jones and William Kent the young Scot spent some years studying in Italy. He was the second son of the successful Edinburgh architect, William Adam.

After the death of William Kent in 1748, fashion, especially as regards home decoration, became quite eclectic and diverse. A re-discovery of "gothick" – as it was spelt in the 18th Century – had been espoused by Kent as early as the 1730's for his Hampton Court Clock Court Gateway of 1732. But the exotic Chinese-influenced flummery enjoyed a brief fashion during the late 1750's and 60's while the French vogue for curly, curvilinear rococo was popular during the same period. It was possible to see all of these styles within one house which may also have observed Palladian rules for its exterior architecture. They were just decorative styles after all. But with Robert Adam it was different. In the words of the furniture historian Ralph Edwards, Adam "was one of those who believed that the minutiae of decoration and furnishing were within the province of the architect, and that only thus could a complete and consistent result be obtained."

Robert Adam's father died in 1748 and he went into partnership with his elder brother John, to continue their father's architectural practice. Almost immediately the brothers were involved with the building and repair of Highland forts after the 1745 Jacobite Rebellion. They had been appointed Royal master masons and were therefore the contractors for the imposing Fort George, near Inverness, and, as part of this project, Robert Adam met the water colourist Paul Sandby. Sandby was drawing master at Woolwich Arsenal. Drawing landscapes and topography was a vital skill for 18th and 19th Century military engineers and artillerymen, as it taught them to look closely at geography to better place encampments and site their guns. From Sandby, Adam learnt about the "Picturesque" ideas in landscape as a concept for architecture, and the style had a great impact and influence upon Adam.

The next stage in Robert Adam's education was to go to Italy, which he did aged 26 in 1754. Reaching Rome in 1755, he stayed there until 1757. He fell in with a group of men attached to the French Academy in Rome, notably Charles-Louis Clérisseau, Jean-Baptiste Lallemand, Laurent-Benôit Dewez and to a lesser extent the architect/engraver G. B. Piranesi. Adam, in particular with Clérisseau, went on many sketching trips to see the Classical Roman sites around southern Italy. Adam was keen to be thought of as a dilettanti gentleman-of-means rather than a working architect with a practice in Edinburgh, thinking that he could learn more than someone who might become a rival artist.

Adam returned to Britain and in 1758 set up a London office in Lower Grosvenor Street, close to ultra-fashionable Grosvenor Square and Bond Street. No longer the provincial Scottish architect, Adam was now a man of fashion who was going places, to create "the Antique, the Noble & Stupendous". Years later in 1812, Sir John Soane said in a lecture,

"The light and elegant ornaments, the varied compartments in the ceilings of Mr Adam, imitated from Ancient Works in the Baths and Villas of the Romans, were soon applied in designs for chairs, tables, carpets and in every other species of furniture. To Mr Adam's taste in the ornament of his buildings and furniture we stand indebted, inasmuch as manufacturers of every kind felt, as it were, the electric power of this revolution in art."

Robert Adam was given the nickname "Bob the Roman". All the various mixed styles, rococo, chinoiserie, gothick, rustic etc., were soon abandoned in favour of the new neo-classical mode; even as the 3rd edition of Chippendale's *Director* was going to print in 1762 many of the designs were out of date!

Amongst the earliest of Robert Adam's furniture designs was a set of two sofas, two stools and six arm-chairs, carved and gilded, made for Sir Lawrence Dundas's house, Moor Park in Hertfordshire, in 1764 by the cabinet-maker James Lawson. Sir Lawrence Dundas

Left:
Sopha for Sir Lawrence Dundas, Baronet. Robert Adam usually supplied his main clients with drawings of his ideas. This fully worked-up water-colour design was executed by one of Adam's team of "articifers" and he charged Dundas £5 for the design in 1764. There were to be four large sofas and eight armchairs for The Great Room, 19 Arlington St, London home of Dundas. The suite was made by Thomas Chippendale and on 9th July 1765 he charged Dundas £216 for the four sofas; this at a time when a curate was paid £30 a year, a footman half that and Chippendale himself might charge 1/- for a pine stool. Courtesy of Sir John Soane's Museum.

Opposite:
The Great Drawing Room, Audley End, near Saffron Walden, Essex. Designed by Robert Adam in 1763-65 for Sir John Griffin Griffin. The superb neo-classical plaster ceiling was made by Joseph Rose who worked on many of Adam's projects. Courtesy of English Heritage. J960205

(1712-1781) was an established Edinburgh wine-merchant when he became an army contractor at the time of the 1745 Jacobite uprising. He supplied the army with all types of stores, food etc. and made an immense fortune; he acquired the soubriquet "The Nabob of the North". Dundas was prominent in supplying the troops at Fort George at the same time that it was being built by Robert Adam and his brother. By 1763 Dundas had earned even more money from various military adventures on the Continent and had set about establishing himself. Thus he acquired the Moor Park estate close to London for £25,000 and a London house in Arlington Street, St James's, for £15,000, both considerable sums for their day. Dundas then employed his old acquaintance Robert Adam to design new, fashionable furniture for the late 17th Century Moor Park and to update the London house. Thus Adam produced a set of neo-classically ornamented seat furniture to fit into the baroque Palladian Banqueting Hall of Moor Park, with its painted and panelled walls and ceilings.

Adam's design was both advanced in concept and backward-looking in shape and classical embellishment. The chairs' shape leant heavily on the then current patterns for large upholstered chairs but with an overlay of neo-classical ornament, such as the bold rams, heads set on top of the front legs, which themselves end in brass cloven sheep's hoof feet. The chairs do look quite odd and have unusual proportions, being wide and shallow in depth. The sofas have humped backs and scrolled arms and were fitted with loose cylindrical cushions. The stools have no backs; they are really what we call today window seats for they were designed to fit into the recesses of the window bays within the room.

The chairs are made from carved and gilded softwood, probably pine imported from the Baltic. The applied decoration of a gilded running, or continuous guilloche is carved from limewood. The hidden seat-rails are of beech, the favoured secondary timber for chairs; it is rarely used as a primary wood as beech has no figure or pattern and is thus rather dull unless it is painted to look like a more expensive wood. The feet have castors hidden inside the brass hooves; this was a most unusual feature as it meant that the chairs were originally designed to be moved around the room and not left in an almost static position, as was the norm. As befits dining room furniture, the upholstery was originally of blue leather, as leather does not pick up the smell of cooked foods as fabric can do. Although originally described in the 1764 receipt as "Turkey leather", the skins used on the upholstery were from large goats that were bred in North Africa and as such, was also sometimes described as Morocco leather. No springs were used in the upholstery of the seats for the simple reason that metal springs for general upholstery did not appear until after 1840 with the introduction of the appropriate metal technology.

James Lawson charged Dundas the considerable sum of £12-10s-5d per chair and the total bill for the whole suite was £187-5s-0d. This was a time when a simple pine stool might cost 1/- (5p) from Thomas Chippendale and a cook might be paid around £6 a year, while a skilled tradesman might be on 2/- (10p) per 12 hour day. Lawson then went on to charge £9-13s to make large packing cases for the suite and £1-16s for a "Man sent to Moor Park to unpack" from his Covent Garden workshop. Little is known of James Lawson as a cabinet-maker. Surviving bills and receipts show him not to have been at the

Robert Adam, an oil painting attributed to George Willison. c.1773. Seated on a close nailed "Gainsborough" library chair, upholstered in blue damask Adam is revealed at the height of his fame, wearing a plain, lapelled frock coat, a double breasted silk waist-coat edged with gold braid. This is a slightly more formal portrait than that of William Kent, as Adam is also wearing a pointed toupee wig with single curls, a style popular for some ten years when he sat for this picture. National Portrait Gallery

forefront of fashion; rather he supplied furnishings for lesser rooms but still for clients such as Dundas at his London and Yorkshire properties, and for Sir Edward Knatchbull at Mersham-le-Hatch, also designed by Adam and for which Chippendale, Samuel Norman and other front rank cabinet-makers made furniture. Lawson must have been trusted though by both Adam as designer and Dundas as client to make such a valuable suite of furniture. Dundas may have been exceedingly wealthy, but he was well aware of the dangers of being over-charged. Indeed he successfully disputed a large bill put in by Samuel Norman in 1763. Norman had submitted a bill for £2,700 but Dundas had it reduced by nearly £300 when it was inspected by independent assessors, amongst whom was Thomas Chippendale.

From Moor Park, Adam went on to design famous pure neo-classical interiors such as the Library at Kenwood at Hampstead, now in London, for another Scotsman, the Lord Chief Justice Lord Mansfield in 1764 and the drastic alteration of the 16th Century house at Osterley, Middlesex, for the Child family from 1761 to 1777 with most of the interior work during the period 1767-72. The Dundas connection may also have introduced Adam to Yorkshire, for he had an important house, Aske Hall, for which Adam supplied designs and went on to create other neo-classical houses in that county, especially at Nostell Priory, Newby and Harewood. For these houses the Yorkshireman Thomas Chippendale supplied much of the furniture.

Robert Adam's late work was mostly in Scotland where he developed his picturesque style that he had seen with Paul Sandby over 30 years before. He did little in England other than develop, with his brothers, the Fitzroy Square area of London, known today as Fitzrovia. He died, aged only 64, in March 1792, in Albemarle Street Piccadilly, quite possibly from a stomach ulcer. Amongst the pall-bearers at his funeral in Westminster Abbey were a duke, two earls and two lords – a sign of Adam's standing in society.

Adam was a hugely influential architect/designer, but not everyone was enamoured. Even during his lifetime there was criticism and after his death the fashion for the neo-classical continued, but often in much debased form. His style is instantly recognisable but is not that easy to copy. By the late 19th Century there grew up a watered-down, emasculated form still known as "Adams" and the misunderstanding is still common 200 years after his death.

Thus from Adam's career it is possible to see how 18th Century patronage worked, both up and down the social scale. Scottish connections helped him to go to Italy and then helped when he returned to Britain. Then Scotland helped again, as it were, to introduce him to Yorkshire. While Adam could find the commissions, he still needed the craftsmen to execute the designs and again Scottish connections were useful, for example his designs for cast iron fire-places etc. were made in Falkirk by Carron & Co, while from Yorkshire, of course, there came Thomas Chippendale.

A fine gilt-wood arm-chair in the French style, made by Gordon & Tait, c.1773. The upholstery is a modern copy of the original three coloured silk damask. Note how the pattern of the fabric runs, almost seamlessly up the chair, and onto the wall covering. The Great Drawing Room, Audley End, Essex. Courtesy of English Heritage. J860060

One of the Moor Park Suite chairs, designed by Robert Adam, made by James Lawson in 1764 for the Entrance Hall-cum-Banqueting Hall of Sir Lawrence Dundas' Moor Park, Hertfordshire. This shows the chair as recovered in blue leather as per the original receipt. Courtesy of English Heritage. J890404

Detail of a Moor Park chair. The rams head was carved separately and then applied over the upholstery as were the "running guilloche" decoration on the seat rail and the curving, pierced entrelac band on the arms. Courtesy of English Heritage. J890405

Back of one of the Moor Park chairs with the outer covering of later upholstery removed to reveal the 1764 work. It is just possible to see one of the blue threads from the original tufting. Also of interest, in view of their considerable cost in 1764, is the rather crude woodwork of the top rail. Courtesy of English Heritage.

Detail of the original 1764 upholstery from one of the Moor Park chairs. Note the striped webbing, typical of eighteenth century English upholstery. See also the extensive damage to the wooden frame caused by the tacks used to fix later upholstery. Courtesy of English Heritage. Moor Pk 4004

Sketch for a scroll sofa by Robert Adam. This sketch is almost certainly an early proposal for the furniture to be made for Sir Lawrence Dundas's house, Moor Park, Hertfordshire. The detail of the moulding is the type of detail that would have been added to the design as used by the maker. c.1763. Courtesy of Sir John Soane's Museum.

Gilded beech and softwood sofa, part of the large set of two sofas, six armchairs and two scroll-ended stools designed by Robert Adam for Sir Lawrence Dundas in 1764. As befitted furniture to be used in a dining room the suite was upholstered in leather, a material that does not pick-up the smell of cooking as ordinary cloth will do. Courtesy of English Heritage. J920203

One of the "2 large carved and gilt scroll stools, at £20-2s-6d each" by James Lawson to Robert Adam's design in 1764 for Sir Lawrence Dundas. Courtesy of English Heritage. Moor Pk 2002

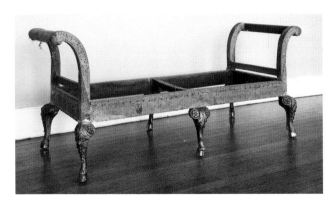

Beech wood frame of the sofa with all the upholstery removed prior to conservation. Courtesy of English Heritage. Moor Pk 3003

A pair of gilt chairs, in the French manner, made by Thomas Chippendale for the 1st Lord Melbourne's Brocket Hall, Hertfordshire, c.1733. These chairs have what Christopher Gilbert, in his Life and Works of Thomas Chippendale, 1978, defined as the "uniform character" of Chippendale's chairs. They have the constructional features thought to be characteristic of his workshop, that is, exposed back struts behind the upholstered backs, cramp-cuts for gluing and batten holes for fixing the chair into a packing case. Furthermore, although Chippendale used a basic array of decorative elements for chairs at this period, 1765-75, he never repeated the same permutation twice. Courtesy of Christie's. Lot No 106 Sale No 6648

Biography:

Thomas Chippendale
(1718-1779)

Mahogany hall chair, c.1765

Mahogany breakfast table, c.1770

Mahogany serpentine commode with ormolu mounts, c.1770

Mahogany library chair "in the Chinese Manner", c.1760

Thomas Chippendale's
Furnishing Commissions 1747-1779

1. **Alscot Park**, Warks. for James West 1760-67

2. **Appuldurcombe House**, Isle of Wight for Sir Richard Worsley 1776-78

3. **Arniston**, Midlothian for Lord Arniston 1757

4. **Aske Hall**, Yorks. for Sir Laurence Dundas 1763-66 also his London house at 19 Arlington St.

5. **Audley End**, Essex for Sir John Griffin Griffin 1774

6. **Badminton House**, Glos. for the Duchess of Beaufort 1764

7. **Blair Castle**, Perthshire for the Duke of Athol 1758

8. **Boreham House**, Essex for Richard Hoare 1767-76

9. **Boynton Hall**, Yorks. for George Strickland 1767

10. **Brighton**, Castle Hotel Assembly Room 1777

11. **Brockenhurst Park**, Hants. for Edward Morant 1769

12. **Brocket Hall**, Herts. for Lord Melbourne 1771-76

13. **Burton Constable**, Yorks. for William Constable 1768-79 also his London house in Mansfield St.

14. **Cannon Hall**, Yorks. for John Spencer 1768

15. **Christ Church College**, Oxford 1764

16. **Claydon House**, Bucks. for Earl Verney 1766.71

17. **Corsham Court**, Wilts. for Paul Methuen 1779

18. **Cranford Park**, Middlx. for the Countess of Berkeley 1761

19. **Croome Court**, Worcs. for the Earl of Coventry 1764-70 and his London house 29 Piccadilly

20. **Dalmahoy**, Midlothian for the 14th Earl of Morton 1762

21. **Dalton Hall**, Yorks. for Sir Charles Hotham-Thompson 1777

22. **Denton Hall**, Yorks. for James Ibbetson c1778

23. **Dumfries House**, Ayrshire for the 5th Earl of Dumfries 1759-66

24. **East Sutton Park**, Kent for Sir Brook Bridges 1765

25. **Foremark Hall**, Debs. for Sir Robert Burdett 1766-74

26. **Goldsborough Hall**, Yorks. for Daniel Lascelles 1771-76

27. **Goodnestone**, Kent for Sir Brook Bridges 1765

28. **Hampton**, Middlx. for David Garrick's Villa 1768-78

29. **Harewood House**, Yorks. for Edwin Lascelles 1769-76

30. **Hestercombe House**, Somerset for Coplestone Ware Bampfylde nd.

31. **Langton Hall**, Yorks. for Thomas Norcliffe 1767

32. **London**
   - **Burlington House** for 3rd Earl of Burlington 1747 and for the Duke of Portland 1766
   - **Browne's House**, Fulham and Grosvenor Square for Sir Gilbert Heathcote 1768-79
   - **Carlisle House**, Soho Square for Mrs Cornelys 1772
   - **Cleveland Court** for George Selwyn 1772
   - **Gloucester House** for Prince Henry, 1st Duke of Gloucester 1764-66
   - **Landsdowne House** for the Earl of Shelburne 1768-69
   - **Middlesex Hospital** 1767
   - **Melbourne House** for Viscount Melbourne 1771-76
   - **26 Soho Square** and **Glasshouse St.** for Sir William Robinson 1759-65
   - **27 Southampton St.** and **5 Royal Adelphi Terrace** for David Garrick 1768-78

33. **Kenwood House**, Middlx. for the 1st Earl of Mansfield 1769

34. **Mersham Le Hatch**, Kent for Sir Edward Knatchbull 1767-79

35. **Newby Hall**, Yorks. for William Weddell c1772-76

36. **Normanton Hall**, Rutland for Sir Gilbert Heathcote 1768-79

37. **Nostell Priory**, Yorks. for Sir Rowland Winn from 1766-79 and also his London house at 11 St James's Square

38. **Paxton House**, Berwickshire for Ninian Home 1774

39. **Petworth House**, Sussex for the Earl of Egremont 1777-78

40. **Rousham House**, Oxon. for Sir Charles Cotterell-Dormer 1764

41. **Saltram House** Devon for Lord Boringdon 1771

42. **Sandon Hall**, Staffs. for the Earl of Harrowby 1763-77

43. **Sherbourne Castle**, Dorset for Earl Digby 1774

44. **Shetland Is.**, Scotland commission for Thomas Mouat 1775

45. **Stowe House**, Bucks. for Earl Temple 1757

46. **Temple Newsam House**, Yorks. for Viscount Irwin 1774

47. **Thoresby Park**, Notts. For the Duke of Kingston 1770

48. **Wilton House**, Wilts. for the Earl of Pembroke 1762-73, also his London house, Pembroke House

49. **Wimpole Hall**, Cambs. for the Earl of Hardwicke 1777

50. **Wolverley House**, Worcs. for Edward Knight Jr. 1763-69

Thomas Chippendale's Furnishing Commissions, 1747-1779. Thomas Chippendale was prepared to go anywhere if the business required it, but it is noticeable from this map that there are three main clusters; London, where the workshops were, Yorkshire, where he grew up and where one of his first major clients, Sir Lawrence Dundas, had a house and thirdly, Scotland where his first partner, Rannie, came from and where Dundas also had many connections. With a few exceptions the country houses are quite close to navigable water, which substantially reduced transport costs; for example No.47, Saltram House is very close to Plymouth and the house overlooks one of the inlets off Plymouth Sound, while Burton Constable, No.13, is close to Hull. Although Aske Hall, No.4, is some way from navigable water. The Scottish links must have come from principally from James Rannie, once a wine merchant, like the partners grand client Dundas, and the business "tentacles" that came with supplying the gentry with quality merchandise such as wine and spirits. Obviously much of Chippendale's business was in London as it was the centre of political power and fashion. In consequence a number of major commissions were not only for London houses but for their related country seats, for example Lord Melbourne's Brocket Hall, No.12, in Hertfordshire, and Melbourne House, Piccadilly, while for Sir Lawrence Dundas Chippendale furnished 19 Arlington St, Piccadilly, and Aske Hall, in Yorkshire but interestingly not Moor Park, Hertfordshire, another grand Dundas house, close to London.

Left:

A mahogany tripod table with an octagonal, galleried top. The dark coloured timber from which this table is made illustrates very well why mahogany became so popular, for the wood carves easily but is also hard and takes a superb, lustrous wax polish. The pieced fret-work gallery is unusual for a tripod table. The gallery was made by gluing together three strips of mahogany, to create a laminate. The central strip is set with the grain lying vertically to give it strength. The pattern is then fretted out using a special saw. This particular pattern is close to Plate VII of J. Crunden's The Joyner and Cabinet-Maker's Darling, 1765. Chippendale and others provided many variations for fret and blind-fret patterns, often either gothick or chinoiserie in style. c.1765. 30" H; 28¹/₂" W. Courtesy of Norman Adams.

Opposite Page:

Detail of the fluted column and acanthus leaf carved baluster of the galleried tripod table. Courtesy of Norman Adams

Right:

An almost severely plain, but very handsome mahogany pedestal cupboard; the only decoration is bold gadroon edge to the top. Possibly one of a pair, such a cupboard, masquerading as a narrow chest of drawers, would have stood either side of a sideboard, supporting urn-shaped knife cases. The top three "drawers" swing out to reveal cupboard space while the lower two combine with the plinth to slide forward on castors exposing a deep drawer with a removable oak liner. This may have been intended to take the dirty plates and cutlery before carrying them down to the scullery. c.1760. 27¹/₂₄" H; 16¹/₂" sq. Courtesy of Norman Adams.

Thomas Chippendale is a name which stands out as a byword for almost all 18th Century English – and American – furniture. There is even a statue of him on the façade of the Victoria & Albert Museum in South Kensington.

He was born the son of a village joiner in Otley, West Yorkshire (it is intriguing how very strong the influence of that county was upon English furniture history). Relatively little is known of his early life until 1748 when he was married to Catherine Redshaw at St. George's Chapel, Mayfair. Unlike the designers and architects of his generation (William Kent, Sir William Chambers, Robert Adam, etc.) Chippendale never went abroad to Italy, but he did visit France at least once and had business contacts there. Despite this he went on to become the owner of a considerable business, catering to a wide section of society. Although he was never an appointed Royal Cabinet-maker, he supplied many members of the aristocracy, especially in his native county, Yorkshire. He had extensive workshops in St Martin's Lane, close to what is now Trafalgar Square, London.

Chippendale was an excellent practical cabinet-maker who knew well how to make furniture. It is likely that he served an apprenticeship in York before coming down to London where, on his arrival, he may also have had drawing tuition from the noted engraver Mathias Darley. In one real sense it is for Chippendale's design and draughtsmanship skills that his name is still so well known. In 1754 with a financial partner, James Rannie, he published a large folio volume *The Gentleman & Cabinet-Maker's Director*. A second edition came out a year later and the most important 3rd edition was published as a part-work between 1759 and 1762.

In 1747 Chippendale received payment of £6-16s from Lord Burlington; sadly the items were not specified, but the furniture was probably for Chiswick House. This was a year before William Kent died and is perhaps evidence that a Yorkshire association was at work; Kent was from Bridlington, East Yorkshire and Lord Burlington had his principle country seat at Londesborough, near Bridlington. There is a suggestion that Burlington is an old form of pronunciation for Bridlington. Burlington designed the York Assembly Rooms in 1731-2,

A mahogany and fustic breakfast table. The basic form of this table can be seen in Pl. LVII of the 1764 3rd edition of Chippendale's Director. Henry VIII had a "brekefaste table of walnutree" as long ago as 1544 but the concept regained some measure of popularity via Chippendale's book. The cage beneath the drop-leaf top was either a wooden fretwork – often chinoiserie in style – or of twisted wire-work, usually in a honeycomb pattern. It is probable that such items were part of the furnishings of a "Lady's boudoir"(George Smith, Household Furniture, 1808). c.1770. 28" H; 42" W open; 24" D Courtesy of Christie's. Lot No 20 Sale No 6045

at the time that Chippendale was probably apprenticed to a York cabinet-maker Richard Wood, who years later would subscribe to eight copies if the 1st edition of the *Director* in 1754. The fact that as early as 1747 Chippendale was already supplying "Persons of Distinction", may well indicate his ambition to succeed in London.

By 1754 Chippendale was established in St Martin's Lane, a site that he and his eldest son, also Thomas, kept on for nearly 60 years. He had by then entered into partnership with a Scottish merchant, James Rannie. It was Rannie who provided the capital that was so necessary to run any business. By 1755 Chippendale and Rannie had a substantial enterprise, due in no small part to the success of the *Director*.

However in 1766 Rannie died and his executors withdrew his capital, plunging Chippendale into dire straits. He was forced to hold an auction in St Martin's Lane of all the partnership's stock including

"a great Variety of fine Mahogany and Tulip Wood, Cabinets, Desks, and Book-Cases, Cloathes Presses, double Chests of Drawers, Commodes, Buroes, fine Library, Writing, Card, Dining and other

Tables, Turkey and other Carpets, one of which is 13 Feet by 19 Feet six, fine Pattern chairs, and sundry other Pieces of Curious Cabinet Work, a large Parcel of fine Season'd Feathers; as also the large unwrought stock of fine Mahogany and other Woods, in Plank, Boards, Vanier, and Wainscot."

This enforced sale almost broke Chippendale but he survived and took on as a new partner Thomas Haig, who had been Rannie's book-keeper and so was someone who knew intimately how the business was run and organised. Haig stayed in London looking after the business and money while Chippendale went out to see clients in London and all over the country, as well as keeping an eye on the quality of work being done in the workshops. However, years later, when Haig died in 1804 and Chippendale's son, Thomas Junior, was running the firm, lightening struck again, but this time Thomas Junior was forced into bankruptcy. The firm did survive again however to close down finally in 1823 with Thomas Junior's death. Such financial precariousness was common in the 18th Century due in many cases to cash-flow problems

The Tool Chest of Benjamin Seaton, 1797. This remarkable survival of an almost complete eighteenth century tool box was made by Seaton to house a set of tools given to him by his father, Joseph, a cabinet maker in Chatham, Kent. The tools cost the considerable sum of £15-10s-4d and Seaton junior made an inventory of them all with the cost of each item. He then spent some weeks making the chest with a softwood exterior and a mahogany veneered and crossbanded interior, so typical of skilled tradesmen's tool boxes, the source of their livelihood. In the picture can be seen the six saws held in place within the lid. A plough plane and five moulding planes sit upon the inlaid sliding till which holds many more tools such as chisels etc. On the floor in front of the chest are a jointer and a try plane, two smoothing planes, a button chuck brace, two marking gauges, another moulding plane, a cock bead fillister and a chisel. There were about 200 tools and Benjamin Seaton added another 60, some of which he had made himself. Family tradition has it that the tools were a gift toward Benjamin immigrating to the Untied States, but for some reason he never went and the chest stayed together and did not suffer the usual fate of such boxes, being worked to destruction. The chest may be seen today in the Guildhall Museum, Rochester, Kent. Photography courtesy of the Tools & Trades History Society.

and a lack of financial expertise. It was endemic in the cabinet-making and upholstery world for clients to be slow in settling debts and it is known from surviving letters that occasionally Chippendale did not have the cash to pay his men on a Saturday, so tight were his reserves.

The 1766 sale reveals Thomas Chippendale's wide ranging business. The frontage on to St Martin's Lane was three houses wide: no. 62 for James Rannie, no. 61 was a shop, while Chippendale and his family lived in no. 60. There was a covered wagon-way between nos. 60 and 61 which led into a courtyard of considerable size with two and three storey brick and clapboard buildings. Such complexes were once quite common in the Soho, Covent Garden and Tottenham Court Road areas of London, but have now been developed out of existence since the 1960's. This hidden world of 18th Century commerce was in part revealed when a fire burnt out part of the site in 1755 – two months after insurance had been taken out with the Sun Office. Nothing should be read into this as fire was a constant risk to all cabinet-makers due to the dust, dry timber, boiling pots of glue on stoves etc. The Sun paid out £847-12s-6d but 22 tool-chests were lost. Each tradesman had his own tool-chest, usually made by the man himself and often with very fine interiors full of perhaps 50 to 100 planes of various shapes, hammers, saws, chisels and special tools also made by the owner. Therefore to lose such a chest was to lose one's livelihood. Chippendale and Rannie organised a fund to raise money for the men as the chests were not insured. They advertised in coffee-houses in the City and West End asking for donations.

The loss of the 22 tool-chests probably represents about half the workforce employed by Chippendale. It appears that there were few apprentices; only three are known. This may have been because these young men were notoriously unruly; there was the perception that too often they were fighting other apprentices, or rioting about one thing or another, even playing football. Masters of any trade demanded a fee for apprenticeship that usually reflected the level of potential earnings. About £10 to £20 was normal for a cabinet-maker, from £20 to £50 for upholsterers, while Mayhew & Ince were once paid a huge £210 in fees by Samuel Hemingway in 1775.

To keep 40 to 50 journeyman cabinet-makers in work required many things; after orders from clients, there must come a good supply of timber. Here Chippendale's large yard was a boon. He arranged for the timber stock to be stored on the roof of one of the workshops which in turn was covered over. While the forced sale of timber after Rannie's death might have helped in reducing the stock of second-hand furniture, it must have been hard to have sold off his reserve of precious inlays, veneers (spelt "vaniers" in the auction advertisement) and other choice woods. Most of the timber, such as mahogany and tulipwood was of course imported, but Chippendale was quite happy to buy "walnut tree slabs" from one of his customers, Sir Edward

Knatchbull, in 1770 at 7d a foot. Softwood for some carved work and a base wood for veneering, was also imported, usually from Norway or the Baltic area.

The yard was split into a number of specialist "shops". There was a cabinet shop, a chair room, a carving and gilding shop, a glass store (where glass could be stored and cut) a metalwork shop, plus other store-rooms for marble slabs, china and glassware, wallpapers, carpets, feathers, and upholstery work-rooms for setting up beds, curtains etc. Chippendale needed large airy rooms to carry out much of his business. There would also have been a "counting house" or office, where Rannie, and later Haig, would keep track of sending out bills and receipts for work.

The cabinet shop was in a sense the heart of the business; it was here that the tables and cabinet-pieces were made, the chests of drawers, bureaux, clothes presses etc. However fine marquetry and veneering were done in a different area. As marquetry was a specialist trade it is quite possible that Chippendale sub-contracted such work. For example, the difference between two Chippendale supplied pieces like the extraordinarily fine work on the so-called "Diana & Minerva Commode" at Harewood in Yorkshire, compared to a rather pedestrian inlaid table at Burton Constable, also Yorkshire, make one wonder who actually made the items. Was the commode sub-contracted to the best craftsman in London while the table was a cheap, in-house piece that lacked careful supervision, or vice versa?

The quality of journeyman employed by Chippendale was high. It is a sad reflection on English cabinet-making that we know so little about the actual makers of the furniture, less even than almost the masters. However we do know something of Chippendale's men; in particular we know of William Benson who lived in Cross Lane, Long Acre, near Covent Garden. He was a subscriber to the *Director* and he had served an apprenticeship with Chippendale's old master, Richard Wood of York. During the 1760's and 1770's he was Senior Foreman. We know of other tradesmen where they signed receipts concerning work finished and their names have survived in country house archives.

Furniture was not always made to order and it was possible to buy "ready-made" items from the shop at 61 St Martin's Lane. Chippendale, like other firms, also hired out furniture; the renting out could be for a long period, such as the London Season, or for a short time such as for a ball, or "rout" as they were often called. Items for this part of the business could be made during slack periods of work. Patterns for tables, cabinets, and chairs were kept in store, along with handles, locks etc. There were guide-books available on how much any set item should cost; for example a 36in wide mahogany bureau would cost about £4. Any deviation from the standard, larger or smaller, would cost more, as of course would extra inlay or decoration.

Chair-making was another separate trade, so therefore had a separate workshop. Chairs are difficult to make (and repair); great skill goes into making the frames so that they will withstand the strains imposed on them by upholstery and also the even greater stresses from use. Such painstaking work is not always realised by the customer, until they break due to faulty workmanship. It is probable that Chippendale had a special skill in chair-making for he chose a chair as his shop-sign, rather than the more common variation on the three tents of the Upholsterer's Company. Large signs hung above all shops in the 18th Century as street numbers were not completely introduced until after c.1775. Thomas Sheraton observed in *The Cabinet Dictionary* in 1803, that there were often considerable differences among a set of chairs made by different chair-makers in the same shop. This is something that one can still see today if one looks closely at a set of antique chairs. It was quite common practice to make pattern chairs to shew clients – as was revealed in the 1766 auction advertisement. Some clients would buy one chair and then have a set made up in the provinces, or even by the estate joiner, with some very high quality results.

Carvers and gilders were yet another distinct trade, but it appears that they used part of the cabinet shop in Chippendale's yard. Furniture-related carvers either did shallow, low relief work such as on picture frames, chairs and bed-posts, while more sculptural carvers carried out bolder, more three-dimensional work, for example curtain and bed cornices, torchères, and large mirrors. It is interesting to look at a large, heavily-carved 18th Century mirror frame, like the ornate Chinese Chippendale mirrors, and see how the detail declines as one looks closely above eye-level: Chippendale was good at saving time and client's money on what one does not see, as it were.

Gilding is always the associated trade with carvers. There are two principle methods of covering wooden furniture with gold – water and oil gilding. Water gilding involves placing gold leaf on a prepared surface covered with glue size. The resultant surface can then be highly burnished. However it is quite fragile and was normally used for wall-mounted mirrors and picture frames and occasionally for very sculptural items such as the Dolphin sofas at Kedleston, Derbyshire, made by John Linnell for Lord Scarsdale to designs by Robert Adam in 1765. Oil gilding was more robust and hard-wearing and thus used more often for chairs and tables. Chippendale's gilded furniture, in particular chairs, is often very plain when viewed from behind. This, like the declining top-half quality of large mirrors, is due to the fact that they were not usually seen, unless by the staff, and so Chippendale was in effect, saving his clients money and certainly not skimping over work.

The provision of large mirrors appears to have been something of a Chippendale speciality. It was, in the 18th Century, technically extremely difficult to make large sheets of glass although it was a skill at which the French excelled. Nonetheless the silvered backing was highly prone to damage during transit, especially during any sea voyage such as crossing the Channel, so Chippendale would usually carry out this process in London. The procedure was to polish the glass and then smear an amalgam containing mercury over the back. This was then burnt off, incidentally releasing highly toxic mercury oxide fume, but producing a mirror with a deeply flattering darkish colour. The mirror makers often eventually suffered from mercury poisoning from which they appeared to be mad like the Mad Hatter in *Alice in Wonderland*, for the reason that mercury was also used by 19th Century hat-makers.

Chippendale supplied ten sheets of "French Plate Glass in London Silver'd and Ready to be put up" at a cost of £340 in 1769 for Lord Mansfield's library at Kenwood in Hampstead. The frames, designed by Adam, were made by William France and not by Chippendale. A different type of glass was also sold by the firm and that was crown glass. The best crown glass was Newcastle and was made by blowing a very large bubble of molten glass and then spinning it in front of an exceedingly hot, open furnace. The bubble would pop out into a large disc, about six feet in diameter, the centre of which produces a glass bulls-eye. These are often seen today in fake Georgian doors and windows but would never have been seen in 18th Century originals. Crown glass has a fine, fire-polished surface but can have slight curved ripples and is rarely flat. In consequence it was used for lanterns, book-cases, and, in the best houses, sash windows.

Chippendale would certainly have kept a large stock of hardware – handles, locks, castors, candle sconces etc. What is less certain is how much, if any, he had made on the premises or whether it was all bought in. As there was a forge within the yard and listed on the insurance plan, he may well have had special mounts made on site for particular commissions. In consequence there may have been a brass-worker, or brazier, on the pay-roll.

Marble slabs for tables were often acquired by gentlemen on the Grand Tour; Lord Burlington acquired two in Genoa in 1719, to be used eventually on a pair of gilded tables for Chiswick House. Chippendale was known to supply expensive slabs, as these ornate marble table tops were called, and also to make their supporting tables. In 1767, at the considerable cost of £40, he provided such a pair of tables for James West of Alscot Park, Warwickshire.

In many respects Chippendale & Co.'s business was the 18th Century forerunner of the modern interior decorator. For example plain dressing tables could be supplied and also the drapes and "Petticoats" to cover them and the glass and china to decorate them. Such a table made from deal was supplied to Ninian Home of Paxton, Berwickshire in Scotland, for 12/- on 7th June 1774. However the "marcela quilted petticoat & cover" were nearly four time the price at £2-6s. "Marcela quilt" was a white quilted fabric from Marseilles in France. As one might guess from the fact that feathers are mentioned in the 1766 auction list, beds, pillows and cushions were a significant aspect of the trade. In the 18th Century the word "bed" had two meanings: firstly it could mean a feather bed or what we might understand today as an eiderdown or quilt. They needed constant attention and Chippendale frequently billed clients for house visits by his workmen to clean and refill the feather beds. Secondly of course it meant what we understand now as a bed, but the word always has an adjective describing its type, such as a field bed, (a bed that can fold up and be taken on campaign), or a French Couch Bedstead, (a bed in the French style that often fitted lengthwise against a wall or in an alcove). Likewise the word "furniture" usually referred to the set of textile curtains and valances. Hence a field bed might have "throw over furniture of muslin".

Beds came with a whole set of valences, counterpanes, testers, headboards, curtains, draw-strings and tassels and were so complex that Chippendale advised any upholsterer to construct a full-scale trial in cheap material before cutting the costly silk brocade, damask or cut Genoese velvet. This advice is still followed today. All bedrooms, even if quite plain, were fitted up with curtains and pelmets that matched the bed-hangings. Setting up bedrooms, and indeed other rooms, was often so intricate that Chippendale usually sent out one or more of his workmen to facilitate the process. All goods were carefully packed; in the case of gilded chairs, they were screwed to a sub-frame in the packing case and the resultant screw-holes are, amongst other things, evidence that a piece was made by Chippendale. The cases were then dispatched at the client's expense either by sea, which was quicker and cheaper but there was a danger of water damage, or by wagon, which was much slower and fairly expensive. When Chippendale sent furniture to Mersham-le-Hatch, near Ashford, Kent, it was sent by sea. While out on site visits the men were paid about £1 a week and the client provided board and lodging. The men often did little extra jobs when on site, for example fitting "A new handle to a Silver Coffee Pot" for Sir Edward Knatchbull at Mersham. Little tasks like this helped the relationship between shop and client, which in this case was often quite strained.

The wide range of work carried out by Chippendale & Co. was fairly typical of one of the larger firms. While Chippendale may have done little work for the Royal family and his was not the largest establishment in London, (for example, Sheraton stated that in 1786 George Seddon employed 400 tradesmen), he was certainly at the top end of his trade and the scope of his firm's activities may be considered typical.

Chippendale's *The Gentleman and Cabinet-Maker's Director* is possibly the most famous pattern book in the world. The growth of urban areas during the 18th Century, and especially in London, led to a huge rise in the demand for furniture and in consequence a need for potential new customers to know more about what was fashionable and how houses should be arranged; the *Director* went a long way to fulfilling that demand.

The *Director* was what is called today a "part-work"; that is the plates and descriptions were published weekly and could then be bound together. To help ensure success of the 1st edition, Chippendale gathered a subscription list of 308 names. Of these, 49 were gentry while the rest were working cabinet-makers and upholsterers. It was surely this aspect that guaranteed the book's success, for it influenced a whole generation of practitioners through a combination of instruction and education. The 3rd and best edition consisted of 200 folio-sized plates. The first eight plates dealt with the five classical orders of architecture and three plates shewing how to draw and measure various mouldings; then came some 192 plates of chairs, sofas, table, picture frames etc. Many of the plates, especially those for chairs, show two designs on one chair, i.e. the design is split vertically into two halves, one half being more richly decorated and the other half-fitted, for example, with an arm; thus if one put a small mirror on the middle, the whole design would be revealed. By this method Chippendale increased the number of designs.

The three editions of the *Director* were enormously influential and there was even a French edition. It is really through the book that Chippendale's name has stayed at the forefront of English furniture studies. That is not to say that there weren't other pattern books, for there were: notably George Hepplewhite's *The Cabinet-Maker and Upholsterer's Guide*, published posthumously in 1788 and Thomas Sheraton's *The Cabinet-Maker and Upholsterer's Drawing Book*, 1791-3, and his fascinating *Cabinet Dictionary*, 1803. There were other books and all of them played a huge part in spreading knowledge of English furniture design, on the Continent and in the new United States of America (and the preceding colonies).

Thomas Chippendale Senior, died in November 1779, of consumption, (i.e. Tuberculosis), possibly the result of hard work in a dusty atmosphere and long hours travelling over trying road conditions; for he was only 61.

Opposite:
A fine ormolu-mounted, mahogany serpentine commode. This elegant French-influenced chest-of-drawers, for that is what a commode is, is a superb example of what English provincial tradesmen could produce. Almost certainly it was made by Henry Hill (fl. 1740 - d.1778) of Marlborough, Wiltshire. It is a simplified version of one at the Lady Lever Art Gallery, Merseyside, but the metal ormolu mounts are almost identical. The commode was probably made for the 9th Duke of Somerset for his house at Maiden Bradley, near Marlborough. It is known that Hill's clients were mostly prosperous Wiltshire landowners. The design is derived from Chippendale's 1754 1st edition of the Director, Pl. XLIII and XLIV. Commodes became popular by the mid-eighteenth century and really no smart, fashionable drawing-room was complete without one, or more. c.1770. 33" H; 43¹/₂" W; 22¹/₄" D. Courtesy of Christie's. Lot No 120 Sale No 6648

Pair of mahogany hall chairs attributed to Mayhew & Ince. Designed by Sir William Chambers for the Entrance/Banqueting Hall of Peper Harow, Sussex for Lord Midleton in the 1770's; the painted central oval contains a viscounts coronet. John Mayhew (1736-1811) and William Ince (d.1804) were cabinet makers in Golden Sq, Soho, London, and were the authors of one of the numerous, but more original, pattern books, The Universal System of Household Furniture, 1762. The partnership was long lived from c.1759 until Ince's death in 1804, and was also amongst the most prominent; the firm may have prospered so long due to the fact that Mayhew was the administrator while Ince looked after the technical, cabinet-making side. Despite such a long existence little can be firmly attributed to the two men; what can be is because of country house archives containing receipts etc. They certainly supplied Lord Coventry's Croome Court, Worcs., Sir John Griffin Griffin's Audley End, Essex, and Lord Shelburne's house in Berkeley Sq, London, all houses that Robert Adam was involved with. Courtesy of Christie's. Lot No 5 Sale No 6077

A pair of mahogany arm chairs in the French style attributed to Mayhew & Ince; these chairs are similar to a set from Warwick Castle whose owner, Lord Warwick was a client of the firm's. the similarity lies in the way that the arms sweep gracefully, and seemingly continuously into the tops of the front legs. There are also constructional similarities with well known Chippendale chairs, see Brocket Hall Chairs. Courtesy of Christie's. Lot No 84 Sale No 6045

A mahogany ormolu-mounted serpentine commode. Like the Henry Hill commode, (Lot 120 Sale No 6648), this piece is in the French manner. However it was intended to stand in front of the pier between two windows, and it probably had a related, but not matched, pier glass. As a "pier commode" it has ornate front doors which open to reveal four mahogany-lined drawers inside; often these pieces of fine display furniture show little or no signs of ever having had the drawers used. The prominent, crossbanded oval on the top and the front are considered by some to be rather a pointer towards manufacture by the Royal cabinet-makers Vile & Cobb; they supplied pieces to George III and his wife, Queen Charlotte, for Buckingham Palace c.1761-70. As an item made by such makers it is in the height of fashion and probably dates to about 1760-65. 33½" H; 43" W; 22½" D. Courtesy of Christie's.
Lot No 100 Sale No 1146

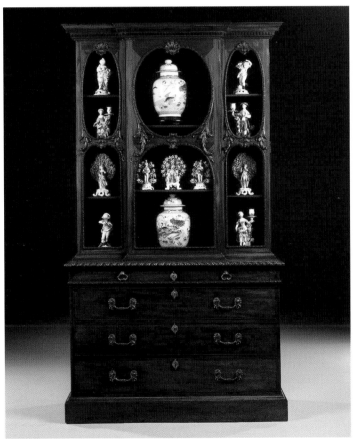

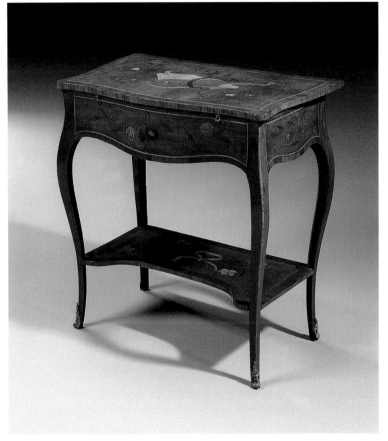

A mahogany china cabinet. The collecting of china had long been popular with women of fashion - Hogarth poked fun at it in Plates II and IV of Marriage à la Mode - and especially fine cabinets were often made for display collections. The large central door, of the upper breakfront section, has a glazed oval surrounded by finely carved mouldings and rococo acanthus leaves. This detail may point to an attribution to the workshop of Vile & Cobb; although it is possible that such carved features may have been supplied by a specialist carver to various cabinet-makers. However the boldly carved gadrooned edge of the lower section is strongly reminiscent of other more securely attributed Vile & Cobb pieces. The handles and escutcheons are of fine quality, but sadly, rarely are they much help in identifying the work of individual makers. c.1760-65. 92" H; 52" W; 21" D. Courtesy of Christie's. Lot No 90 Sale No 6045.

A ladies writing table, in the French manner, possibly made by John Cobb. The timber used in the construction is harewood and sabicu; harewood is, in reality, sycamore that was stained, with oxide of iron, to a green-grey colour – nearly always completely faded today. Sabicu comes from Central America, another of the West Indian trade imports. The whole table is cross banded and has stringing, outlining, and emphasising , the shape. The top is inlaid with a violin and sheet music. This French style of this table was considered correct for the boudoir, a female equivalent of the library and study. It was introduced by the expatriate cabinet-maker, Pierre Langlois, in the 1750's and the style was taken up by John Cobb, as well as other top makers. c.1770. 28¼" H; 26" W; 16" D. Courtesy of Christie's. Lot No 94 Sale No 5879.

A group of painted and gilt pelmets. There is, in the Gillows Estimate Sketch Book in the Westminster City Library, a page of water-colour designs for pelmets for which there is a strong possibility that they were drawn by Thomas Sheraton. The two sets of painted pelmets in the illustration are remarkably similar. The supply of pelmets was a staple product of upholsterers and they would make them to carry the running mechanism for the drapes; these could be pulleys for draw-up, festoon curtains or so-called French rods for horizontal closure. Painted pelmets were a feature of many late eighteenth century houses, not only grand country homes; they would have been common in London for example. c.1800. 68^{1}/$_{2}$" W. Courtesy of Christie's. Lot No 1 Sale No 7013

Biography:

Thomas Sheraton (1751-1806)

Set of three "knife cases", c.1770

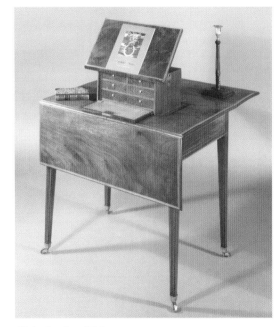

Harlequin table, c.1795

Pair of painted beechwood armchairs, c.1795

Set of "quartetto" tables, c.1800

Thomas Sheraton was another trained cabinet-maker, who turned drawing-master, designer and author. Like George Hepplewhite, he also came from County Durham and was the son of a schoolmaster.

Almost certainly Sheraton had received an education from his father. He became a devout Baptist and wrote a religious tract in his early 30's by which time he must have received a thorough training in cabinet-making, probably near to where he was born. There were, in the 18th and 19th centuries, independent cabinet-makers all over the country, even in quite small villages; they were part of the rural economy, like shoemakers, joiners, wheelwrights and blacksmiths, that existed before the outbreak of the First World War. It appears as though he never set up shop on his own, preferring, as Sheraton himself later said, to work "for many years as (a) journeyman cabinet-maker."

In 1790, aged 39, Sheraton took the momentous step of moving, with his wife and two children, to London where he set up as a drawing-master and draughtsman in Soho and may have then ceased practical cabinet-making. It is quite probable that this was the time that Sheraton also supplied fully worked-up furniture designs in water-colour to nearby furniture makers such as Gillows of Lancaster's Oxford Street shop; it is known that the Lancaster firm had designs and cabinet-making sundries sent up from London. One of these designs survives in the Gillow Archive and it bears an uncanny similarity to one of the designs in *The Cabinet-Maker and Upholster's Drawing-Book*. Sheraton capitalised on these commissions, facilitated no doubt by the precariousness of setting up his school, and set about producing the most influential pattern book after Chippendale's *Director*.

He assembled 717 subscribers for his proposed book, all of whom were, or had been, practising cabinet-makers from all over England and Scotland, as well as London. One of his Soho neighbours, Peter Nicholson, was a subscriber. He also ran a drawing school and was himself about to publish *The Carpenter's New Guide* and went on to publish the highly influential *New Practical Builder* in 1823, amongst other books. Nicholson, like Sheraton, was a trained cabinet-maker who had had a good education and was a gifted mathematician, an important skill for joiners and furniture makers. It was this base of practical men that, in part, accounted for the spread of Sheraton's designs. Also, like the *Director*, Sheraton's book was a part-work. It was made up of 42 sections, published every fortnight for 1/- each, and was in print from 1791-93. A 2nd, larger edition appeared in 1794 and a 3rd in 1802, while a German edition came out in Leipzig in 1794. Many copies also went out to America. Again like the *Director*, Parts I & II of the *Drawing Book* were treatises on geometry, perspective and the five Orders of Architecture, while the rest contained Sheraton's designs for furniture. He had a strong desire to help improve the education of his fellow cabinet-makers, a strong element of British Non-Conformism. He was also keen to give credit to a small number of colleagues whose designs he sometimes used, instead of taking all the glory himself, as was the usual scenario.

In 1799 Sheraton returned north and was ordained a Baptist minister, but three years later he had returned to London and in 1803 published *The Cabinet Dictionary*, a fascinating, instructive book on all aspects of the furniture and upholstery trade. Sheraton then embarked on a third book, *The Cabinet-Maker, Upholsterer, and General Artist's Encyclopaedia*, another part-work intended to be 125 sections in length, but only 30 had come out by the time Sheraton died in 1806, aged only 55.

The *Drawing Book* was very influential, aimed at and supported as it was, by fellow tradesmen. Sheraton's designs were not particularly aristocratic or fashionable but reflected the taste and less flamboyant fashions of people "of the middling sort". This is one reason why the designs remained in manufacture for over 25 years. It is one reason why collectors see so much furniture in antiques shops and sale-rooms today that is dated "c.1790". Another reason is that there was a considerable expansion in housing, especially in London, and of course new houses needed to be furnished. The Sheraton style was neat and plain but could still carry extra enrichment without looking ostentatious. It was perfect for the row upon row of late 18th and early 19th Century homes that were sprouting up all over the country; surprisingly perhaps, considering that Britain was still in the grip of a war with Napoleon that lasted for 21 years.

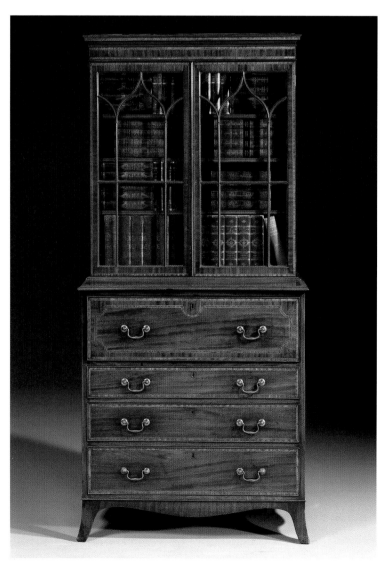

Left:
A mahogany and satinwood secretaire bookcase. By the late eighteenth century this type of useful furniture had come down, as it were, from the bedroom/dressing room and was placed in the drawing room, certainly of the London house. The piece is made from mahogany crossbanded in satinwood, with box and ebony lines; the doors have graceful astragals in the gothick style. The deep, top drawer is a fitted secretaire for writing - probably with no secret drawers by this date and has a sweeping, serpentine apron and finished with French feet. c.1790. 78" H; 37" W; 20½" D. Courtesy of Christie's. Lot No 149 Sale No 5879.

Opposite:
Metamorphic furniture: pieces that are not always what they appear to be. Here an apparent side table can be made to unfold into an elaborate set of library steps. The table is made from mahogany with blind-fret decoration. It was made by an as yet unknown cabinet-maker in about 1770-80. The design idea was drawn-up in Sheraton's Drawing Book, 1791-3. Now at Kenwood House, Hampstead, London. Courtesy of English Heritage. J920229

A painted satinwood pier table. Painted satinwood furniture was popular in the late eighteenth century though not seen so much today - possibly due to the decoration being stripped off to accommodate modern taste. This rectangular table with exaggerated concave corners is veneered with satinwood, with boxwood stringing, crossbanding of amaranth and painted with swags, pendants and wreaths of coloured flowers. It is similar to one illustrated in Hepplewhite's 1788 1st edition of his Guide; it is possible that this table may have been made by Seddon, Sons & Shackleton, another of the more prominent London upholsters during the period 1770-1840. Satinwood was a yellow timber with darker streaks that was imported from both the East and West Indies and very popular during the late eighteenth century after which it was replaced by rosewood; amaranth was another exotic tropical timber imported in small quantities. c.1790. 35³/₄" H; 47¹/₂" W; 19¹/₂" D.
Courtesy of Christie's. Lot No 184 Sale No 6019

George Hepplewhite
(1727-1786)

Mahogany urn stand, c.1790

Painted satinwood pembroke table, c.1785

Mahogany night-table or pot cupboard, c.1790

Mahogany bow-front chest of drawers, c.1800

George Hepplewhite was a cabinet-maker and designer who came, originally from County Durham. Little is known of his early years but he must have served an apprenticeship as a cabinet-maker, probably in the North of England. By 1768 he was married with four children and living in Clerkenwell, London. In November 1785 Hepplewhite and his son, also George, set up a business at 48 Red Cross Street, Cripplegate in the City of London. Less than a year later he was dead.

Hepplewhite's fame lies almost completely with his *The Cabinet-Maker and Upholsterer's Guide*, posthumously published in1788 in the name of his widow Alice. The *Guide* consisted of 126 plates containing almost 300 designs for chairs, sofas, mirrors, tables etc. No such large scale pattern book had been published since Chippendale's 3rd edition of the *Director*. The designs are by no means avant-garde and probably represent the stock-in-trade patterns of Hepplewhite and his son's small scale business on the edge of the City.

Typically the designs are neo-classical, owing much to the work of Robert Adam. Hepplewhite's book, and its two slightly later editions, did have some influence on the Continent, for example in Denmark, but also in Germany where his designs were pirated by a German publisher in 1795. Copying of other people's work was a great problem for designers in the late 18th and early 19th centuries, until effective copyright laws were enforced.

To a large extent Hepplewhite's modern reputation rests upon an 1897 reprint of the *Guide* which came out at a time when there was a great deal of interest in, and a revival of, late 18th Century furniture designs. Many copies were made by firms like Edwards & Roberts, Wright and Mansfield, and even Waring & Gillow.

An oval painted satinwood pembroke table. The drop-leaf pembroke table is one of the great late eighteenth century designs; the difference between the often confused pembroke and sofa table is that on a sofa table the leaves drop at the short ends of the rectangular table. Oval pembroke's, such as this are illustrated in Hepplewhite's Guide, 1788, and also in the Gillow of Lancaster Estimate Sketch Book. Sheraton believed that they were called after a lady, possibly the Countess of Pembroke, ordered one. This especially fine example is made from a variety of exotic timbers, mahogany, tulipwood, amaranth and box. The crossbanded top has an oval floral design painted onto it. Of particular note are the elliptical silver Sheffield-plated handles. c.1785. 28³/₄" H; 39¹/₄" W; 30¹/₄" D. Courtesy of Christie's. Lot No 113 Sale No 5879.

A mahogany urn-stand. Urn-stands were part of the mid-Georgian paraphernalia for making tea and were used in rooms frequented by the women of the house. This example is similar to those illustrated in Hepplewhite's Cabinet-Maker's and Upholsterers Guide of 1788, with the addition of shaped stretchers. A hot water urn was set upon the stand and the small tea-pots of the period put upon the small slide fixed just below the solid, waved gallery. c.1790. 26" H; 11³/₄" sq. Courtesy of Christie's. Lot No 137 Sale No 6648

Two of a set of ten dining chairs. These are classic shield-back chair, with waisted-block feet, that are so often labelled 'Hepplewhite', after his published designs of 1788. However the pattern appears in Gillows of Lancaster manuscript Estimate Sketch Books in the early 1780's described as 'camel back' chairs. The original upholstery would have been either leather or woven horse-hair. Courtesy of Christie's. Lot No 24 Sale No 6045

A pair of pot cupboards. Similar to [Lot No 144 Sale No 7013] but the cupboards have tambour fronts; these were made by gluing rib-moulded strips of mahogany vertically onto a canvas backing. Thus the cabinet-maker could produce a sliding door that could turn through 90° curve. c.1790. 30" H; 20" W; 17" D. Courtesy of Christie's. Lot No 53 Sale No 6045

A linen, or clothes press. Made from mahogany the two doors have crossbanded ovals of "flame" figured veneer. The upper part will have a number of slides upon which clothes were laid flat; dresses were sometimes hung by two loops from horizontal pegs but were mostly laid flat. Clothes hangers were not invented until the late nineteenth century. Shirts, stocks, shifts, caps, aprons, tippets and all the other items of clothing considered necessary; household linen, sheets, napkins etc, would have been kept elsewhere. Described in Hepplewhite's Guide under Wardrobe's they are, and remain, the quintessential late eighteenth century bedroom/dressing room piece. This particular press was probably made by Gillows of Lancaster as it contains a fragmentary label inscribed "Mr Samuel Rawlinson Manchester", a known customer of the firm whose name appears in the Estimate Sketch Book. c.1788. 79" H; 50¹/₄" W; 25¹/₄" D. Courtesy of Christie's. Lot No 74 Sale No 6933

Biography:

Gillows of Lancaster (1728-1961)

Mahogany toilet-mirror, or "dressing glass", c.1797

Mahogany davenport desk, c.1795

A mahogany bowfront chest-of-drawers

When looking at English furniture and reading about its history, it is easy to think that everything came from London. While this was true to an extent, there were some notable firms of cabinet-makers working out of town. For example, Wakefield in Yorkshire was the home of Wright & Elwick, one of the leading provincial companies. Edward Elwick advocated furniture of, as he put it, "neat plainness". By this he meant plain, well-made, well-proportioned, useful furniture, often made from mahogany, but not exclusively. In the colonies of New England and Virginia one come across the similar term "neat and plain". Elwick rather abhorred excessive display in furnishings and his views once attracted scornful comments from Thomas Chippendale. Nonetheless the firm of Wright & Elwick supplied many clients in the North of England on both sides of the Pennines.

However by far the largest of provincial cabinet-makers was Gillows. They were certainly the longest-running firm of furniture makers ever, for although they started in 1728 in Lancaster, by 1770 they had a shop in Oxford Street. in London. They became Waring & Gillow in 1897, being based in that street until the after the middle of the 20th Century.

Robert Gillow (1702/3 -1772) was the founder of the firm in the county town of Lancaster in 1728. The Gillows were devout Catholics and Lancashire was still a centre of Catholicism. Lancaster was also a seaport that had close links to the West Indies and Gillow was able to tap into these two strands of possible business. Not only did he supply the Catholic gentry in the colonies, but he developed a trade of sending out small items packed into his furniture. So successful was this that he was sending out far more brought-in goods than his own furniture. A chest of drawers could be packed with many things. From the return voyages Gillow had access to mahogany and rare timbers for veneers. Using these commercial and religious link the Gillow family built up a substantial business which was carried on by a succession of sons and nephews until the family sold out in 1813 and became gentry themselves. The company name however was kept on by the new partners as it was so well known.

The company was one of the very few 18th Century British cabinet-makers who stamped their name on their furniture, in the manner that Frenchmen did. Gillows started marking in about 1785 and GILLOWS • LANCASTER was stamped prominently, for example on the top of a drawer front or beneath a table top.

Gillows were often ahead of fashion, using designs before similar ones were published by Sheraton or Hepplewhite in their pattern books. There are designs, especially of pier tables and matching mirrors, in the Gillow Archive in Westminster City Library that are identical to ones in Sheraton's Drawing Book. This archive is an extraordinary survival of a set of almost complete company records from 1733 to 1928.

It is very likely that Gillows "invented" the Davenport desk. A Davenport is a square-shaped desk with four vertical drawers that open to one side and, a top with a writing slope that slides forwards, enabling the user to sit and write in comfort. There is an entry from the late 18th Century, in the Archive recording that such a desk was made for one "Capt. Davenport"!

Gillows rarely used ornate inlay, preferring plain banding and simple stringing to emphasise outline. They also were very sparing of most carved ornament. However they did make a great deal of painted furniture; this was usually made from plain beech and often painted with pretty neo-classical ornament. To use the American term, Gillows' furniture was the epitome of "neat and plain".

A set of late eighteenth century made by Gillows of Lancaster. One of the chairs is signed by one of Gillows presumed tradesmen, "Collins". The design is related to one by Hepplewhite but the exact pattern is in the Estimate Sketch Book. These chairs have their original leather upholstery. Courtesy of Christie's. Lot No 30 Sale No 6933

A mahogany bowfront chest-of-drawers. A pattern for this chest appears in Pl 76 of the 1788 1st edition of Hepplewhite's Guide. However a design, heightened in water-colour, of a satinwood example, puffed-up by being described as a commode, appears in Gillows Estimate Sketch Book dated 24th October 1789. This piece is attributed to Gillow but probably dates to about 1800. 35³/₄" H; 42³/₄" W; 23¹/₄" D. Courtesy of Christie's. Lot No 46 Sale No 6933

A late eighteenth century mahogany dressing-mirror. Attributed to Gillows of Lancaster due to its similarity to one illustrated in the Estimate Sketch Book of 1797. 23" H; 17¹/₄" W; 9" D. Courtesy of Christie's. Lot No 2 Sale No 6933

A mahogany davenport writing desk. This is probably the archetype Gillows piece of furniture. The writing slope slides forward s that one can sit at it comfortably; often a pen and ink tray draws out from the top to pivot horizontally and sit parallel to the desk. Originally made for a "Capt. Davenport" by Gillows subsequent pieces were recorded in the Estimate Sketch Book under the name of the original customer; no more is really known about the Captain. c.1800. 33" H; 21¹/₄" W; 23" D. Courtesy of Christie's. Lot No 206 Sale No 6019

Further Reading

Adam Bowett
English Furniture 1660-1714.
Woodbridge Antique Collectors Club, 2002

Victor Chinnery
Oak Furniture the British Tradition.
Woodbridge Antique Collectors Club, 1979

Clive Edwards
Eighteenth Century Furniture.
Manchester University Press. 1996

Ralph Edwards
Dictionary of English Furniture.
Woodbridge Antique Collectors Club, 1983
Originally published in 1923 and reprinted in 1954

this three volume work is the best reference book if it can be found. There is also a one volume version, The Shorter Dictionary of English Furniture, which may be easier to obtain.

John Fowler & John Cornforth
English Decoration in the Eighteenth Century.
London. Barrie & Jenkins. 1974
Still one of the few books on the history of interior decoration.

Christopher Gilbert
The Life and Work of Thomas Chippendale.
2 Vols. London. MacMillan. 1978

Christopher Gilbert
English Vernacular Furniture.
New Haven & London. Yale. 1991

John C. Rogers
English Furniture. London. Country Life. 1964 ed.
This is an old book published originally in the 1920's but there are modern editions and it is still an excellent introduction, with outline drawings, of how furniture was made.

Joining the Furniture History Society, with its annual journal, visits and conferences is a must if one becomes serious about the history of English and Continental Furniture.

The Antique Collectors Club has a monthly magazine and publishes widely on all aspects of antiques, not just furniture.

IV

The Nineteenth Century

Jonathan Meyer F.R.I.C.S.

Jonathan Meyer is currently a director of Sotheby's and Head of the Furniture Dept at Sotheby's Olympia. He has also been in charge of 19th Century Furniture since 1994. He was a past chairman of the RICS, Fine Arts and Antiques Faculty and has helped organise several of their annual conferences. He is currently researching furniture shown at the series of International Exhibitions between 1851 and 1904. He has a degree in Theology from Oxford University and is also training for ordination as a non-stipendiary priest in the Church of England. He lectures regularly and has contributed to several publications.

Design Style during the Period

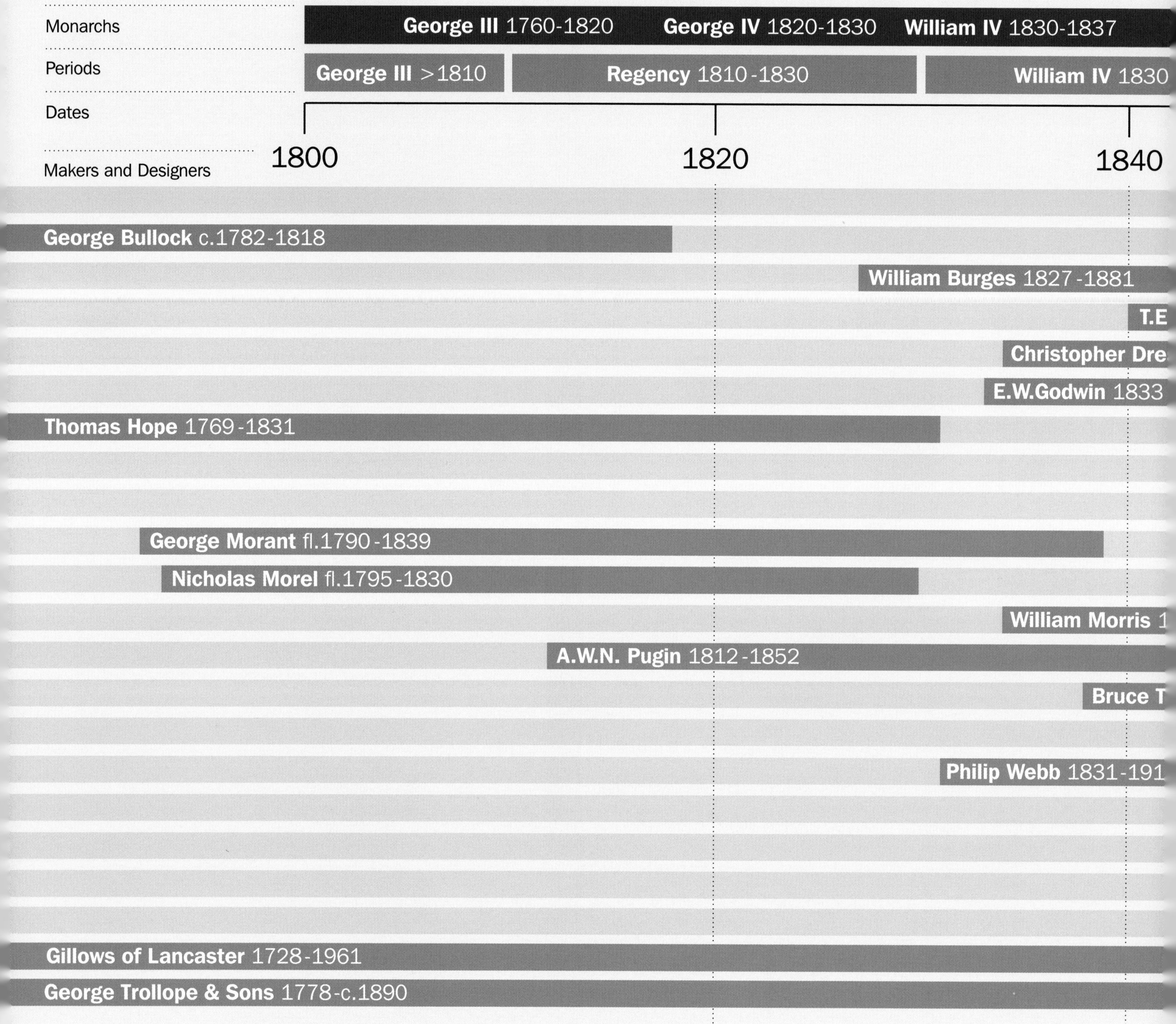

Monarchs	George III 1760-1820	George IV 1820-1830	William IV 1830-1837
Periods	George III >1810	Regency 1810-1830	William IV 1830

Dates

1800   **1820**   **1840**

Makers and Designers

George Bullock c.1782-1818

William Burges 1827-1881

T.E

Christopher Dre

E.W.Godwin 1833

Thomas Hope 1769-1831

George Morant fl.1790-1839

Nicholas Morel fl.1795-1830

William Morris 1

A.W.N. Pugin 1812-1852

Bruce T

Philip Webb 1831-191

Gillows of Lancaster 1728-1961

George Trollope & Sons 1778-c.1890

Regency brass inlaid rosewood and gilded side table c.1810

Regency brass inlaid rosewood sofa table c.1820

Early Victorian papier mache centre table c.1850

Cast iron hall chair in the style of Christopher Dresser and probably by Coalbrookdale Co. c.1875

Victoria 1837-1901

Victorian 1845-1895

1860	1880	1900

C.R. Ashbee 1863-1942

840-1924

1904

W.R. Lethaby 1857-1931

A.H Mackmurdo 1851-1942

-1881

C.F.A. Voysey 1857-1941

George Walton 1867-1933

Edward Lutyens 1869-1944

Ernest William Gimson 1864-1919

& Sons 1843-1908

IV

The Nineteenth Century
Empire and Eclecticism
Jonathan Meyer

To categorise man's contribution to the decorative arts, or any other human activity for that matter, within the arbitrary framework of each century, is never entirely satisfactory. The 19th Century is no exception in this respect. To the historian and collector its mention will elicit thoughts of the Victorian period. Victoria's reign dominated the century, stretching from 1837 to 1901. However in design terms, the true Victorian style, if there be such a thing, doesn't really commence until 1845 and by the end of the century the Arts and Crafts Movement (to be discussed separately in this book), together with the seeds of modernism, had taken root. In 1801, George III was still on the throne and design followed on seamlessly from the developments of the previous century. If we are to break up the century, Regency style spans the years from around 1810 until about 1830; William IV furniture, hardly distinctive in itself, modified much of the opulence of the Regency period and heralded the rather confused early Victorian era. High Victorian style was a complicated web of different strands, most of them revivals of one kind or another.

Like many makers of the 18th Century, Regency designers turned to the past for their inspiration. Greek and Roman architecture provided key sources. What characterised the Regency classical style was a boldness and more solid architectural element, which were lacking from much of the earlier Classical Revival.

The growth of Empire encouraged the search for more exotic styles; Egypt, India and China also influenced makers. The Royal

A George IV mahogany library writing table, stamped GILLOWS LANCASTER.

Opposite: *A brown oak, oak and holly circular centre, 1817 made for Tew Park*

Pavilion in Brighton, created by the Regent later to be George IV, combines an Indian exterior with sumptuous Chinese interiors together with furniture to compliment it. Thomas Hope's *Household Furniture and Decoration* 1807, showed interiors at his own Duchess Street mansion, which included an Egyptian and Indian room as well as a room dedicated to Thomas Flaxman, the sculptor and exponent of classic Greek taste. Neither can the French influence be ignored. In spite of the Napoleonic Wars, which dominated the early years of the century, George IV admired the French style, and furniture in Louis XVI and Empire styles was much in vogue. Marsh and Tatham supplied furniture in the French manner for Thomas Whitbread at Southill, Bedfordshire. The French designs of Percier and Fontaine from the Empire period also provided ideas for fashionable makers. Alongside all this, the native Gothic style, first re-explored at Strawberry Hill by Horace Walpole, was examined again by designers like Wyatt and Soane or William Porden at Eaton Hall. Elizabethan and Jacobean revivals developed from the work of William Bullock and Richard Bridgens. Thomas Hopper re-created a Norman style at Penryhn Castle in North Wales. Augustus Charles Pugin published *Gothic Furniture* in 1827; his son's version of the Gothic style was to become more refined and serious as the century developed.

Broadly speaking, the years up to 1840 did not see a radical change in the clientele or the means of construction, but during what we consider as the Victorian period, external influences on design and manufacture were extensive. Changes in the structure of society

Opposite:
The Dressing table from the Bedroom suite exhibited in Paris in 1878. By Holland & Son

Below:
A Regency Mahogany Carlton House Desk, early 19th Century

and the growth of industrialisation and mass production had a profound influence on the type of furniture being produced. By the early Victorian period the industrial revolution had created a wealthy middle class eager to show off their riches. New wealth permeated society to a far greater extent than it had in the past. The Manchester showroom of Lamb, for example, took account of this by organising stock on three floors, each of differing quality, aimed at different strata within the newly emerging society. Lamb is interesting as a maker because he had inherited a business which specialised in building factories and mills, and seeing the opportunity to supply his newly wealthy clients with aspirations to be men of taste, he turned to furniture making.

Alongside the commercial aspect was that of education. The Art Union of London was set up to make art, in the form of two-dimensional work as well as sculpture, available to the masses. Although this did not extend specifically to furniture, it helps us see the great desire people had to acquire ready-made "taste" and this certainly did extend to the buying of fashionable furniture. Wealth had been created by machines and they in turn changed the way furniture was made and allowed for mass production. As well as these factors, there was the Anglo-Catholic revival inspired by the Oxford Movement, which invigorated the Gothic Revival, both in church building and furniture making. Pugin was profoundly affected by it, as were architects such as Street, who also designed furniture.

Whereas in the Regency period we turn to the design books, such as Ackermann's *Repository of the Arts*, to identify designs of the period, for the second half of the century the series of International Exhibitions, commencing with the "Great Exhibition" in London in 1851, supply rich sources for style. After 1851 international exhibitions burgeoned throughout Europe and the rest of the world. Those in London in 1851 and 1862, and those in Paris in 1855, 1867, 1878, 1889 and 1900, provide an insight into the most popular furniture of the time. But exhibitions in America (New York in 1853, Philadelphia in 1876, and Chicago in 1893), as well as other parts of Europe, are also useful. British makers took part in all of them. An essay by Algenon Wornum, which appeared in the illustrated catalogue of the Exhibition published in the *Art Journal* gives some idea of the proliferation of styles to be seen. "We shall find that nine will comprise the whole number of the great characteristic developments which have had any influence on European civilisation; namely three ancient, the Egyptian, the Greek, and the Roman; three middle-age, the Byzantine, the Saracenic, and the Gothic; and three modern, the Renaissance, the Cinquecento, and the Louis Quatorze. All styles are different ways of using the same language, that of ornament."

The most important lesson to emerge from the exhibition was the prevalence of French design and workmanship, which was acknowledged even by the British commentators, and the relative inadequacy of British furniture. In the few years since the end of the 18th Century and the vigorous Regency style, design in Britain had lost its way.

Wornum wrote, "there is nothing new in the Exhibition in ornamental design; not a scheme, not a detail that has not been treated over and over again in ages that are gone; that the taste of the producers generally is uneducated, and that in nearly all cases where this is not so, the influence of France is paramount in the European productions". The need to follow French methods was well understood; both the design schools and the South Kensington Museum, later the Victoria and Albert Museum, were a response to this.

The exhibitions of 1851 and 1862 in London highlighted the range of design. It is important to understand that 19th Century makers whom we revere today, such as Pugin who dominated the Medieval Court at the 1851 Exhibition, were not highly rated at the time. On the whole, Pugin's work was laughed at. In 1862, William Burges was primarily responsible for the Eccesiological Court, which was similarly derided. The makers who were most highly thought of were those such as Wright and Mansfield, George Trollope and Son, Holland & Sons, Jackson and Graham and Lamb of Manchester.

William Morris, only a schoolboy of seventeen at the time of the Great Exhibition, lamented the advent of the mechanical age. Its importance was in its novelty and that it marked the true beginning of the industrial age. He greatly resented the decline in traditional crafts and local industry and with his socialist zeal saw the future evils that the new industrial age would inflict on ordinary people. In spite of this, his newly formed company Morris, Marshall, Faulkner and Co. exhibited several pieces at the 1862 Exhibition. Clearly he came to see the commercial advantages which could come from such national and international exposure.

Much has been made of the development of technology, but in truth the best furniture was still finished by hand; only the carcass woods were sawn by machines. Many techniques are recorded in some detail in exhibition catalogues, but it is difficult to find evidence of them in general use. The carving machines tended to rout out the basic outline but the product was then finished by hand. Techniques for marquetry cutting were based on better quality mechanical saws and did not radically affect the appearance of the finished product, but they did mean that it was possible to produce higher volumes more cheaply. There was great excitement regarding the use of electrolysis which was mostly applied to plating silver but also used by furniture makers to produce electrotypes of mounts. Designs could be impressed or burnt into wood, although pieces of this nature tend to be of low value today and not worthy of much attention. Lamination was also used, a process not new by any means as it was incorporated by makers in the 18th Century, but now it could be put to use in techniques of mass production. It is especially evident in some of the American chair companies.

Making sense of the later 19th Century is not simple. The variety of styles are endless. Not only were they revived and re-interpreted but there was also a market for reproductions as we know from the production of makers like Blake, who supplied some accurate copies of French pieces to Richard Wallace, the Marquess of Hertford. In general, design was often over-cluttered or ornamented but quality of workmanship on the better pieces can be very high indeed. To consider interiors as a statement of new-found wealth and to a degree as a symbol of British power and confidence in the world, helps put much of it in perspective. But at the same time this power and confidence could allow talented and individual makers and designers to flourish on the fringe. Today many of them, such as Pugin, Burges, Talbert and Norman Shaw are much more highly regarded than those with whom they competed at the time: firms like Jackson and Graham, Wright and Mansfield and Holland & Sons.

Right:
The Vita Nova washstand by Burges, 1880

Opposite:
A pair of oak and holly window seats
by Bullock, 1817

A bergère chair made for Northumberland House, described as, "from the antique of your Grace's aburra wood, highly polished and richly carved and gilt with ornamental trusses, foliage leaves, scroll sides and tablets back seats stuffed with the best horse hair in canvas, standing on brass socket castors." They cost £225 16s for the pair. As the description indicates, they were inspired by designs for the classical world and architectural detail has been incorporated into the design. They still have a strong French feel and undoubtedly owe something to the designs of Percier and Fontaine. Courtesy of the Trustees of the Victoria and Albert Museum

Nicholas Morel
(fl.1795-1830)

A sofa from the Windsor Castle suite. By kind permission of Her Majesty Queen Elizabeth II

An armchair made for the Library at Windsor Castle. By kind permission of Her Majesty Queen Elizabeth II

A giltwood armchair made for the Small Drawing Room at Windsor. By kind permission of Her Majesty Queen Elizabeth II

A maple and purplewood wardrobe. By kind permission of Her Majesty Queen Elizabeth II

The cabinet-maker Nicholas Morel first came to notice at the end of the 18th Century. He was associated with two partners, achieving considerable success with each, firstly with Robert Hughes and secondly with George Seddon, the third of that name to be involved in the furniture trade. He first appears working for Henry Holland with a group of French craftsmen engaged in decorating Carlton House which the Prince of Wales, later to be George IV, had been given in 1783. The architect Henry Holland was given the chance to remodel the building. In keeping with the fashion of the time and the aspirations of the Prince of Wales, he turned to France for inspiration. The reference to Morel occurs in the accounts for 1795; typically parts of his account were paid in arrears.

Unfortunately it has not been possible to identify any of the furniture he made, but it is clear that he was associated with the leaders of French taste in England; he may have been of French descent himself. This association led to work for Sir Thomas Whitbread at Southill, Bedfordshire, but again, individual pieces cannot be identified with certainty. What is clear however is that these early commissions were steeped in the prevalent French taste of the period. If Morel was indeed French, which seems likely, he would have brought a French feel to this and later work, a typical strand within Regency furniture, through the influence of Percier and Fontaine and others.

Henry Holland drew on the Neo-classicism of the last years of the reign of Louis XVI. Furniture design returned to clean lines, incorporating simple fluted legs; the curvaceous forms of the Rococo disappeared. Gilt bronze was used, not in the form of flamboyant figural mounts, but in discrete mouldings, finely finished. French style was embraced by others like the Duke of Devonshire. Through Daguerre, the celebrated Paris supplier, Holland was in touch with makers such as Adam Weisweiller and Georges Jacob. The great French maker Jacob-Desmalter, who was later employed at Windsor Castle, was also associated with this group. These influences were to help form what became a Regency style with French roots.

By 1802 Morel was listed at 13 Great Marlborough Street, London and from 1805 he was joined by Robert Hughes. The partnership continued to supply furniture to the Prince of Wales, both at Carlton House and Brighton Pavilion. Information on the commission comes from accounts but much of the furniture itself remains unidentified. In 1810 it is recorded that a mahogany sideboard with bronzed mounts and griffin supports was supplied for the New Dining Room at Carlton House, the cost being the considerable sum of £182 16s.

Amongst other commissions was work for the Earl of Bradford at Weston Park in Staffordshire, where again the furniture has very strong French parallels. They also worked for the Duke of Buccleuch

Left:
An inventory stamp and label from the burr elm and parcelgilt secretaire by Morel and Seddon supplied to George IV in 1828. Courtesy Sotheby's

Above:
A centre table in amboyna and giltwood attributed to Morel and Seddon. This centre table is very similar to an example in the Royal Collection delivered in 1828 for the Large Drawing Room. The rich Boulle border with mother of pearl, cut brass and tortoiseshell is reminiscent of the work of George Bullock and typical of Regency Boulle. Courtesy Sotheby's.

Above:
Giltwood Armchair made for the Duke of Northumberland at Alnwick Castle. By permission of His Grace the Duke of Northumberland

Above:
Stool by Morel and Hughes, Alnwick Castle.
By permission of His Grace the Duke of Northumberland

Above:
A Burr Elm and Parcel-gilt secretaire by Morel and Seddon. Supplied for the Royal apartments at Windsor Castle in 1828, this piece has the Victorian inventory number and Windsor Castle label. Some furniture from the Royal collection was sold during the last century and appears on the market from time to time. This piece exhibits simple and architectural characteristics, similar to early 19th Century French work. Courtesy Sotheby's.

Left:
Sofa by Morel and Hughes, Alnwick Castle. By permission of His Grace the Duke of Northumberland

at 75 South Audley Street, London, did repairs to a piece for the Duke of Bedford and carried out work at Longleat for the Marquess of Bath. This string of noble clients indicates that the firm was extremely fashionable and clearly attracted high class commissions. Unfortunately many of the pieces recorded cannot be traced and in the absence of a signature, it is impossible to be absolutely sure what is actually the work of the firm. It is common to see pieces catalogued "in the manner of" Morel and Hughes, but not always possible to attribute them with certainty.

Probably their most important commission was for the 3rd Duke of Northumberland at Northumberland House in the Strand. Much of this furniture can be traced. In 1820 the Duke had commissioned Thomas Cundy to work on the south wing of Northumberland House and at that time all the rooms were refitted, the total cost being the enormous figure of £34,111 9s. 7d. The furniture for the so-called Glass Drawing Room comprised a pair of gilt fire screens, a pair of gilt footstools, a Turkish divan and an aburra and canary wood sofa table. The sofa table can now be seen at Syon House, while some of the seat furniture is at Alnwick Castle; their Northumberland home, and a bergère from the set is in the Victoria and Albert Museum. The rooms were opened to London Society on 14th May 1824 and the work of the partnership was much admired.

On the 3rd July 1826 Morel secured his most prestigious commission. Doubtless the work he had carried out for the Prince Regent at Carlton House twenty or so years earlier helped him gain the instruction to furnish the King's Apartments at Windsor. Queen Charlotte had detested what she called the coldest house in England and it was a project of the new king to refurbish the Castle in a manner fit for a monarch of extravagant tastes. Morel was aware that in partnership with Hughes he did not have sufficiently large premises or a workshop to carry out a commission of this size and at some time before May of 1827 the partnership was dissolved.

Hughes seems to have carried on working on his own for several years. Morel sought an established maker; George Seddon seemed a perfect partner. The family of Seddon had been involved in the furniture since the second half of the 18th Century and their business was located in Aldersgate Street. The partnership retained the Marlborough Street address as their head-quarters but the workshops of the Seddon family remained as the centre of production.

Morel had started work himself up to a year before the partnership was established. During that time he was involved in recording many of the existing items in the Royal Collection in the form of watercolours, as well as designing schemes for the interiors. The intention was to incorporate some of the existing furniture, which was indeed done, the firm undertaking restoration, regilding and other alterations which may have been necessary. It was during this period that the elder Pugin was among those carrying out the work and A.W.N.Pugin, only fifteen at the time, was also employed. There is an extremely full account of this commission in *For the King's Pleasure – The Furnishing and Decoration of George IV's Apartments at Windsor Castle*, by Hugh Roberts, published by The Royal Collection Enterprises Ltd in 2001.

The range of styles used by Morel was extensive. They included the more traditionally French taste of the Carlton House years, and it is fascinating to note that he was paid by the Treasury to travel to France to seek inspiration for his designs. They also drew on the Gothic taste, as well as the more robust Regency style which owes so much to the inspiration from Greece and Rome, as seen in the Northumberland commission. All the work was approved by the King and the expense was prodigious. In the light of the unpopularity of the monarchy at the time and George's love of French taste, the Treasury tried to encourage as much use of native craftsmen and materials as possible, and the high costs proved an enormous difficulty. The final account, originally for £200,000, was eventually approved by a select committee after the death of the King.

Right:
An armchair with a giltwood border made for the Library at Windsor Castle, the boldly shaped back and x-form front legs are very striking. By kind permission of Her Majesty Queen Elizabeth II

Above:
*An ebony and giltwood centre table made for the Large
Drawing Room at Windsor Castle, the double scroll legs
have a strong French feel and the border is richly applied
with anthemia, which are brilliantly set off by the ebony
ground veneer. By kind permission of Her Majesty Queen
Elizabeth II*

It is worth drawing attention to several of the pieces so as to give some idea of the range and quality of the work. As has been noted, in the absence of signatures it is impossible to be certain of work carried out by Morel in either of his partnerships unless accompanied by original accounts or other documentary evidence. Consequently comparison with pieces in the Royal Collection in particular, is a valuable means of making attributions with some confidence. Amongst furniture in the Crimson or Large Drawing Room is an extensive suite of gilted furniture originally numbering fifty-six pieces. The design is somewhat reminiscent of George Smith and incorporates laurel leaves and fan ornament with typically masculine lion mask arms and claw feet. In the same room were two large centre tables appearing in the original account as,

"large circular tables of fine amboyna wood, highly polished, the tops with handsome buhl borders of pearl and metals inlaid in tortoiseshell with richly chased ormolu Grecian egg and shell mouldings on the edges the frieze of each elaborately carved chased ormolu husk and fluted coved moulding, supported by a massive pillar in the centre (*sic*) with finely carved water lily and ivy foliage also 4 handsome antique carved chimeras with wings..."

These are wonderful tables, the Buhl border typical of the Regency or early George IV period, the mother of pearl adding a lightness of touch.

A dressing table in purplewood and satinwood from the King's Bedroom gives an idea of the range of the commission. This piece, which has taken a form not to be found in the 18th Century, is applied with gilt-bronze mounts in the French Empire style. The use of these contrasting woods is rather unusual. In the bathroom there were some much more ordinary chairs indicating that the firm was capable of a more practical simplicity.

The commission to supply furniture for Lord Stafford at Stafford House, now Lancaster House, was carried out from 1828 and has been well documented by James Yorke in "The Furnishing of Stafford House", *Furniture History*, 1996. In keeping with other work much of the furniture supplied was in the French manner, although not a great deal remains. Following this commission and the work at Windsor, there is little else recorded regarding Morel and he died soon afterwards. A reference to him in a letter from Thomas Grenville to the 2nd Duke of Sutherland in September 1833 points to an unsatisfactory demise: "I am sorry that poor Morel was swindled into bankruptcy by Seddon, for he worked with excellent taste and your father did not think his charges unreasonable; I never heard what became of him but he may be worth your hunting out if he is again in business..."

Furniture that is very close to the work of documented commissions can be found on the market and it is very likely that much of it was supplied by him; unfortunately he did not sign his pieces. His contribution to furniture design, and in particular the French taste in the first years of the 19th Century, was enormous, although it did represent a taste which was only within reach of the richest patrons.

Left:
A sofa from the same suite made for Windsor Castle. By kind permission of Her Majesty Queen Elizabeth II

Biography:

George Bullock (1782-1818)

A marble-topped cabinet, c.1815. Courtesy Sotheby's.

A Regency oak and holly chest, 1817, for Tew Park. Courtesy Christies

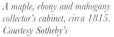

A maple, ebony and mahogany collector's cabinet, circa 1815. Courtesy Sotheby's

A brown oak, oak and holly circular centre table, 1817 made for Tew Park.

Opposite: *A rosewood and brass inlaid side cabinet. With its fine porphyry top, this cabinet is typical of Bullock's work and has parallels with the cabinets at Blair Atholl – courtesy of Sotheby's.*

George Bullock was something of a polyglot. He achieved considerable renown in his relatively short life, although his work was almost completely forgotten until his career was rediscovered by Brian Reade and reassessed in *Regency Antiques* in 1953. Anthony Coleridge extended the range of knowledge of this individual maker in 1965 by drawing attention to bills for his work and attributable furniture, notably at Blair Castle, the home of the Dukes of Atholl, which started the quest to outline his oeuvre with greater certainty. Subsequent to this pioneering work, the sale conducted by Messrs Christie's at Tew Park, Oxfordshire, 27th-29th May 1987, made the name of Bullock widely known in circles of dealers and auctioneers. The collection contained numerous pieces made for Tew Park and supplied by Bullock to Matthew Robinson Boulton. An exhibition entitled "George Bullock, Cabinet Maker" at H.Blairman and Sons and the Sudley Art Gallery in Liverpool early in 1988, helped cement interest in this talented and unusual man. Research has continued since then. Because of a lack of original material such as accounts or day books, which sometimes exist, the opportunities for discovering more about this fascinating man are limited.

There are two major sources, one being the Christie's sale of the stock from Bullock's London premises carried out after his death, over three days from May 3rd 1819. The second significant source is the collection of tracings in an album now in the City Museum and Art Gallery, Birmingham, entitled, *Tracings by Thomas Wilkinson, from the designs of the Late Mr George Bullock 1820*. This curious collection contains a number of designs for furniture, room settings and marquetry in various styles. Alongside these documents we have isolated bills of sale, records of commissions and collections with a known connection such as Tew Park.

Bullock's life was short and little is known of him prior to his emergence in Liverpool as a sculptor. He died in 1818 and if his age of 35 was correctly recorded, he would have been born in 1782 or 1783. A note from *A Century of Birmingham Life 1868* records "August 27th 1798 Mr Bullock the young artist who gained such great repute in Birmingham returning to London, the statue business not answering his expectation." Apart from this and a small sculpture in wax of the celebrated Henry Blundell of Ince, signed G.Bullock and dated 1801, now in the Leeds City Art Gallery, there are no clues as to his early life. All we can surmise is that he gained notoriety at a very young age and frequented London as well as Birmingham. It also suggests that he may have been the son of the wax modeller Mrs Bullock, who was known to be working in Birmingham in the 1790s. In 1804 he exhibited a marble bust of Blundell at the Royal Academy.

Left:
A maple, ebony and mahogany collector's cabinet, circa 1815. This piece is unsigned and has no provenance to firmly establish authorship, but it can be attributed with reasonable certainty based on close parallels with the Wilkinson Tracings. Courtesy Sotheby's

Right:
A Regency oak and holly chest, 1817. Part of the commission for Tew Park and a good example of the simpler furniture Bullock made. There is nevertheless a strong architectural feel to the piece. Courtesy Christies

Left:
A Regency brown oak and holly footstool. This small stool came from Tew Park furnished for Matthew Boulton by Bullock in 1817. It is typical for its use of native timbers and a strong Regency form. A very similar footstool was part of the commission for Longwood. Courtesy Christies

Trade directories record his presence in Liverpool in 1804 where he is listed as a "Modeller and Sculptor" in Lord Street. By the following year he had gone into partnership with William Stoakes, when the entry appears as "Bullock and Stoakes Cabinet Makers, General Furnishers and Marble Workers 48 Church St". The Liverpool Chronicle finds him advertising his "Grecian Rooms at Mr Stokes Looking Glass Manufactory ...this day re-opened where are the most extensive collection of Bronze and Bronzed Figures, Marble tables, Chimney Pieces, see the Rich Gothic Furniture, Armour &c which he has designed and executed for Cholmondeley Castle." The partnership did not survive beyond June 1807, by which time his "Grecian Room" had been set up at 23 Bold Street. But around 1809 he was in partnership with the architect Joseph Gandy. They described themselves as " architects, modellers, sculptors, marble masons, cabinet makers and upholsterers." The partnership did not endure and by 1810 Bullock moved to London where he established his "museum" in the Egyptian Hall in Piccadilly. By 1814 he was recorded at the address where he died on May 1st 1818, 4 Tenterden Street, Hanover Square, although he appeared in Liverpool Trade Directories in 1813 and 1814, suggesting that he may have retained premises there for some time. After his death the artist Benjamin Robert Haydon wrote, "George Bullock was one of those extraordinary beings who receive great good fortune and are never benefited by it,

and suffer great evils, and are never ruined, always afloat but never in harbour, always energetic, always scheming." His energetic character is matched by the range of the work he produced, whether it be the medium used or the style worked in.

Around him the style we recognise as Regency predominated, relying on Egyptian and Grecian masculine forms, derived from antiquity. While much of his work was classical in inspiration and relied on timbers such as mahogany and rosewood as we expect from the period, he also explored other styles, such as Gothic, Elizabethan and Jacobean. Towards the end of his career he tended to make use of native timbers, partly out of necessity because of the restrictions imposed by the Napoleonic wars but also for aesthetic reasons. The *Repository* of 1815 pays tribute to his work, "designed for execution in our native woods, relieved by inlaid metal ornaments; a style happily introduced both in respect of taste and true patriotism. There are no woods more beautiful, or better suited to the purpose of cabinet embellishment than those indigenous to our own country." He incorporated decorative forms derived from native flora, such as cornflowers and hops, rather than simply reproducing the natural forms used in classical times. He also employed native marbles, making use of Mona marble, from his own quarries on the island of Anglesey, as well as marble from Scotland.

Above:

*A Regency brass and tortoiseshell circular ink-stand.
This is attributed on the strength of parallels with the
Wilkinson tracings. The trails of the native honeysuckle
intertwined with vine leaves are very distinctive.*

Right:
A pair of brass-inlaid and ormolu-mounted
rosewood and ebony torcheres. A torchere is
a stand for a candelabrum or oil-lamp.
A similar pair of torcheres is recorded in
George Bullock's posthumous sale on May
3rd 1819. They are conceived in the French
manner and are clearly inspired by classical
prototypes. They are made in première partie
and contre partie, meaning that the cut brass
marquetry is taken from a single cutting, one
being positive, the other negative.

Above Top:

A marble-topped cabinet, circa 1815. The design for this cabinet exists in the Wilkinson Tracings, the scagliola columns are especially striking. Courtesy Sotheby's.

Above Middle:

An oak and ebony-inlaid four-pillar dining table, circa 1815. This particular table came from Greystoke Castle, the home of the Howard family in 1939. It is of a type very similar to that supplied for Napoleon's use at Longwood.

Above Bottom:

A Regency mahogany and ebony inlaid desk, probably from Longwood. Courtesy Sotheby's.

A brief review of some of his commissions will help illustrate the nature and scope of his *oeuvre*. His earliest ones naturally date from the time when he was established in Liverpool. Of these his work at Cholmondeley Castle in Cheshire is perhaps the most significant. His first contact with Lord Cholmondeley dates from late in 1804, when he was helping with the Gothic alterations being made to the Castle under the direction of the architect William Turner of Whitchurch. Among the furniture known to have been supplied by William Bullock was a bed in Regency taste, a brass chandelier originally in the dining room and a collection of ceramic armour made to decorate the Great Hall. The decorative armour is specially engaging as it highlights the interest in creating a romantic medieval style, which Bullock was to do later at Abbotsford for Sir Walter Scott. Another commission, which reflects the interest in what at the time was seen as "medieval", was the work carried out at Speke Hall, near Liverpool. As we have noted in connection with the decorative armour for the Great Hall at Cholmondeley, Bullock, like many furniture makers, was involved with the decoration as a whole as well as the architectural scheme on which he was associated with Joseph Candy and William Atkinson. Unfortunately the furniture was sold in 1812. The advertisement of the sale tantalisingly describes:

"a large set of curious Oak Dining Tables, with a large Sarcophagus with Bronzed Ornaments of peculiar beauty and Design, Gothic Lamps, suspended from the ceiling, and elegant Candelabra, with Patent Lamps, Antique Fire Dog (admirable design) light elegant Armed Oak Chairs, Antique Couch, Crimson Curtains, and Cushions round the seats of the Hall, Footstools, &c, &c... Designed after much study and attention to suit the Antique Costume in true Baronial Magnificence, has been executed by, and under the direction of Mr George Bullock."

None of it can be traced but the chimneypiece in the Great Hall is a fine example of Bullock's idea of a romantic Gothic interior. To a degree he is a designer who linked the whimsical Gothic revival of Walpole's Strawberry Hill with that of Pugin and Burges to come later in the century.

In a different vein he carried out work at Blair Castle in Perthshire for the Duke of Atholl and bills from the firm dating from 1814-1819 are preserved in the castle's records. The 4th Duke of Atholl was known as the "planting Duke" on account of his great interest in forestry. Bullock reflected this passion in the choice of wood on a pair of cabinets supplied, being executed in larchwood, a tree widely planted by the Duke. Larchwood is found only very rarely in furniture, the soft yellow veneers with marked striations reminiscent of, but more subtle than, pitch pine, contrasting well with ebony, gilt-bronze and gilded mounts. The overall appearance is classically Regency in conception but more monumental and architectural than one would normally expect. The marble for the tops came from the quarry of Glen Tilt. The cut-brass inlay is characteristic of Bullock and of the period, being referred to as "English Buhl" after the great French cabinet maker, Charles Andre Boulle, who first introduced the technique. Bullock also supplied circular tables in larchwood and a sofa table of a more traditional form with little ornamentation. Among other pieces was a tripod table in bog oak. Of typical form, it is distinctive for a stylised tulip border to the top, with a triform base applied with characteristic rosettes punctuating the rim. The choice of timber is significant in that it came from the Isle of Man, where the Dukes had been hereditary Lords until the time of the 1745 rising. The three legs probably reflect the "legs of Man". Bullock seems to have carried out a number of commissions on Scotland and there are

Above:

*A brown oak, oak and holly circular
centre table, 1817 made for Tew Park.
The inlay and the bosses punctuating
the base are typical of Bullock.
Courtesy Sotheby's*

Left:

*Detail showing the inlay in the border.
Courtesy Sotheby's*

pieces, which can firmly be attributed to him at Scone Palace, which is only about 40 miles from Blair Atholl. Here we find an octagonal library table of rosewood in mainstream Regency style but with a very distinctive and individual cut-brass band of thistles and acorns. A second table, of rectangular form with canted angles, is veneered in burr-elm, a timber favoured by Bullock but not widely used at the time.

Another great Scottish house to which I referred earlier is Abbotsford. Here Bullock returned to the recreation of a romantic Gothic, pseudo-medieval interior. He had been introduced to Sir Walter Scott by J.B.S.Morritt of Rokeby in Yorkshire and knew him personally. Sir Walter Scott was the quintessential medievalist. He was renowned for his poetry and his romantic novels; he had starting collecting items for his armoury several years earlier and was immersed in a romantic idea of the past. At Abbotsford he intended to create a house which reflected these themes. These ideas were very much in tune with those of Bullock and he collaborated with some of the decorative schemes, which endevoured to create a baronial interior as he had at Cholmondeley. The two most notable pieces were a stand for the silver urn, containing bones removed from Athens in 1811, which was given to Scott by Lord Byron, and a plaster bust of Shakespeare, on a rectangular plinth with a cut-brass wreath.

Bullock was also employed by the British Government to supply furnishings for Longwood, a house on St Helena for Napoleon in exile. The commission is exceptionally well documented and has been recorded in detail by Martin Levy in *Furniture History* 1998. It was the intention of the Government to treat Napoleon with respect and indeed the furnishings were given great thought – Bullock was one of the most fashionable designers of his day. After Napoleon's death, the furniture and other effects were transported back to London and sold by auction at the Session House over ten days between 1st April and 12th August 1822. Furniture from this commission is sometimes traced and has appeared on the London market from time to time.

As we noted at the outset, Bullock was an individualist and this was reflected in the vast range of designs he produced, in spite of his short life. He had worked with Richard Bridgens who contributed to the work at Abbotsford. A volume entitled *Furniture with Candelabra and Interior Decoration* designed by Bridgens was published in 1838. This seems to be a late edition of an earlier work of around 1825, which, although produced after Bullock's death, reflected the influence of his designs, in particular some of his Elizabethan and Jacobean Revival pieces made for Aston Hall, the home of James Watt just south of Birmingham. It serves to underline the continuing influence of Bullock after his death. Much of Bullock's work was in the main stream of Regency design and is recognisable as such, but he gave it a boldness and confidence sometimes lacking in other designers. Yet alongside this he began to explore other sources, and his use of native timbers and his fascination with the Gothic style in some ways anticipate the work of Pugin and others later in the century.

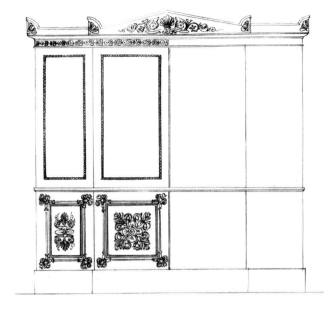

Above:
Designs for the desk from Longwood, for a bookcase and for two stools. The Wilkinson Tracings, Birmingham City Art Gallery.

Biography:

Gillows of Lancaster (1728-1961)

A George IV mahogany library writing table, stamped GILLOWS LANCASTER. Courtesy Sotheby's

A Mahogany library Bergère, c.1820, stamped GILLOWS LANCASTER. Courtesy Sotheby's

A Gothic revival oak extending drum-top table, stamped GILLOWS LANCASTER. Courtesy Sotheby's

A Burr Walnut Kidney-shaped writing desk, c.1840. Courtesy Sotheby's

Opposite: *A pair of Aesthetic movement satinwood side cabinets, stamped L4967. Characteristic of the later 19th Century and made around 1880, these cabinets show a wider use of materials with the combination of satinwood and amboyna as well as the painted panels. Courtesy Sotheby's*

Gillows and Co was arguably the greatest furniture making firm in England. Their history begins in the middle of the 18th Century and continues until the middle of the 20th. Thus they span the whole of the 19th Century. Certainly they play an important part in the history of furniture making in the latter part of the 18th Century but they did not reach real dominance until the early 1800's and a hundred years later they played a major role in fitting out the Royal Pavilion for the Prince of Wales at one of the last truly great international exhibitions in Paris in 1900.

The company were really furniture makers rather than designers. Although they did design furniture, they never produced a design book as such, like Sheraton or Hepplewhite. Certainly they made use of other makers' designs and over the period worked with many different designers, including Wyatt (in the 18th Century), Pugin and Bruce Talbert. They contributed work to most of the international exhibitions since 1851. The business was essentially a commercial enterprise. Ivan Hall, in the *Dictionary of Furniture Makers*, sums up their success; "The firm astutely realised the huge market possibilities

Below:
A Regency Mahogany Carlton House Desk, early 19th Century. The original Gillow's design for this was produced in 1796 based on Hepplewhite's design for a Gentleman's Writing table published in 1793. Both are based on the desk made for the Prince Regent in 1790 as part of the furnishings for Carlton House. The clean simple architectural design remained popular and a number of versions exist. They were produced throughout the whole of the century, both by Gillow's and other makers.

offered by the middle and upper-middle class households of the later Georgian and early Victorian eras. They foresaw this demand as that for well made items of good materials, and in a style that would remain acceptable when the immediate fashion had waned; that is, in their designs they achieved a satisfactory mean between the merely conservative and the ultra-fashionable. This is one reason for their survival. No firm gained a wider geographical spread of patronage, though with greater concentration in North West England, and in those parts better served by the steadily improving land or water carriage".

Robert Gillow started his business in Lancaster in the late 1720's and continued with his two sons Richard and Robert. By 1769 premises were opened in London at 176 Oxford Road, now Oxford Street. Richard's son, also Richard, was born in 1772 and became the major force in the firm. He purchased Leighton Hall in 1827 and was persuaded by his wife to retire from trade in 1830, at which time his son Richard Thomas also left the business. Like many firms its registered name changed repeatedly, being "Gillow and Taylor" in 1772, by 1776 solely Gillow, by 1790 Robert Gillow and Company, and by 1811 G. and R. Gillow and Company. For a short time it

became Redmayne, Whiteside and Ferguson, late Gillow and Co., but the simpler name "Gillow and Co." was reverted to for most of the 19th Century. At the end of the century, in 1897, they took over the distinguished business of Collinson and Lock and, as has been noted, merged with Warings in 1903 after collaborating with them for some years. For a short time they also had a branch in Paris.

It is fortunate that an excellent record of the firm has been preserved. Most of their output is documented in the form of letter books, ledgers, waste books and estimate sketch books, the latter being the most useful. They are a record of the design for a particular piece, together with the estimated cost of making the article, usually down the last farthing for screws or other minor materials. Most of the books have an index in the back recording for whom each design was made. It would seem that prospective clients could use the estimate sketch books as a form of catalogue, from which to choose a design that they liked. These invaluable resources are preserved in the Westminster City Archive and on microfilm in the University of Lancaster. The record is not continuous but there is very good representation from the late 18th Century well into the 19th.

The quality of work they produced contributed to their success. In the 18th Century, west coast ports like Liverpool, Lancaster and even Whitehaven benefitted from trade with the Americas and imports of fine mahogany were key to the furniture trade. In the early days the company was exporting furniture to patrons in the West Indies. Their furniture is characterised by the use of West Indian mahogany, dense and dark in colour with a tendency to figure more than some of the timbers used earlier in the century. Gillows' work is usually very well finished; examination of a moulding or cockbead on to a drawer, will often show attention to detail. The turning on a chair leg may have fine secondary mouldings which heighten the definition. This sort of attention to detail would have cost more at the time and always indicates quality.

Gillows tended to respond to fashion; they were not revolutionary or original in terms of design but simply responded to demand. This was the key to their success. At the end of the 18th Century they popularised the circular library table, usually with a revolving leather top and fitted with frieze drawers. This design, first produced in the 1795, endured until at least 1820 and is often seen. Snap tables, usually referred to as tripod or breakfast tables today depending on their size, were also a standard design enduring well into the reign of George IV. Work tables, "Sideboard Tables", bookcases and small cabinet furniture such as bonheur de jours; were all staples of the firm.

In 1800 they patented a design for an "Imperial Dining Table". This consisted of a dining table on pedestals, which fitted together and may have been interposed by further leaves. These tables may have had up to five or six pedestals, usually with four splayed legs for the central sections and three for each end. They are sometimes described as "sets of dining tables" in the Estimate Sketch Books. Chests, washstands and bedroom furniture were all part of the repertoire; indeed the firm was capable of providing furnishings for a whole house and frequently did so. Gillows' commissions are so extensive that this is not the place to list them all, but amongst those using their services from 1800 were the Earl of Westminster at Eaton Hall, where much furniture, some of it the Gothic Revival taste, was supplied around the time of Porden's adaptions to the building from about 1815; large amounts of furniture were supplied to the Tempests at Broughton Hall in Yorkshire, new furnishings were supplied in the 1820's to Tatton Park for the Egerton family, as well as to Dunham Massey.

There was no "house style" for the firm; they adapted well to change and by the Victorian period were producing a very wide range of furniture from small Davenports in satinwood, an adaption of earlier designs, to walnut furniture applied with gilt bronze mounts in the French manner. The firm was responsible for some of the furniture Pugin designed for the Palace of Westminster and they continued to make furniture to Pugin's designs into the 1880's. They contributed a library table of shaped outline carved with Chimerae at the angles, and a sideboard supported by massive carved eagles to the 1851 Exhibition. The latter was described as showing "a freedom from too great slavishness of idea, a determination to get rid of the trammels of conventional style, which is very cheering to all who have felt its primary importance to native interests". At the 1862 Exhibition they showed a walnut sideboard in Renaissance style thought to be "one of the gems of the exhibition" by the *Illustrated London News*. By the 1870's they had responded to changing taste by working to designs by the emerging Arts and Crafts designer, Bruce Talbert, whose sideboard had been made by the rival firm of Holland and Sons for the Paris Exhibition of 1867. A note from *The Cabinet Maker* in 1880 underlines the scope of the firm, which reflected the eclectic tastes of the time.

Above:
A Mahogany library Bergère, circa 1820, stamped GILLOWS LANCASTER. Good quality library furniture of this type is typical of Gillows. The reeded legs and uprights to the arms as well as the moulded frame are very distinctive. The fineness of he reeding is a key to dating pieces, the heavy bolder models are usually later. Courtesy Sotheby's

Above:
A Rosewood card table, circa 1835, stamped GILLOWS LANCASTER. This table is from the reign of William IV, the leaf carved baluster supports and the scrolled moulded legs are more typical of this period. Rosewood was used throughout the Regency period and is highly sought after. Courtesy Sotheby's

Above:
A George IV mahogany library writing table, stamped GILLOWS LANCASTER. The slightly heavier design and scroll feet indicate at date at the end of the Regency period. Courtesy Sotheby's

Left:
A pair of George IV mahogany side cabinets, stamped GILLOWS LANCASTER. Small cabinets of this type were produced in larger numbers to satisfy the demand of more modest houses, the gadrooned base and leaf carved acanthus corbels are typical of later Georgian work by Gillows. Courtesy Sotheby's

"The workshops above the machine department afford plenty of opportunity for the display of skill on the part of the talented cabinet makers and various articles we saw in Jacobean, Queen Anne and Chippendale and every other fashionable style gave evidence that all kinds of work were within the grasp of these Lancashire artisans. The modellers and carvers of the establishment have an apartment well-lighted, admirably kept and profusely decorated with casts of ancient and modern decorative art. Gillows have a name for high class carving, including Renaissance work, but no foreigners are employed."

Finally a note should be made regarding the Gillows stamp, which appeared on some furniture. It was not typical for 18th Century English makers to stamp their furniture, in contrast to French craftsmen who were obliged to do so to comply with the guild regulations. It is more common to find signatures on English furniture from the middle of the 19th Century. In the case of Gillows, the simple stamp GILLOWS LANCASTER appeared between about 1770 and 1780 but by 1800 it had acquired a mullet or stop mark, GILLOWS·LANCASTER.

It usually appears on the top of a drawer front but is by no means universal. For example, furniture made for the Tempest family, although identifiable from accounts, is not stamped. It has been suggested that only furniture sold in one of the showrooms was stamped and that work for special patrons was left unsigned, although this does not seem to consistent. By the 1870s there was also an L followed by a four digit number, indicating the design in the Estimate Sketch Book, and the end of the century the name GILLOW & CO was used. It has to be added that a fake stamp has also been used in the last 20 years or so. Evidently this has been applied to some pieces which were probably made by Gillows but left unstamped, at the time but it also appears on later pieces or pieces which are not of sufficient quality to have been made by the firm. Lindsay Boynton further suggests that after the merger with Waring, when the company became something of a High Street name, it became rather unfashionable to have furniture by Gillows and that some genuine stamps were erased by owners anxious to preserve their social standing.

Left:
A pair of Oak bookcases. These bookcases are not signed by they can be firmly attributed to Gillows as the provenance is known and they are recorded in the original design books. They were made for Sir James Ramsden for Abbots Wood, his house in Barrow-in-Furness. They show Pugin's influence. Courtesy Sotheby's

Right:
A George III style mahogany desk, stamped GILLOWS, circa 1900. Revival or reproduction furniture became very popular towards the end of the century, this desk is based on a Chippendale design. Many other firms produced furniture of this type, Gillows generally maintained a high quality. Courtesy Sotheby's

Left:
A Gothic revival oak extending drum-top table, stamped GILLOWS LANCASTER. This table is typical of work carried out in the Gothic revival style championed by Pugin. Courtesy Sotheby's

Left:
A side cabinet typical of the later work of Gillow's, stamped GILLOWS 16321. This is typical of the later work of Gillows and is similar to the work of Collinson and Lock, acquired by Gillows at the end of the 19th Century. It owes its inspiration to 17th Century cabinets made in Paris and the Low Countries. Courtesy Blairman's. Courtesy Sotheby's

Biography:

Augustus Welby Northmore Pugin (1812-1852)

A plain oak writing table made to a Pugin design c.1846. Courtesy of the Trustees of the Victoria and Albert Museum

An armchair probably designed by Pugin for Eaton Hall. Courtesy of the Trustees of the Victoria and Albert Museum

A bench carved in oak, c.1835. Courtesy Fine Art Society

The centre table made for John Naylor of Leighton Hall by Crace and Co.

Opposite: A gilded side chair. This chair emerged at a house sale in Berkshire. It is made to the same pattern as chairs made for the new Palace of Westminster in 1846, where it is now. Courtesy Blairmans

The Nineteenth Century   145

Pugin's great cross, unveiled at the Great Exhibition, caused something of a minor political crisis at the time. It towered over the celebrated Medieval Court and dominated the aisle of the Crystal Palace. There were suspicions that it represented a secret attempt to persuade the nation to turn its religious affiliation again to Rome. Lord Granville, the Prime Minister, had to defuse the row by arranging for it to lowered somewhat so as to be less dominant. Pugin himself had become a Roman Catholic in 1835. His commitment as a Christian was matched by his passion as an architect and designer. Gothic was the style in which he had been raised; his father, a refugee from France, had worked with John Nash and later with Rudolph Ackermann who published *Gothic Furniture*. Augustus Welby Northmore Pugin was born on 1st March 1812 and must have grown up steeped in "Gothic". His passion was religious and artistic: a prolific designer of churches, ecclesiastical metalwork, and furniture, both secular and religious.

It is remarkable that the work of a man who had designed most of the furniture for the Houses of Parliament should have remained almost completely forgotten until the 1960's. He had a prolific influence on architects and designers throughout the 19th Century. William Burges, described him as that "wonderful man".

He influenced a whole generation, including Owen Jones, Christopher Dresser, William Morris, Philip Webb and Richard Norman Shaw, as well as Gimson and Voysey in the next generation. By some he has been called the Father of the Modern Movement. In the way in which Pre-Raphaelite painters sought to return to be pure principals of the early Renaissance, he strove for a pure Gothic revival and thus made it possible for the architectural forms of the medieval period to be incorporated in domestic architecture and furniture as well as metalwork and ceramics.

Pugin was something of a bridge after the more whimsical "gothick" revival of the late 18th and early years of the 19th Century. His earliest work had been to cooperate with his father on furniture for Windsor Castle at the extremely young age of fifteen. A suite of chairs, probably designed by Pugin and made by the firm of Morel and Seddon, are in rosewood, partially gilded and with gilt-bronze mounts. It has been suggested recently by Hugh Roberts that Pugin somewhat exaggerated his contribution in this respect. These pieces have elements far closer to the early gothick revival. Essentially they simply copy forms from medieval architecture and incorporate them into "modern" pieces. As Pugin matured he stuck to two overriding principals: firstly that design should always serve some purpose, and secondly that details

Right:
An armchair probably designed by Pugin for Eaton Hall. This chair has broken away from the purely decorative and whimsical Gothic associated with Horace Walpole and Strawberry Hill but it still lacks the seriousness of Pugin's later work. Courtesy of the Trustees of the Victoria and Albert Museum

should not merely appear for their own sake but be "essential either for convenience or propriety". In later life he criticised his own part in the design of the furniture for Windsor Castle in 1827 and the Regency form of Gothic: "everything is crocketed with angular projections, sharp ornaments and turreted extremities". The type of Gothic revival espoused by Pugin was deeply serious; it was associated with a moral educational purpose as well as being imbued with a religious fervour. The evangelical and Anglo-Catholic revivals of the 19th Century were a reaction against the moral turpitude of the 18th Century. This point is important for the understanding of Pugin's architecture and furniture, and to some degree it accounts for the reaction against his furniture and the Victorian age in general, which characterised the first half of the twentieth century.

Pugin grew up in London, living in a house in Gower Street. From here he had easy access to the British Museum and made special use of the Print Room and the Reading Room. He was an accomplished draughtsman and watercolourist from an early age. He had a passion for antiques shops and considerable expertise. Edward Hull, who owned the "Ancient Furniture Warehouse" in Wardour Street, supplied old pieces to him and his clients and made new furniture to his designs. He also worked with Edward Holmes

Baldock, who was well known as a decorator and supplied him with Jacobean furniture. Baldock also purchased pieces in France, which was a favourite hunting ground for Pugin himself. He spoke fluent French and frequently sailed to France in his own boat.

John Webb of Bond Street was another dealer who specialised in very high quality furniture. He made pieces for Lord Hertford, now in the Wallace Collection, and supplied some of the grander Pugin pieces for the Palace of Westminster. It is very important to understand that Pugin did not make furniture himself, apart from for a very short period. Amongst those who carried out work to his designs other than John Webb, were the celebrated firm of Crace and Co, George Myers, Gillows, and Holland and Sons. Hardman's of Birmingham executed most of his designs for metalwork; not only for free-standing candelabra or chandeliers, but also for hinges and lockplates which appeared on the furniture itself.

It is not clear whether Pugin worked with his father on the early designs, published by Rudolph Ackermann in *The Repository of the Arts*. In 1829 he turned to a much more massive style and set up business at 12 Hart Street. This lead to commissions at Murthly Castle in Scotland, which showed a clear Jacobean influence. Designs for a series of stools date from this period; they are characterised by what

Left:
A design for the sideboard at Windsor Castle, 1827 showing the early Gothic style, which has more in common with the Gothic revival work of the 18th Century than Pugin's own work ten years later. Courtesy of the Trustees of the Victoria and Albert Museum

Left:
A plate from Ackermann's Repository of the Arts showing a Gothic table and chair, published on 1st June 1827. Courtesy of the Trustees of the Victoria and Albert Museum

is sometimes called Jacobethan style. It combines many elements taken from Elizabethan and Jacobean design, largely because the distinction was not properly understood. A communion table in mahogany made for Christchurch Priory comes from the same period. The choice of timber is important: most of the later work by Pugin and designers who followed him was in oak which was thought to be a more natural, honest and British material. Because of the high standards of workmanship which he insisted on, the business went bankrupt in 1831 and only one piece stamped A.Pugin, now in the Victoria and Albert Museum, is known. Although the business was short-lived it had given him practical experience, which was to prove useful in the future. In common with many Victorian designers, Pugin made use of a variety of styles. Early chairs often show barley-twist turned supports which derive from Jacobean and sometimes Batavian or Indo-Dutch chairs, which were thought to be Elizabethan at the time.

By the 1840s he was producing some very simple pieces. They are in marked contrast to the earlier Regency gothick. They are characterised by simple members, usually straight although sometimes of curved form, generally chamfered and the tops with a simple moulding. The so-called "tusked tenon" joint is typical on chairs and tables of this period. This refers to a rounded joint formed by a tenon protruding through a flat surface and pegged, so as to be part of the design. The refectory table for St Mary's, Oscott, as well as Pugin's own dining table, are fine examples of this type.

As mentioned earlier, Pugin played a significant part in the Medieval Court at the Great Exhibition in 1851. He was not universally popular in his lifetime and this is reflected in some of the comments written about this display. Algernon Wornum, who wrote an introduction to the *Art Journal's* illustrated catalogue of the Exhibition, warned against the inferiority of Gothic as compared with the Renaissance style. He wrote, "the profusion of vertical and diagonal lines, in the same relation, is fatiguing and palling to the mind, as is well illustrated in by the peculiar assemblage in the so-called medieval court, which stands there as a warning to us against making this style familiar in our dwelling houses." There were favourable reviews too and Queen Victoria herself spent forty-five minutes with Crace and Minton on her second visit to the Exhibition on May 7th, showing considerable interest and asking if the bookcase was sold. The *Illustrated London News*, wrote, "To Mr Pugin, then, who furnished the design for this gorgeous combination, is the highest honour due; and he has marvellously fulfiled his own intention of demonstrating the applicability of Medieval art in all its richness and variety to the uses of the present day." Assessments as favourable as this seem to have been rather uncommon, although the Court itself was a great source of interest.

Below:
A bench carved in oak, circa 1835. This bench is an unusual example of Pugin's early Gothic furniture. It is stamped HEIRLOOM/SUTTON PLACE and the crest is probably that of the Salvin family, who inherited Sutton Place. The panels on the back are based on a 15th Century panel owned by Pugin.
Courtesy Fine Art Society

The most important furniture was made by Crace to Pugin's designs, and amongst it was the carved oak sideboard hung with a scarlet cloth emblazoned with the heraldic devices of the House of Talbot and intended for Alton Towers, the seat of the Earl of Shrewsbury. Crace also supplied a small praying desk surrounded by a triptych and made for C.R. Scott Murray of Danesfield. There were other tables in oak of simple design, gilded chairs with supports and velvet covers. Mr Crace also supplied the hangings and, in the centre of the display, a cheval screen, carved with the rose, the shamrock and the thistle. The cabinet or bookcase was purchased by the Board of Trade for £154 and is now in the Victoria and Albert Museum.

Probably the most celebrated piece was the octagonal centre table in marquetry, designed by Pugin and made by the firm of J.G.Crace. It is now in the Library at Lincoln's Inn. Unusually, it is in walnut with a wonderful marquetry border and central rosette. The cusped legs are carved with foliage and masks in Perpendicular manner. There are several versions of this table: Crace made one in 1853 for James Watts at Abney Hall and a version made for John Naylor of Leighton Hall, Welshpool appeared on the market recently. Work of this type seems to have been taken up by makers such as Trollope and it may be that he first saw it in 1851.

A jewel-like room was created at Eastnor Castle in Herefordshire in 1849. It survives intact with the furniture, encaustic tiles and a wonderful chandelier by Hardman. The furniture is mostly walnut with polychromatic marquetry and detailed carving, and was made by Crace & Co. The firm of Crace & Co had been established in 1768. They specialised in decorating and worked with every British monarch from George III to Victoria. They had formed a house-decorating partnership with Pugin in 1844, when he was working for Lord Shrewsbury at Alton Towers. The firm of Myers also showed pieces which they had made to Pugin's designs. They had their names and the nature of their work on banners on each side of the display.

The furniture for the House of Lords ranges from simple chairs with octagonal legs joined by chamfered squared sections, to much more elaborate pieces such as the celebrated Clerk's table made by the Bond Street maker John Webb and the throne modelled on the Coronation Chair in Westminster Abbey by the same maker. The State Bed, sold in the early years of the last century and returned in 1986, was made by Holland and Sons in 1857.

Below:
Designs for a bookcase and a table dated 1832 from a sketchbook entitled Contrasted Domestic Architecture. Courtesy of the Trustees of the Victoria and Albert Museum

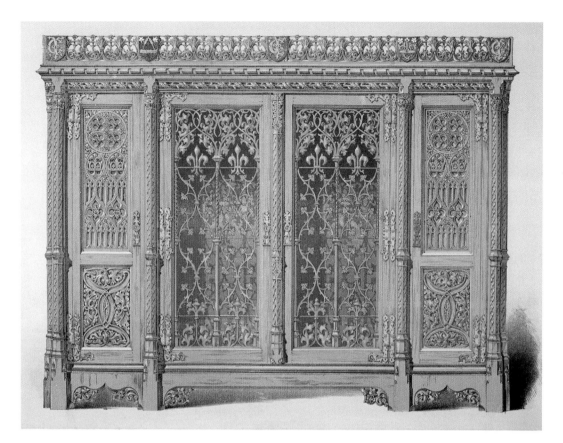

Pugin died at the early age of 40 on 14th September 1852, having suffered from mental illness during the last months of his life, probably brought on by extreme hard work. He was known for his boundless energy and would travel for many hours by train, seeing two or three clients in a day. His influence lasted many years after his death, not only through his son Edward Welby Pugin who took over the practice at that time, but also through other makers. As we have seen, Crace produced a copy of the marquetry table for Abney Hall in 1853, Holland continued work to his designs as noted above, and makers such as C. and R. Light were publishing and taking orders to his designs as late as 1880.

What characterised his work, especially of the later period, was a simplicity of material. He tended to use oak as a primary timber, apart from isolated examples such as the marquetry table by Crace. Ornamentation was mainly carved, or in simple brass metalwork or relatively restrained gilding. In spite of his dictum that features of design should be useful, he applied medieval features such as foliage, tracery and linenfold carving as decoration. To the modern eye this may seem superfluous, but seen in the context of over-ornamentation so much complained about at the time of the 1851 Exhibition, it shows considerable restraint and Pugin would surely have claimed that it showed "propriety" within its context. His legacy was not simply to have recreated a style, but to have taken a very English strand of design and reinvented it. He distilled what he saw as a quintessential style, which looked back to before the Reformation; that it represented an England once in communion with Rome was no accident. He laid the way for the Arts and Crafts and Modern Movements, rooted in a respect for human values, a wholesome morality and, to a degree, pointed to the birth of Socialism so beloved of men like William Morris.

Below:
The Medieval Court at the Crystal Palace, 1851. Chromolithograph from Dickenson's Comprehensive Pictures of the Great Exhibition, after Nash, Haghe and Roberts, Plate 12. This image gives an idea of the Gothic element at the Exhibition. Pugin's cross can be seen in its lowered position in the background and the top of the oak cabinet can just be seen to right at the back.

Above:
The centre table made for John Naylor of Leighton Hall by Crace and Co. This wonderful table shows fine carving and the greater use of colour, which Crace encouraged. The marquetry has faded and would have been much brighter when the table was first delivered.

Above:
A plain oak writing table made to a Pugin design almost certainly after his death. The simple chamfered central and end supports are typical as are the "tusked tenons" at each side. Washstands of this type were supplied to The Earl and Countess of Dunraven, Adare Manor, Co Limerick around 1846. Courtesy of the Trustees of the Victoria and Albert Museum

Right:
An oak side table made by John Webb, the simple design incorporating subtle carved foliage and the so-called tusked tenons are very characteristic.

Opposite Page:
A satinwood, painted and parcel-gilt side cabinet. This small cabinet to a Pugin design is similar to furniture made for Scarisbrick. Courtesy Blairmans.

A painted chest of drawers showing clean and dirty clothes. Burges'
light-hearted approach and sense of humour show through in this
piece. It was eventually used at the Tower House and is now in the
City of Manchester Art Gallery

Biography:

William Burges
(1827-1881)

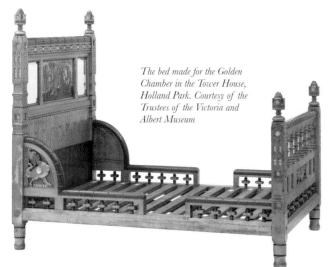

The bed made for the Golden Chamber in the Tower House, Holland Park. Courtesy of the Trustees of the Victoria and Albert Museum

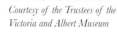

The Vita Nova Washstand. Courtesy of the Trustees of the Victoria and Albert Museum

The Industry and Idleness Cabinet. Courtesy of Christies

Detail of The Industry and Idleness Cabinet.

Like many furniture designers, William Burges was primarily an architect; not only the exterior, the structure and the decorative embellishments of a building concerned him, but also its interior, ranging from hangings and wallpaper to the furniture. He extended his range to ceramics, jewellery and metalwork so as to create a complete dream world. Unlike Pugin, Burges had little interest in making furniture for commercial gain and consequently his furniture is rare and highly prized. This is partly because it was often highly decorated and painted by distinguished artists, so that it was not possible to reproduce it in the same way that a maker might work from a Pugin design. Unlike Pugin he did not have such a busy practice and no son to take on the business when he died.

He was born on 2nd December 1827 and educated at Kings College School in London, where he was a near contemporary of D.G.Rossetti, the Pre-Raphaelite painter. He continued his studies at Kings College as an undergraduate, commencing an engineering course which he gave up after a year. He then joined the office of the architect Edward Blore, which set him on course for his future career. For him Pugin was a formative influence from an early age. At the time of the Great Exhibition, towards the end of Pugin's career, Burges was assisting Matthew Digby Wyatt in preparations for its opening. He must have been entranced by the Medieval Court, combining its veneration for the past with an emerging love of ritual and the delicate designs derived from Gothic style. At the time of the International Exhibition held in London in 1862 on the site where the Natural History Museum now stands, he organised a second Medieval Court for the Ecclesiological Society. As Burges developed, he venerated the 13th Century above all and, as is recorded by the Builder magazine, he stuck fiercely to that style even when many of his contemporaries were beginning to turn to the Queen Anne style for inspiration. "I have been brought up in the 13th Century belief, and in that belief I intend to die", he stated.

In fact his style was extremely eclectic, often incorporating Renaissance, Pompeian, Japanese, Assyrian and Islamic strands. His version of Gothic or what is sometimes referred to as painted Gothic, goes beyond the Perpendicular style of the late 15th Century and incorporates the earlier Norman or Romanesque style of the 12th Century. Surfaces are often highly painted and jewelled; certainly early furniture was painted, although most that is extant now lacks its decorated surface. Burges contrasts with Pugin in this respect: he better understood the use of colour in earlier times and reproduced it in what to some may seem an almost garish manner.

Above:

The Yatman Cabinet, Chromolithograph Plate 155, Masterpieces of Industrial Art and Sculpture 1862 - J.B.Waring. Designed for Herbert George Yatman in 1858 and made by the firm of Harland and Fisher. It is one of Burges' earliest pieces of painted furniture and was described as the only truly painted piece of painted furniture mad in England since the middle ages. Made from pine and mahogany and decorated with scenes from the story of Cadmus, suitable for an escritoire, as Cadmus was the hero who brought the alphabet to ancient Greece. It can be called the first piece of Pre-Raphaelite furniture. Now in the Victoria and Albert Museum.

Above:

A walnut and painted chair made by Seddon and Co. This chair can be seen in the photograph of the medieval court and although it is not by Burges, it is possible that he decorated the surround with distinctive penwork, similar to that on the King René Honeymoon chest, which was also made by Seddon. On that piece the additions are thought to be by Burges.

At the time of the 1862 Exhibition he wrote two articles for the *Gentleman's Magazine* which discussed the exhibition as a whole and the Japanese Court in particular. He makes the general comment that by 1862, Gothic, which had been regarded as an eccentric style restricted to a very few makers like Pugin in 1851, had become virtually a national style.

The interest shown by Burges in the Japanese Court is important in two respects. Firstly this was the first significant display of Japanese goods in Europe since the ending of the isolationist policy, which had endured since the seventeenth century. Secondly many of the styles and techniques were copied by craftsmen in England and France; in particular they were adopted by the generation which followed Burges and Morris, eventually giving birth to the Anglo-Japanese style. Burges considered the study of Western European medievalism as highly problematical due to the marked changes and development in society. He looked on Middle Eastern and Islamic cultures as being closer to true medievalism by virtue of their more conservative and under-industrialised way of life.

It is easy to understand why he admired Japanese works of art so much. There was a strong influence from natural forms, a striking use of colour and a slightly quirky stylised sense of design, which equated

Below:
The Medieval Court at the International Exhibition in London in 1862. The exhibition buildings stood where the Natural History Museum now is. The vast building was divided into national and international spaces. The Medieval Court following on from Pugin's of 1851 contained pieces by Burges and others. The Yatman cabinet can be seen, as can a chest which was discovered recently and the chair by Seddon & Co. illustrated opposite

Left:
The Industry and Idleness Cabinet,
probably made by Harland and Fisher
and originally in Burges' own office.
It is likely that the source for both this
piece and the Yatman cabinet were
medieval armoires preserved at Bayeux
and Noyon. The latter was illustrated
by Viollet-le-Duc in his Dictionary of
French Furniture published in 1858.
Both are in a strong architectural form,
favoured by Burges. The cupboard is
painted with four figures emblematic of
the seasons, with personifications of Day
and Night to the sides. On one side there
is a shepherd shown tending his sheep,
inscribed "Industry', on the other a
shepherd sleeps inscribed, "Idleness".
Courtesy of Christies.

well with his own. He was impressed by the quality of bronzes and metalwork and made special mention of copper hinges and fastenings for the cabinets, which were tinned or covered with Venetian lacquer, engraved and the recesses then gilded. The characteristic of attention to detail and colour can be seen in Burges' own work. His enthusiasm for the section is evident throughout. He ends, "I hope I have said enough to show the student of our reviving arts of the thirteenth century, that an hour, or even a day or two, spent in the Japanese department will by no means be lost time, for these hitherto unknown barbarians appear not only to know all that the Middle Ages knew, but in some respects are beyond them and us as well."

Burges' active life was short; his first major architectural commission was for Cork Cathedral in 1863 and he died only eighteen years later. As far as furniture was concerned, his most important patrons were the fabulously wealthy 3rd Marquess of Bute and A.J.Beresford Hope. His most important work was carried out for Lord Bute at Mount

Stewart, Cardiff Castle and Castell Coch, all of which contain furniture. He also designed furniture for his own dwelling, Tower House, 9 Melbury Road in Holland Park, London. He was financially secure and this allowed him to indulge in fantasy, without any real financial concerns. His furniture is scarce and most of it is now accounted for. Because of its highly idiosyncratic nature it did not allow for designs to be reproduced after his death as in the case of Pugin. J. Mordaunt Crook's summary of his furniture cannot be improved on: "More that most of his generation, Burges despised Georgian and Regency furniture. Veneering he regarded with suspicion; upholstery he hated. His furniture therefore, boxy and perpendicular, painted with heraldic colours and Pre-Raphaelite panels, was conceived as the ultimate answer to the dark ages of Georgian joinery. Drawing on the talents of a veritable galaxy of artistic friends, Burges in effect created the perfect medium for his talents: the art of Pre-Raphaelite furniture."

Above:
Detail of The Industry
and Idleness Cabinet.

Above:
Ebonised & Hardstone Inlaid Dressing Mirror 1858. A very similar design for the Reverend Yatman given as a gift at the time of his marriage to Anna Hamilton in 1858. Courtesy of Christies

Above:

*The Wine and Beers Sideboard, 1859, shown at the 1862
exhibition, it was apparently commissioned by James Nicholson,
although it was sold at the end of the exhibition to someone else.
It is painted by Sir Edwin Poynter and shows the combat
between Sir Bacchus and Sir John Barleycorn, each are supported
by figures of Burgundy, Hock and Champagne and Porter, Pale
Ale and Scotch Ale respectively. There are also six portraits on the
outside and figures of Ginger Beer, Lemonade, Seltzer Water and
Soda Water on the interior.*

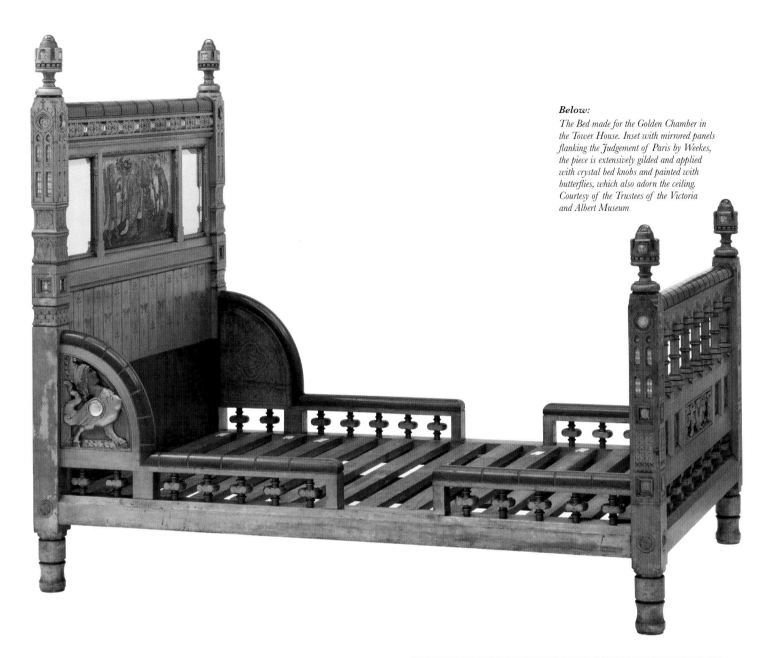

Below:
The Bed made for the Golden Chamber in the Tower House. Inset with mirrored panels flanking the Judgement of Paris by Weekes, the piece is extensively gilded and applied with crystal bed knobs and painted with butterflies, which also adorn the ceiling. Courtesy of the Trustees of the Victoria and Albert Museum

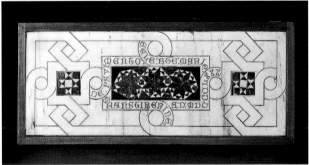

Above:
A mosaic inlaid marble pier table, 1879-80. This table was made for the Golden Chamber or the Guest bedroom in the Tower House. The table described as a dressing table in 1880 was one of the last pieces of furniture designed before Burges died. The marble top prepared by the firm of Burke and Co reputedly incorporates marble for the floor of the Basilica of Santa Maria in Trastevere, in Rome, taken from the spot where St Paul preached. A contemporary description of the room gives some idea the fantasy created, "What bedrooms! The guest chamber is made of fire and flowers... the bed, toilet-table, washstand, cabinets, are all plain gold. The shutters are plain gold. The windows glow with the colours of Alhambra... Through Moorish trellis work these colours shine, the subjects being only visible by scrutiny. What is not pure gold is crystal; the knobs on the bedpost, the shelves of the tables, scintillate with facets. The whole room is like an ancient shrine or reliquary." Courtesy Sotheby's

Above:
A detail of the upper part of The Vita Nova Washstand. Courtesy of the Trustees of the Victoria and Albert Museum

Opposite:
The Vita Nova Washstand, also made for the Golden Chamber. Mrs Haweis, who described the pier table wrote, "Up to now a washstand has seemed an impertinent sort of affair, to be kept out of sight, but here we have a gem fit to splash at all day in poetic enjoyment." It is gilded inset with hardstones and shells, finely carved with flowers. There are marble plates for the soap and a bronze bull's head through which the water emerges. The jewel like details and fine gilded work recall the Japanese lacquer, which so fascinated Burges at the 1862 exhibition. Courtesy of the Trustees of the Victoria and Albert Museum

An impressive cabinet on stand, exhibited at the 1862 International Exhibition in London. This illustration comes from the Art Journal record of the exhibition.

Trollope & Sons (1778- c.1890)

A cabinet detail showing a
porcelain portrait of Raphael

A walnut centre table applied with
gilt-bronze mouldings exhibited at
the Paris Exhibition of 1867

Cabinet detail in high quality
enamel. Courtesy Sotheby's

A carved walnut sideboard of
massive proportions shown at
the Paris exhibition of 1867

Trollope and Sons are by no means the best known of Victorian makers but they exemplify what one might call mainstream Victorian cabinet-making. They combined high quality workmanship with a lively eclectic style, drawing on many different strands from the past for their inspiration. They fused their interests as builders with their skills as interior decorators. The commercial practicality of having links with a building business and being able to carry out the decoration of interior, had obvious benefits. While they are not considered important today for their innovative designs, as Pugin or Burges, are they represent what would have been the overwhelmingly popular taste of the period. Many of their better pieces were exhibited at the series of International Exhibitions both in London and Paris as well as elsewhere, and this is a very useful way in which to approach their work.

Although Trollope and Sons did not become widely known until the second half of the 19th Century, the business was founded by Joseph Trollope in 1778 and established at 15 Parliament Street, London. The family had originally come from Louth in Lincolnshire. By 1843 the business was registered as George Trollope and Son and extended to "and Sons" in 1846. Although we are not primarily concerned with

their early work there is an in-house letter book preserved for the years 1787-1808, which records work for distinguished clients, giving some idea of the standing the firm. Amongst the addresses mentioned are Kingston Maurwood, The Vyne, Vale Royal, Burghley and Shugborough. Interestingly they were associated with Thomas Cubitt, the architect, and had an agreement to let his houses for a 1% commission, (the normal commission was 5%.) After Cubitt's death in 1857 they took several sites from his executors including the north side of Eccleston Square, which they completed between 1857 and 1859. These contacts would probably have helped them find clients. As Thomas Cubitt was one of the commissioners of the Great Exhibition, their contact might well have encouraged them to take part. It is difficult to establish how important the cabinet-making arm of the firm was by 1851, but judging from the reports and the furniture illustrated, they were not considered as highly as they were by the mid-1860s, following the 1862 Exhibition. By 1864 they had taken premises at West Halkin Street in the heart of Belgravia, which would have given them an excellent base to attract new clients settling in Cubitt's new developments. An entry in the diary of Lady Frederick Cavendish for December 13th, 1864 also indicates the standing of the firm. "Thence to our

Right:

A chest and toilet mirror exhibited by Trollope at the 1851 Exhibition. This chromolithograph was published by Wyatt in his record of the Exhibition. These records often provide a way of identifying pieces and give a good idea of what was popular at the time

BED ROOM FURNITURE IN MARQUETERIE BY TROLLOPE OF LONDON

splendid mansion No 21 Carlton House Terrace, where we met my old Meries and Mr Talbot and Trollope, the builder and furnisher's man. And we have settled the whole painting of the house, chosen all the papers and the principal grates and discussed many other points." In the following year they had four separate premises: their original address at Parliament Street, West Halkin Street, the Belgrave Works and Grosvenor Street West. They added a fifth in 1870 in the High Street, Vauxhall.

For the Great Exhibition of 1851 the catalogue records them as showing a "sideboard elaborately carved in oak representing hunting and fishing". This piece is illustrated in the *Art Journal*, where it is described as having "rich and elaborate carving". The wood employed is not clear from the engraving, although the detailed work would suggest walnut. In comparison with much of the over-carved and heavy sideboards exhibited, especially in the English section, this piece shows a lightness of touch rather in advance of its time. Although not mentioned in the catalogue, the jury reports refer to "bed and toilet furniture", which is reproduced in chromolithograph by Digby Wyatt in *Industrial Arts of the XIXth Century at the Great Exhibition 1851*. The toilet mirror and chest incorporate marquetry work which was highly praised by Wyatt, who observes that much contemporary marquetry employed artificially stained woods which were not usually durable, were too brightly coloured and poorly assembled in garish combinations. Trollope, he says, has tried to overcome these difficulties and did not use artificial colours. He hopes "that they will improve and mellow with time. Original beauty may be restored with scraping". This last statement suggests that he considered even the natural colours rather bright. The reference to "scraping" gives an insight into Victorian attitudes to restoration: he must mean that when the colours have faded they can at least be recovered – something which could not be achieved with artificial colours. Again it is not clear what the primary wood may be, perhaps walnut, satinwood or Russian maple. Above twenty different woods were incorporated including, "holly, cornwood, tulip, sandal, purplewood, ebony, Barbary wood, Russian maple, mulberry, kingwood, amboyna,walnut and porcupine wood".

British cabinet-makers did not take full advantage of the first opportunity to exhibit furniture at an international exhibition. in Paris in 1855. Trollope and Sons showed alongside Crace, Banting, Jackson and Graham, Gillows, Levien, Morant and Boyd, Holland and Sons and J.Webb. Under Trollope the catalogue simply lists "marquetry furniture of stained woods".

The firm attracted great interest and acclaim at the second International Exhibition in London in 1862. The period following the exhibition seems to have lead to the firm's expansion; at the time of the Exhibition they are still recorded at Parliament Street, but, as we have seen, by 1864 they were at four separate addresses. Literature and reports of the Exhibition indicate their standing with the public had been enhanced and their range of work together with the expense of the materials employed supports this. Recently a cabinet shown at the exhibition came to light. It was carved in solid ebony and incorporated marquetry panels and lion masks in gilt bronze. There were porcelain ovals by Copeland showing Benvenuto Cellini, Bernard Palissy, Rafaello Sanzio and Michaelangelo Buonarotti. The piece had been designed by Richard Beavis, formerly a pupil of Marlborough Howe School, and the carving carried out by Mark Rogers, who served as the foreman of Trollope's carvers. The piece is a departure from the earlier work of the firm, monumental in design and in the use of solid ebony, sparing no expense. The use of ebony

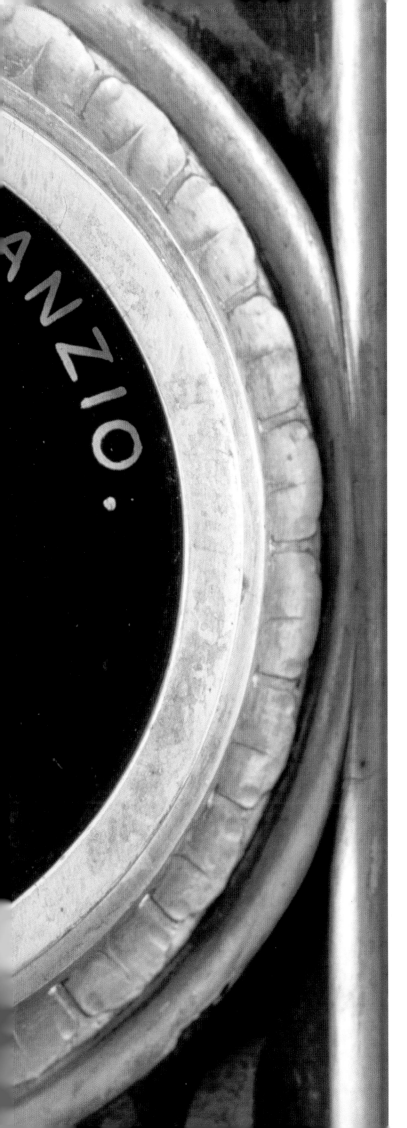

in this and works shown in Paris in 1867, was a specific attempt to rival French makers who favoured the material. The jury reports on the Exhibition read, "with regard to the ebony cabinet, if objection may be made to the arrangement of the lower part, the beauty of execution fully compensates for this defect of the elegance and simplicity of the general form; the inlaid woods, the carving of the figures on the pediment, the enamelled paintings are treated with great care, and cause this cabinet to be regarded as a quite exceptional work, superior even to the other productions of the same exhibitors".

The *Illustrated London News* praises the piece very highly, even rating it above the work of the celebrated Paris maker Fourdinois. The style is described as Cinquecento, the marquetry "wrought by wood inlays; red, yellow, cream, and grey woods being inserted in the ebony." On inspection of the piece today, this suggests that the colours did not have the permanency hoped for as they do not contrast in such a striking way. The writer also refers to the "electro-gilt" mounts in such away as to draw attention to the technique, which today might be played down. The use of electrolysis was considered a great advance and an important contribution to the industrial arts. The writer considered it "one of the most exalted works of its class brought before us in the exhibition". A chimneypiece in the same exhibition demonstrates both the range of the firm and its roots in the building trade. The design is again by Beavis in the "Lombardo-Gothic" style and the modelling by Mark Rogers. The frieze has medallions of red sparl on a black marble ground. The clock within the central pediment was supplied by Dent. The whole of the mantle and the superstructure was in oak, inlaid with bands of ebony and a darker stained oak. The central section, which appears filled with a patterned paper, was intended to contain a picture. The wooden panels were carved with foliage and busts of Homer, Virgil, Dante and Petrarch, with Apollo in the central panel at the top.

Another piece was first shown at the 1865 Exhibition in Dublin and from the catalogue it would appear that it was the only piece the firm sent. It was not uncommon for the same piece to be shown at different exhibitions and subsequently it was at the Paris Exhibition of 1867. The cabinet is related to one made to a very similar design, which is applied with vignettes of Milton and Raphael, which can be seen in an engraving made at the time. The Cabinet is clearly related to the piece illustrated and described in more detail in the reports. It has an identical frieze and columns, although the doors and lower section are different. The reports describe it as "Renaissance style". It incorporated flat areas of marble in the lower section, above a drawer centred by a lion mask similar to the one which appeared on the 1862 cabinet.

Left:
A detail showing a porcelain portrait of Raphael. Vignettes showing artists of the past were popular and often appeared on pieces. This practice was linked with the desire to educate people about the arts in general as well as acknowledge a debt to artists of the past.

PLATE 64

A table described as "a salon table" in ebony with gilt bronze and ivory inlay is shown in the *Art Journal* for the 1867 Exhibition. This table, or an almost identical example, was sold at auction in 1996. The basic model was repeated by the firm and similar versions have been on the market since. A buffet in "modern Renaissance" style is typical of Victorian furniture. It was in walnut and considered rather too heavy by the writers of the jury reports. Large Victorian furniture of this type, although often made to very high standards, was not at all popular during the middle years of the last century and much of was destroyed or dismantled.

The firm declined towards the end of the 19th Century and, although they did show pieces at the Paris Exhibition of 1878, they are not mentioned as much in the jury reports. They still had a showroom in Liverpool in 1890 but there is no work recorded from that period. Although not associated with leading designers, their links with the building trade and their understanding of what the emerging middle class wanted, makes them a good mirror of popular taste. They are also accredited with introducing several new techniques such as xylotechnograpy and sgraffito. The former was a means of applying colour to wood, the latter borrowed from ceramics, whereby a veneer was applied and then part-engraved to reveal the contrasting timber beneath.

Above:

An ebony, marble and enamel cabinet shown at the Dublin Exhibition of 1865 and the Paris Exhibition of 1867. Courtesy Sotheby's

Above:

A detail from the cabinet. High quality enamel plaques embellished this piece. They are probably French and indicate that many London makers would have looked to Paris for decorative detail. They are inspired by the enamel work from Limoges, which had been produced since the 16th Century. Courtesy Sotheby's

Above:

An ebony cabinet shown at Paris in 1867 related to cabinet far left.

Opposite:

A design for a chimney-piece shown at the 1862 Exhibition. It shows the range that the firm was capable of, concentrating here on a decorative scheme for an interior. It combines contrasting materials and styles, making use of a strong sense of colour. Plate 64 from Burney's work on the 1862 Exhibition. Courtesy Sotheby's

Right:

A walnut centre table applied with gilt-bronze mouldings and finely carved. This table is identical to a design for one exhibited at the Paris Exhibition of 1867. Tables based on this model and of varying quality do appear from time to time. Courtesy Sotheby's

Right, Below:

A detail showing the carved end support of the centre table. Courtesy Sotheby's

Holland & Sons
(1843-1968)

*A bird's eye maple
Davenport, c.1845*

*A burr walnut and parcel-gilt
library table, c.1860 stamped
HOLLAND & SONS*

*A marquetry side cabinet applied
with gilt-bronze mounts c.1860*

*A Victorian mahogany
library writing table stamped
HOLLAND & SONS*

Opposite: *A section of a bookcase and chimneypiece shown at the Great Exhibition in London in 1851. This shows the high Renaissance style combined with a richness of materials; the piece is predominantly carved in walnut with cut brass doors and applied with marble. It is typical of the rich and eclectic style of the period.*

Although the history of the firm spans most of the century, they were not attracting major commissions until the second quarter. Early records suggest a partnership in the names of Stephen Taprell and William Holland from as early as 1803. Taprell was evidently the senior partner, and was probably the same as the Taprell recorded as subscribing to Sheraton's Cabinet Dictionary in 1803. Whether William Holland was related to the celebrated architect and designer of Carlton House, Henry Holland, remains uncertain. From 1835 the firm traded as Taprell, Holland and Son and, following Taprell's death in 1843, as Holland and Sons, later to be William Holland and Sons. The firm finally went into receivership in 1968. After collaborating with Thomas Dowbiggin on the royal commission at Osborne House, they took over his business at 23 Mount Street in 1853.

Unlike many firms of the period the Holland archive has survived largely intact. It runs from 1824 to 1942, but unfortunately lacks the years from 1826 to 1835, when the firm became Taprell, Holland and Son. This extensive and invaluable record includes Property records, ledgers for non-government and government contracts, account books, day books for clients funeral books. It is preserved in the National Art Collections Archive and, as well as giving an insight into the internal workings of the firm, it can be a very useful research tool. Commissions are recorded meticulously by date and by name. That Holland & Sons arranged the State Funeral for the Duke of Wellington in 1853 and supplied the Coronation throne for Edward VII in 1902, testifies to their status throughout the second half of the 19th Century. They worked with many leading designers, sent exhibits to international exhibitions in London in 1851 and 1862, Paris in 1855, 1867, 1878 and 1900, as well as Vienna in 1873. They also undertook extensive commissions for many London clubs and worked for the Royal Family.

Amongst early commissions were those for a series of London clubs, beginning with the Union Club in 1823, where they supplied chairs and tables. Furnishing the Athenaeum Club, beginning in the following

Above:

Two pairs of early Victorian mahogany hall benches from The Subscription Room, Tattersalls, Knightsbridge. These benches came from Tattersall's premises and probably date from around the middle of the century. Holland's success at furnishing clubs would have made them an obvious choice for work of this type. Courtesy Sotheby's

Above:

A Victorian mahogany library writing table stamped HOLLAND & SONS on a frieze drawer a writing table made to a very high standard. The quality of the mahogany can be seen from the figuring, which gives this piece great character. Courtesy Sotheby's

Opposite:

From Masterpieces of Industrial Art & Sculpture 1862, by John Burney, chromolithograph. The table is centred by a spider's web in silver and ivory done in marquetry by Mr Rosenburg and decorated with roundels showing the artists, Titian, Raphael, Rubens, Velaquez, Claude Lorraine, Rembrandt and Hogarth. The style represents a somewhat restrained version of Louis XVI. French taste has always been revered throughout the world and its exposure in London in 1851 and 1862 made it very popular at that time. It was also praised for a better standard of design and workmanship. Courtesy Sotheby's

year and continuing with work until 1838, was perhaps their most distinguished early commission. It has been discussed in some detail by Simon Jervis in the *Furniture History Society Journal* for 1970. For temporary premises twenty tables and five dozen chairs were ordered, but there were considerable additions until 1830 when the present building, designed by Decimus Burton was completed. The work continued for another eight years and included much dining and library furniture as well as bedroom furniture and more modest pieces for use in the servants quarters. The committee's minutes give some indication of the style of furnishings.

"Ordered Two Books Cases one on each side The Map Room door in the Great Room, the Ottomans to be placed back to back on each side the Centre Table in the Drawing room. A square Plinth three inches high to be affixed to the Books Cases in the Great Room for the acception of the Busts taken from the Brackets. Two Brackets to be placed one on each side the Looking Glass in the Great Room."

In following years other clubs made use of the firm, including the Oxford and Cambridge (1835-40), the United Services, Arthur's, Clarence and Albion.

At the 1851 Exhibition a chimneypiece and bookcases were shown. They were made under the direction of the architect T.R.MacQuoid. The exuberant rich style is typical of the middle of the century. As the *Art Journal Catalogue* states, it is that of the Cinquecento, a broad Renaissance revival popular at the time describes it as "a free adaption of natural forms introduced with judgement and taste. The work is exquisitely carved in walnut wood, and inlaid with green and red marbles; the doors are of perforated brass, and all the materials are of British growth and manufacture."

The production of the firm becomes more varied from the middle of the century. Exposure at the Great Exhibition would have brought a wider clientele and it was around this time that work was carried out for Queen Victoria and Prince Albert at Osborne House, as well as other Royal residences, Sandringham, Balmoral and Marlborough House. Collaboration with distinguished designers was characteristic of the period. An ebony cabinet and stand with gilt-bronze mounts on striking monopodia with claw feet and centred by a porcelain panel by George Gray, was designed by Professor Gottfried Semper and shown at the Paris Exhibition in 1855. On the whole the British section was not much admired at the time, but French commentators made special mention of this piece. It marks a more general eclecticism and use of varied materials, a move away from oak and mahogany to satinwood and walnut or more exotic materials.

A table discovered in a private collection and made for the1862 Exhibition illustrates well the use of foreign timbers. It is fully illustrated as a chromolithograph in *Masterpieces of Industrial Art and Sculpture* 1862, by John Burney Waring and the woods used are described in detail, "Tulipwood, Kingwood, New Zealand spicewood, airwood, box, purpleheart, and orangewood". The table is the style of the Louis XVI period but translated into a very English idiom; somewhat more restrained than the French original might have been. French taste was very much in vogue in the early years of the second half of the 19th Century and much of Holland's furniture reflected this taste. This piece is recorded in detail in the archive under an entry for the International Exhibition of 1862 and so, presumably, it was made for the Exhibition and not to a special commission. The comments made at the time indicate the status the firm had acquired, "Messrs. Holland & Sons by means of employing well qualified designers, by great excellence in technical processes, and by their enterprising character, this firm attained to the highest position as furniture makers, and would certainly have obtained a medal for the

Above:
A bird's eye maple Davenport, circa 1845, with the stencil FROM HOLLAND & SONS, Upholsterers & C. 19 MARYLEBONE ST, ST JAMES'S LONDON. This simple piece shows the use of unusual timbers which began to develop as the century progressed. The strong attractive figure of maple was highly thought of. This type of small desk with an adjustable top is reputed to have a naval origin. Courtesy Sotheby's

Above:

*A burr walnut and parcel-gilt library table, circa 1860 stamped
HOLLAND & SONS. This table makes use of walnut, which
was very popular by the 1860's. The parcel-gilt highlights add
something to the piece and are characteristic of more highly
decorated pieces. Courtesy Sotheby's*

Above:

*A walnut and parcel-gilt folio library desk, circa 1860. This desk came from
Westonbirt House in Gloucestershire and was probably supplied to Robert Staynor
Holford, the patron and collector. It may have been removed from his London
residence, Dorchester House. Courtesy Sotheby's*

finely executed, marqueterie table, but from the fact of Mr. Holland accepted the honorary post of a juror in his class, which as one of the greatest distinctions." The stand was "excellently designed" and consisted of three columns supported on brackets, all decorated with ormolu, which must have had a striking effect. This table is similar to a suite of furniture made for Mr R.N.Thornton of Knowle Cottage, Sidmouth, Devon and illustrated by Symonds and Whineray in *Victorian Furniture*.

Hollands were very aware of the need to make furniture to good designs. The Exhibition of 1851 had highlighted shortcomings in design schools and training for artisans in England. Holland himself stated that, "the principal impediments to the progress of manufacture of elegant cabinetmakers' work in this country are caused by a great want of designers, draughtsmen, and modellers; in fact of all the directors of art. The very few who can assist, demand and are paid with such excessive rates, that their services are dispensed with, except on important occasions." As we have seen, Hollands employed the German Gottfried Semper, who was teaching at the Department of Practical Art at Marlborough House, in 1855. In contrast to the prevailing tastes, but remaining faithful to the principal of working with distinguished designers, they made and exhibited a cabinet in Gothic taste by Bruce Talbert, at the Paris Exhibition of 1867. This striking side cabinet in oak with fruitwood marquetry is embellished with inscriptions, "May good digestion wait on appetite" and "We have all great cause to give great thanks".

By the time of the Paris Exhibition of 1878, the Adam Revival style was well underway and Holland & Sons sent a magnificent painted satinwood bedroom suite, which included a wardrobe, an "Arabian" bedstead, a side cabinet, a dressing table, a writing table, six side chairs, a night table, a pair of bedside cupboards, a bidet, a side table, a toilet mirror and a washstand. The suite was by no means an exact reproduction of an Adam period suite; indeed such an extensive suite would not have existed at the time. It simply drew on the vocabulary of the period, combining high quality painting in the manner of Angelica Kauffman within finely cast gilt bronze borders. It was highly praised at the time of the exhibition both by French and English commentators. It was purchased by Sir Richard Wallace, the collector responsible for the Wallace Collection; as the French publisher Gonse noted, this choice was an excellent certificate of good taste.

Holland & Sons were renowned for the quality of their work. They had introduced machinery at an early stage, but not allowed this to interfere with the standard of work on the finished surface. By the middle of the century they were employing about 350 men. This allowed them to produce work to the highest standard but also to supply pieces to the growing middle class, as well as royalty and the aristocracy. As Digby Wyatt pointed out in his *Industrial Arts of the XIX Century* at the Great Exhibition 1851, "their workshops are so excellent and so well arranged with every appliance for good and cheap production", that the great cabinetmaker Jeanselme of Paris continually and voluntarily refers to the fact that he took his ideas and models from their establishment.

Right:

A marquetry side cabinet applied with gilt-bronze mounts and stamped HOLLAND & SONS, circa 1860. The back is also stamped M.H., referring to Marlborough House, the residence of Edward, Prince of Wales, later Edward VII and Princess Alexandra following their marriage in 1863. Inventory stamps such as the M.H. are not uncommon on furniture and can help considerably in attributing a piece. This exceptionally fine side cabinet underlines the vogue for French taste, followed by the Prince of Wales and the quality shows off the firm at the height of their powers and popularity. Courtesy Sotheby's

Opposite Page:
The dressing table from the bedroom suite at the Paris Exhibition of 1878. Courtesy Sotheby's

Left:
Detail of a winged harpy from the dressing table illustrated, showing the excellent carving and gilded highlights. Courtesy Sotheby's

Below:
The wardrobe from the 1878 Bedroom Suite. Courtesy Sotheby's

V
The Arts and Crafts Movement

Michael Barrington

Mike Barrington's love of anything to do with craft skill started at prep school and centred on model engineering and steam engines in particular. Later, his maternal grandmother, a serious collector of antique furniture, bravely invited her only grandson to mend parts of her collection which he later inherited and had to undo much of the ill-informed work he did some 30 years earlier! MB's first career was in the Army for 26 years as a regular cavalry officer very much involved in equitation, horse trials and the Three Day Event. He was the Regimental Riding Master.

On leaving the service in 1983 he decided to "go into restoration", worked in the antique trade, attended a number of courses on various skills and set up in business, initially working almost entirely within the antique trade. He joined the embryo British Antique Furniture Restorers' Association (BAFRA) in 1984, was editor of their newsletter and became BAFRA's Chairman in 1992 in which appointment he served until 2004. He is now the Association's Chief Executive.

V

The Arts and Crafts Movement

Origins & Ideals

Michael Barrington

Craft skills in furniture design and making in Britain have evolved over a period of some 500 years and they reached their highest levels at the end of the 18th Century. At this time British furniture design and manufacture were very highly respected throughout Europe and further afield. New aspects of design were constantly imported into Britain through inter-marriage and exchanges between Royal Houses, through rich aristocrats' and estate owners' tours in search of works of art and by itinerant craftsmen moving through international labour markets. Added to this, the development and popularity of long distance sea transport, albeit requiring many months of absence, encouraged British designers and craftsmen to visit countries such as Japan, China and India either for their own self-education or in support of British patrons and ex-patriots involved in trade. Foreign craftsmen were actively encouraged to work in Britain and many settled here to establish themselves within existing design and manufacturing businesses while others set up their own enterprises.

The industrial revolution, which was well under way in Britain by the end of the 1830s, was having a debilitating effect on craft industry. For many years previously there had been great activity in the study and revival in the practice of many of the decorative handicrafts neglected in England and America, though on the Continent and throughout the East these were carried on without a break. The machine production of an industrial century had laid

Fronticepiece from Great Exhibition Catalogue produced by the Art Journal

its iron hands upon what had formerly been the exclusive province of the handicraftsman, who in England only lingered on in a few obscure trades and in forgotten corners. The ideal of mechanical perfection dominated workmen, and the factory system, first by extreme division of labour, and then by the further specialisation of the workman under machine production, left no room for individual artistic feeling among craftsmen trained and working under such conditions. The demand of the world-market dictated the character and quality of production, and to the few who would seek some humanity, simplicity of construction or artistic feeling in their domestic decorations and furniture, the only choice was that of the tradesman or salesman, or a plunge into costly and doubtful experiments in original design.

Hand-made furniture became very expensive in comparison with that produced with sophisticated machine tools for moulding, carving, veneer cutting and planing, to mention but a few, all driven by the new phenomenon of the steam engine. Quality of both furniture design and construction were inevitable casualties. Both suffered because of designers' and makers' obligations to meet the technical demands imposed by manufacturers. A gap was created between the designers and manufacturers, and the craftsman was relegated near to obscurity.

A group of theorists, architects and designers in Victorian Britain started to form in the 1840s, seeking to provide relief to the harshness of industrialism which they observed as being responsible for serious declines in manufacturing standards and an accompanying loss of public respect for traditional craft skills, which they saw fast disappearing. The group was also disturbed by the apparently growing gulf between designer and craftsman.

An important fillip to the Movement was the Great Exhibition of 1851 in the Crystal Palace, centred on world-wide recognition and acclaim of Britain's industrial base. The exhibition demonstrated strong proof of the decline in both design and manufacturing standards, widely accepted as the result of divergence of design and craft skill.

However, industrialism was far from being the sole or even the main catalyst for the Movement. Arts and Crafts evolved out of the strict design morality of the Gothic revival in early Victorian Britain, so ably and fervently pursued by the architects and theorists Augustus Welby Pugin (1812-1852), Henry Shaw (1800-1873) and later William Burges (1827-1881), William Butterfield (1814-1900), G. E. Street and others. The school of pre-Raphaelite painters, by their careful and

A. W. N. Pugin.
By courtesy of the Victoria and
Albert Museum

Above:

Full-blown Gothic Revival. The redesigned drawingroom by Augustus Pugin at Eastnor Castle, Herefordshire, a sham Gothic pile designed by Sir Robert Smirke, architect of the British Museum in 1812-1814

Pugin designed the fan vaulting, fireplace, sideboard and chairs in the 1840s – pointers to the Arts and Crafts Movement following some twenty years later

thorough methods, and their sympathy with mediaeval design, were among the first to turn attention to beauty of design, colour and significance in the accessories of daily life, and artists like D. G. Rossetti themselves designed and painted furniture. The most successful and most practical effort towards the revival of sounder ideas of construction and workmanship may be said to have arisen out of the work of this group of artists, and maybe traced to the workshop of William Morris and his associates.

Pugin rejected the early Victorian vogue for classical architecture in favour of medieval Gothic, which he believed reflected the order and stability of Christian faith. Pugin was intensely religious and a convert to Roman Catholicism. He provided the foundation from which the moral aesthetics of the Arts and Crafts evolved during the second half of the century, which he was tragically never to witness because of a seriously curtailed life at the age of 40. Pugin's second most important legacy was his dream of re-uniting craftsman with designer – the "Spiritual with the Everyday", which inspired the movement's founding fathers Ruskin and Morris to forge and develop fiercely idealistic foundations with which a number of highly gifted and multi-talented architects and designers could identify and who were to form this important but relatively short-lived (50 years) movement with eventual almost worldwide recognition.

Pugin was multi-talented to such a degree that there are stories of serious tutorial relationships with craftsmen of varying disciplines during the building of the Palace of Westminster made possible by his very detailed and perhaps even inherited knowledge of a wide range of craft skills and a passion for perfection nurtured by very strong religious convictions. Today it is widely accepted that the quality of the building of Westminster is probably more appropriately attributed to Pugin than to the senior architect Barry. Perhaps as a sign of determination to stamp his authority on the design as well as the quality of building, Pugin left his trademark/monogram "AP" in many parts of the design/decoration of the fabric and furnishings of Westminster, as well as furniture made for his own use.

Pugin is one of the most talented and original furniture designers ever produced by England and, in spite of his very short life, he managed to produce a range of furniture designs from the enormously highly decorated gothic to the simplest and most functional which equalled if not emulated Arts and Crafts ideals. His insistence on a quality of manufacture, which was achieved only in traditional hand craft, work was also fundamental to the Movement born some twenty years after his death.

Above:

This is Pugin's own dining room cabinet made c.1845, probably by Myers who ranked with Gillow, Webb and Crace – the latter two featured importantly in the early days of the Arts and Crafts Movement in association with Morris, Ashbee, Voysey and Godwin. Pugin's passion for and insistence on quality reduced the excellence of his furniture makers' skills to no more than factual importance; the same applied to his other interests in ceramics, metalwork, textiles, interior decoration and many building constructional skills. By courtesy of the Victoria and Albert Museum

Above:

This is his dining table made in about 1845 which, like many Victorian table designs following, is telescopic but hand operated as opposed to later "winched" extending tables operated by a crank handle turning a screw thread, often so long that it had to be made on a version of the gun lathe. By kind permission of the Palace of Westminster

This is one of his simplest designs of a pine table of such startling clarity as to put him in a designer category not seen in Britain before and which was very much a forerunner and pointer to the Arts and Crafts movement to follow. By courtesy of the Victoria and Albert Museum

In his book *True Principles*, Pugin says "the smallest detail should have a meaning or serve a purpose – there should be no features about a building (or its furniture) which are not necessary for convenience, construction or propriety". These principles were basic to the Arts and Crafts Movement and were to be heard repeated by so many of its protagonists, particularly Mackintosh and Walton whose ideals as architects were that a building's function should dictate its design and that it should be built of undisguised materials and contain related interior fittings – a cohesion of design. It is from this belief that we see the significance of the architect's profession in the design of Arts and Crafts furniture.

Extravagance of design was also shared with other leading designers of the period such as Kent, Adam, Hope and Bullock. The use of hitherto untried materials and techniques in furniture design was in purpose-made support of the Movement's ideal of unification of constructional and design skills. Non-ferrous metals such as copper, pewter and tin were introduced as design enhancements which, perhaps in the case of mechanical fittings such as furniture hinges, were at the expense of practical considerations of both strength and longevity. Punched, etched and hand-beaten panels and elaborately carved gesso ornamentation became commonplace. This resulted in some designers abandoning principles of simplicity. An example is the work of William Burges who produced stunningly decorated pieces for wealthier clients, which must have been somewhat of an anathema to the more simplistic doyens such as Voysey and Dresser.

...his bed. By courtesy of the Cecil Higgins Gallery

...his Narcissus washstand. By courtesy of the Cecil Higgins Gallery

However, the use of engraved and hand-beaten metal panels found in Burges' designs was adopted with vigour but in rather more simplistic form by many of the Arts and Crafts designers towards the end of the century, in addition to the use of inlays of organic (animal) materials and carved and coloured gesso panels. Whilst Burges is not generally associated with the Movement, he shared the same passion for gothic design as Pugin and was a contemporary of one of the Movement's earliest models, the artist Dante Gabriel Rossetti whose influence on William Morris was fundamental to the latter's development as a designer and decorator and one of the Movement's founding fathers. Burges was too extreme and too eccentric to be an integral part of the Movement which may be relevant to his lifelong bachelor status and conviction that "marriage would interfere with his beautiful tastes" which, like many Victorian gentlemen of the time, included "ratting" and opium!

William Morris (1834-96), together with his close post-university associates Dante Gabriel Rossetti and John Ruskin supported by a constantly growing number of like-thinking painters and architects, laid the foundations of the new Movement but with a strong bias towards simplicity and the rural vernacular. That simplicity, together with excellence of craftsmanship, persisted throughout the life of the Movement, but a number of designers incorporated flamboyant decoration into their pieces and in some cases it was this decoration which was the designer's principal craft contribution. William Morris was one of these but because of his outstanding, almost universal talent,

Above:
The Red House, built in 1860 by Philip Webb for William Morris at Bexleyheath. Its local materials and unpretentious Gothic influenced style heralded the domestic revival of the 1870s.

Left:
Stained Glass window "Si Je Puis" at The Red House

...his dressing table. By courtesy of the Cecil Higgins Gallery

Left to Right:
Examples of extravagant furniture of William Burges (1827-1881) held in the Cecil Higgins Gallery in Bedford. His bed, his Narcissus washstand, his dressing table

he was able to apply his decorative skills to mediums other than furniture. The same multi-talent virtuosity was common to a number of the Movement's leaders and must be attributed to their common expertise in architecture, tempered by their belief in the oneness of design for purpose and utility.

The exterior designs of buildings complimented exactly their interiors, from wallpapers to fabrics, metalwork fittings, glass and furniture; above all shone the design principal of fitness for intended use. Many of the commissioners of design work were owners of successful businesses in the large cities and centres of burgeoning British industry, such as Glasgow, London and Birmingham. Owners in their quest for design would choose carefully from the wide range of both established and up-and-coming young designers. The success of the owners' enterprises enabled them to take calculated risks in their choice of designers and often the early successes of the young and relatively unknown was quickly established and publicised. Notable in that stream were Glaswegians Rennie Mackintosh and George Walton who were employed by established and highly successful business empires such as publisher Walter Blackie and Miss Cranston, the owner of a number of city tea rooms, to design interiors, furniture and decoration.

Few of the Movement's leaders were furniture makers as such, notable exceptions being the Barnsley brothers, Ernest and Sidney. For the most part furniture designs were put out to cabinet-makers of proven excellence who satisfied the designers' very high expectations. A few of the cabinet-makers such as Peter Waals also exercised their own design skills which, ranked equally with their better-known employers, and must have attracted their acclaim and probable advice. Waals (formerly van der Waals) emigrated from The Hague, Holland in 1870. The same acclaim went for some blacksmiths and glass and pottery craftsmen working within the Movement.

A most important feature of the Movement was its cohesion of principle and quality. Some of the designers formed their own craft guilds and manufacturing companies and others made arrangements with existing well-known furniture manufacturers and retailers such as Heals and Waring & Gillow to make and market their designs.

The burgeoning industrial base of Britain centred in the cities, together with a belief that true craft skills had been driven into the countryside, caused Morris and some of his immediate followers to move out of London and into the countryside, which they epitomised as being Wessex and Gloucestershire in particular. It is there that so much evidence of the Arts and Crafts Movement is to be seen today, where the great furniture designers and makers such as Gimson and the Barnsley brothers produced so much of their work and where so many superb cabinet-makers, potters, metalworkers, glass-makers and others also found inspiration because of them.

In the Movement's early days, simplicity of design in furniture was evident. The use of home-grown woods, finished naturally to foster appreciation of both grain and constructional methods, was fundamental. The high standards of cabinet-making evolved in the preceding century, were retained in the main, although the ideals of "utility, fitness for purpose" and indeed "affordability" did have some side effects on quality and this is discernable in some of Rennie Mackintosh's earlier designs which have been described as "banged together". They were, however, as was his intent, thoroughly practical and fit for purpose. Such faults in construction would have been caused more by his lack of attention to detail during design than ignorance. As a form of demonstration of quality, some furniture designers incorporated visible carcase

Below:
This picture is from a Liberty's of Regent Street, London catalogue. The firm opened in 1875 and marketed furniture, fabrics,, clothes, metalware, carpets and pottery. They boasted an impressive list of craftsmen/designers including George Walton, who had moved from Glasgow and designed much of the furniture while Walter Crane and C F A Voysey were responsible for much of the fabrics sold, while couture, for which Liberty's were famous, was overseen by architect E W Godwin.

Right:

A Shaker Rocking Chair in Cherrywood. William Morris's commitment to functional design and his aversion to useless ornament echoes the philosophy of the Shakers. For them beauty could only exist in the useful

jointing of pieces of furniture as a form of decoration and the display of "dovetail" joints and "through tenons" in particular was common and is a design feature which has been copied many times in 20th Century designs.

Some of the British designers worked abroad, and the Movement spread to Belgium, Germany, Austria and Hungary and to Scandinavia. The Arts and Crafts Movement also spread to America where it formed a strong and long-lasting movement, largely as a result of mid-19th Century American scepticism of European cultural dominance. For example, the Shakers who emigrated under religious persecution from England in the 17th and 18th centuries, had established a number of religious and economic communities which identified closely with the ideals of Arts and Crafts, viz. labour was seen as a sacrament, a view shared by 19th Century John Ruskin, himself a low-church Presbyterian. On a wider view the Movement had a strong and lasting effect on architecture in the more northern states.

Later, towards the end of the 19th and into 20th centuries, there was a serious influx into England of immigrant workers, largely from European states with anti-Semitic policies. With these immigrants came new, or new to Britain, design influences. They spread throughout the industrial cities of Scotland and England and some were to form important parts of the British furniture making industry surviving today such as Ercol (Luciano Ercolani, from Tuscany, born 1888, arrived London 1898) and, much later in 1938 Schreiber (Chaim S.Schreiber from Lwow, Poland, born 1918) many of whose designs in the early 20th Century echoed traditional Arts and Crafts features.

The Arts and Crafts Movement is generally regarded as having come to its end by the start of the Great War (1914). As early as 1907 the British Socialist A.R.Orage, declared that "virtue had gone out of the Movement. The disappearance of sociological ideas has in fact left the craft ideas of the Movement pale and anaemic".

At their most idealistic, the Movement's founding advocates vowed to change society through the transformation of the work process, but even the most radical leaders were unwilling completely to abandon prevailing culture to create a truly oppositional one. Although Orage sounded the Movement's death knell prematurely, the initial crusading spirit had certainly lost its momentum by 1910. But a number of designers and makers successfully perpetuated the Movement's design concepts and the very high standards of skills involved, into the 21st Century. Typical of these was the Barnsley family who eventually settled in Hampshire near Petersfield, where an educational trust in their name carries on the teaching of the very highly developed skills for which the name Barnsley is so famous.

A direct and now in-built contradiction exists today in society's disregard of natural talent and passion for 'qualification' and even the belief in some quarters that "talent" can be taught, rather than inherited, nurtured and developed. This sad reflection of the industrial age for which Arts and Crafts originally aimed to be a palliative, is fortunately well recognised today and serious efforts are made to revive and strengthen craft skill, although "apprenticeship", on which high standards were built for at least 350 years, seems beyond retrieval for purely economic reasons and the modern understanding of apprenticeships proclaimed by politicians hardly relates.

At the same time, modern furniture-making technology, much of it imported, has now developed to an extent to which just about every hand skill can be replicated or replaced with an accompanying very high degree of quality. Modern adhesives replace older forms of jointing, and wood replacement materials and photosynthesised veneers have effectively displaced the associated cabinet makers' skills. Finishing techniques are akin to those used in the motor industry. But in spite of this, the demand for hand-made furniture of the highest quality continues, admittedly at a high financial cost and the many gifted furniture designers and makers working today have full order books and the industry is decidedly competitive.

Proponents of Arts and Crafts were never able to resolve the dichotomy between the quest for democratic art and one which upheld the highest standards of craftsmanship. In Britain, Arts and Crafts was a phenomenon within high culture and in Britain in the 19th Century, high thoughts and class restrictions went together. In 1913, Ambrose Heal's proposal that the Arts and Crafts establish a permanent shop, was rebuffed on the grounds that such commercialism was unacceptable. The British upper-class aversion to trade, coupled with the inherent expense of hand labour using the finest materials, meant that Arts and Crafts products were restricted to an elite. People like William Morris had to fight to make crafts respectable. This reluctance to combine art and commerce resulted in the Movement being directed principally at the broad masses of people through philanthropy or through amateur handicrafts. In America, where there were fewer class restrictions, this conflict was not apparent.

Nevertheless, the failure of the Movement to attain its ambitious but sociologically contradictory goals should not preclude appreciation of its many real achievements. It left important legacies in design education, city planning, the development of industrial art and the continuation of craft studios. The conservative nature of much Arts and Crafts production can be recognised as an integral part of it, which has significantly affected how we judge good design today.

A Broadwood Grand Piano, the case decoration designed by Edward Burne-Jones for the Arts & Crafts Exhibition of 1888 painted for Morris Faulkner by Kate Faulkner. By courtesy of the Victoria and Albert Museum

Biography:

William Morris (1834 - 1896)

Reclining chair by Morris & Co.

The George and Dragon cabinet painted by William Morris

Green painted pine table designed by Morris for his rooms in Red Lion Square

A Sussex chair, "Light moveable chair made of sticks" by Morris & Co.

William Morris is generally regarded as the founder of the Arts and Crafts Movement in Britain, although so involved were the Movement's origins and *raison d'être* that one needs to look carefully into his upbringing and education to realise how his deep and natural relentless enthusiasm was formed. He had an obviously outstanding artistic talent and ability to use his hands – two facets which were to be the basis of his lifelong ambition to bring designer and craftsman together. That ambition was largely fired by what he saw as appalling degradation of craft skills and the isolation of craftsman from designer, both attributable to the industrial revolution and resultant sudden affordability of "luxury" goods. So deep was his dislike, at the age of 17, whilst still at school at Marlborough College, of these "modern trends", that he refused absolutely to take part in a family visit to the Great Exhibition of 1851, describing the exhibits as "wonderfully ugly". Morris was regarded by his schoolmates as something of a solitary character, preferring to ramble in nearby Savernake Forest rather than partake in group activities. At Marlborough he received little formal education, but made good use of the well-stocked library from which he developed interests in archaeology and ecclesiastical architecture. It seems that Marlborough contributed, albeit indirectly, to his extraordinary ability for teaching himself which emerged as such a striking feature of his working life.

Morris went to Oxford (Exeter College), having been withdrawn from Marlborough a year early following a boys' mutiny because of poor school management. For a year, he was privately tutored at home in preparation for the university entrance exam, by a local clerical schoolmaster from Walthamstow, before entering Oxford to study theology. In much the same way as at Marlborough, Morris did not rate the academic tuition he received at university very highly. It was the *genius loci* and the opportunities for self-discovery that were all important to him as an undergraduate. He described Oxford, still very much a medieval city, as "a vision of grey-roofed houses and a long winding street, and the sound of many bells, whose memory has been an abiding influence and pleasure in my life".

At Oxford Morris, although brought up as an evangelical , became a Pusyite and deeply affected by the High Church Movement which presaged Anglo-Catholicism even to a point at which he and his friends considered forming a monastic brotherhood. Instead of the monastic ideal, the brotherhood of the Pre-Raphaelites emerged as a crucial influence, and amongst them Ruskin who was to be undoubtedly one of the most important influences on Morris. A fellow undergraduate, Edward Burne-Jones, the son of a Birmingham picture-framer, became William's closest and life-long friend and introduced him to Charles Faulkner who was later to become a business partner.

A pine (deal) table 55¹/₂" diameter and 28 " high designed for Red Lion Square by Morris. The top is of 5 boards screwed to a brace underneath, painted green over a red-brown layer which is similar to the colour of the base of the St George's cabinet. The table came from Kelmscott Village Hall. The notch in the table top's edge has been attributed to the later fitting of an iron vice, a tempting but unproven theory. By courtesy of Cheltenham Art Gallery

His family had assumed that William would go into the Church., but, to his now widowed mother's intense disappointment, he gave up the idea. After taking his degree, Morris was articled to a leading figure in the Gothic revival, George Edmund Street in Oxford and later London, possibly best known for his work on London's Law Courts. Under Street the breadth of his extraordinary vision as a designer was moulded and he remained passionately interested in architecture throughout his life. Most importantly, Street's vision of the architect as not just as a builder but a painter, glass designer and fabric worker, in other words as an all-round artist, had a lasting effect on the direction in which Morris was heading and was later to be copied and even replicated by men such as Voysey and Mackintosh who were central to the Arts and Crafts Movement. Curiously this all-inclusive approach to design of both the building and its contents did have a downside, and in a few cases excellence of craft skills and even constructional methods suffered – Mackintosh in particular exemplified this. The apprenticeship with Street lasted only a few months when Morris, frustrated by "office work", moved away, having established digs in Bloomsbury with Burne-Jones his close friend from undergraduate days. Their rooms had originally been occupied by Rossetti who taught at the Working Men's College in Great Ormond Street together with the revered Ruskin and this provided the two friends with the opportunity to join Rossetti's Hogarth Club with a most distinguished membership of designers and artists of the time.

An important turning point for Morris as a designer craftsman came when he and Burne-Jones found that they were quite unable to find any furniture they liked sufficiently to furnish their rooms at a new address in Red Lion Square. So they designed their own, thus establishing a trend which would be followed again for the decoration of Morris's next home, The Red House and which would ultimately lead to the formation of the firm of Morris, Marshall, Faulkner and Co. Morris's designs, which could have come straight out of the middle ages, were made by a local carpenter in plain deal, which provided a perfect base for decoration.

The settle which was jointly painted by Rossetti and Burne-Jones with scenes from the story of Dante's love for Beatrice was later moved to The Red House near Bexleyheath in Kent. This, together with a large round table and chairs whose backs were painted by Rossetti, represent the sole extent of Morris's own furniture design. Although Morris and Co was noted for its distinctive furniture, this was never designed by Morris himself, but usually by Philip Webb, later with George Jack.

In 1857 Morris, who had recently decided with some encouragement from Rossetti to abandon architecture and concentrate on painting, was invited to join a team of young painters commissioned by Benjamin Woodward, the architect of Oxford University's Debating Hall, for his latest project. Rossetti assembled the team whose task was to decorate the ten bays between circular windows in the hall's gallery

Above:
The best-known piece of furniture designed for Red Lion Square was an enormous settle with a long seat with three cupboards above

Above:
Chairs possibly designed and certainly painted by Morris.

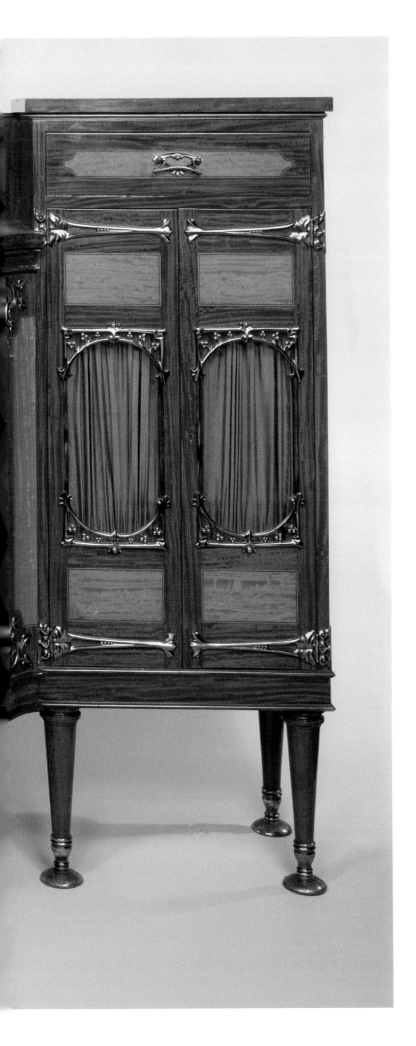

with scenes from Malory's *Morte d'Arthur*. The project was haphazard to say the least: the artists were unpaid except for the costs of materials and the work was conducted in a "light-hearted, convivial atmosphere". The experience, however, enabled Morris to demonstrate an outstanding ability of concentration while working fast to high standards. The project was a forerunner to Morris's later decorative work. The artists in the team used each other as models, a feature he employed later in Morris's stained glass designs. He had a suit of armour made to his own design by a local blacksmith which he could work into his mural, the story of Sir Palomyde's unrequited love for La Belle Iseult. Burne-Jones later recalled Morris getting stuck inside the helmet because he was unable to lift the visor. However, after mastering the mechanism, Morris was so delighted with his armour that he wore it to dinner!

The finished murals were highly acclaimed for their brightness and purity of colour comparable to an illuminated manuscript. However, the effect was somewhat ruined by the team's amateurish approach and enthusiasm, in that the painting had been done straight on to damp untreated plaster and deteriorated very quickly until the murals were virtually unrecognisable. Ironically Morris and Co was asked twenty years later to undertake the redecoration of the roof.

It was while he was working at Oxford that Rossetti introduced him to Jane Burden, the daughter of an Oxford groom and very beautiful. Rossetti had a long-standing affair with Jane whom he drew and painted obsessively, as this painting "The Blue Silk Dress" by him shows. Jane also posed for Morris as Iseult / Guinevere for the debating hall mural.

Although Morris's family disapproved of the match and did not attend their wedding, Morris and Jane married in April 1859 and in the following year moved to the new house built for them The Red House near Bexleyheath designed by Philip Webb and which Burne-Jones described as "The Beautifulest Place on Earth". The house proved a catalyst to Morris's career. He and Jane were immensely happy and it was as a result of his decorative work on the house itself that he found his true vocation as a designer. They had two daughters, Jane (usually known as Jenny) in 1861 and May in 1862, who meant a great deal to Morris and affectionately and proudly described as "very sympathetic with me as to my aims in life".

"Furniture, either depending for its beauty on its own design, on the application of material hitherto overlooked, or in its conjunction with Figure and Pattern Painting. Under this heading is included Embroidery of all kinds, Stamped Leather, and ornamental work in other such materials, besides every article necessary for domestic use. It is only necessary to state further, that work of all the above classes will be estimated for, and executed in a business-like manner; and it is believed that good decoration, involving rather the luxury of taste rather than the luxury of costliness, will be found to be much less expensive than is generally supposed".

Left:
Jane Burden

Opposite Page:
Morris & Co. designed and made furniture of this type based on traditional 18th and early 19th Century styles to satisfy the market's strong attachments to "Classical Design".

St George's Cabinet. Mahogany, Pine and Oak with Copper Mounts. By courtesy of the Victoria and Albert Museum

In the course of their work on The Red House, and Jane also played an important part in its decoration, Morris realised that others must be finding themselves in the same position of being unable to find anything to their taste in terms of house decoration and furnishings. From this growing conviction the firm of Morris, Marshall, Faulkner & Co was established in 1861. It grew spontaneously, rather than as the result of detailed planning, out of the efforts of the friends who helped Morris with decorating and furnishing The Red House. The seven founder members set themselves up as an artists' co-operative with the intention of producing everything necessary to decorate a house. The firm was founded on a shoestring in terms of capital investment with each one of the seven holding shares of £1, later raised to £20. Morris's mother made up the rest with an unsecured loan of £100. Faulkner was the "treasurer" and he and Morris paid themselves a handsome £150 per year. Their first products were ecclesiastical embroideries and stained glass which were later to win them gold medals at the International Exhibition in 1862. Hand-painted tiles, furniture and wallpapers followed and it was not long before the firm was able to offer a complete interior decorating service. In the firm's inaugural literature, amongst the five services provided, the section was subservient to that of stained glass.

After stained glass, furniture was the most important part of the firm's output. *The George and Dragon Cabinet*, designed by Philip Webb and painted by Morris, is one of the best known examples of their work and is now in the V&A Museum's British Galleries.

Made of mahogany and pine and mounted on an oak stand, the painting is a vivid account of the legend of St George which provides evidence of Morris's gift as a story-teller. Jane, his wife, is the Princess. The paintwork incorporates transparent colour over gold and silver while the interior is in deep "dragon's blood" red.

After his early work at Red Lion Square, Morris stopped designing furniture but retained strong preferences for simple, traditional designs in stark contrast to the highly ornate heavy Victorian furniture of the day. He shared these beliefs with Philip Webb, the firm's principal furniture designer who liked plain oak, stained green or black and sometimes decorated with lacquered leather.

Chairs were a predominant part of the firm's repertoire and in particular the so-called "Morris" chair adapted by the firm from a traditional prototype found in Herstmonceaux in Sussex on the premises of an old carpenter Ephraim Coleman. The simple framed reclining chair became tremendously popular and was upholstered in a variety of Morris fabrics in cotton, wool and velvet. It was also copied by Liberty's.

THE SUSSEX RUSH-SEATED CHAIRS

MORRIS AND COMPANY

449 OXFORD STREET, LONDON, W.

"ROSSETTI" ARM-CHAIR. IN BLACK, 16/6.　　SUSSEX CORNER CHAIR. IN BLACK, 10/6.　　SUSSEX SINGLE CHAIR. IN BLACK, 7/-　　SUSSEX ARM-CHAIR. IN BLACK, 9/6.

ROUNDSEAT CHAIR. IN BLACK, 10/6.　　SUSSEX SETTEE, 4 FT. 6 IN. LONG. IN BLACK, 35/-　　ROUND SEAT PIANO CHAIR. IN BLACK, 10/6.

Above:

The Sussex chair was available in different versions as shown in Morris & Company catalogue c. 1911. By courtesy of Cheltenham Art Gallery

Above:

The "Morris" chair. By courtesy of Cheltenham Art Gallery

Below:

The rush seated "Sussex" chair of ash stained black. By courtesy of Cheltenham Art Gallery

Possibly even better known is the rush-seated "Sussex" chair of ash stained black and probably designed by Ford Maddox-Brown and made for Morris & Company. These were made in very large numbers and priced at 9 shillings. The Sussex chair fulfilled Morris's requirement for "light movable chairs made of sticks". The price was evidently approved of by the firm's manager Warrington Taylor whose opinion was "It is a hellish wickedness to spend more than 15/- in a chair, when the poor are starving in the streets".

The negative side of the firm's amateur approach was that the business side was always in a shambles. Warrington Taylor reported a seemingly total failure to cost jobs or organise the flow of work, to charge enough or keep proper accounts or make the best and most economical use of available labour. Taylor did a great deal for Morris in relieving him of much of the burden of the business, but only until Taylor's untimely death from consumption in 1870.

In 1871 Morris moved to the best loved of all his homes, Kelmscott Manor near Lechlade in Gloucestershire. Morris never actually owned Kelmscott – he took out a joint tenancy with Rossetti, the first three years of which were overshadowed by the latter's continuing affair with Jane until he Rossetti left the house in 1874. The house remained Morris's country home until his death 22 years later at the age of 62.

In 1875 "The Firm" was reorganised under Morris's sole direction and its name changed to Morris & Co., with prestigious large showrooms at 449 Oxford Street and North Audley Street. This signalled the start of the most prolific ten years for Morris as a designer. Burne-Jones and Webb ceased to be partners in the new firm but remained to continue designs for both stained glass and furniture.

This Page Below:

Mahogany Secretaire

Opposite:

A mahogany breakfront dresser
A mahogany bookcase

These pieces were designed, made and marketed by William Morris' firm "Morris, Marshall and Co." as a part of Morris' reluctant acceptance of the continuing popularity of the traditional designs from 18th and early 19th Centuries

Below and Opposite:

Kelmscott Manor from the east
The yard and outbuildings on the south side
Kelmscott Church and Tombstone
All by courtesy of Michael Barrington

Morris now immersed himself in the design of wallpapers, fabrics and carpets. Part of his most important achievements lay in dyeing and hand-printing techniques on which he carried out endless research, leading to standards of design and production later to be recognised and admired worldwide and still very much with us in the 21st Century. His first designs for carpets were for such companies as Kidderminster, Wilton and Axminster. By the early 1880s Morris & Co. products were a household word and their reputation was established as far afield as the United States. Most middle class households included some Morris design as part of their decoration. Such distinguished designers as Charles Ricketts, Charles Shannon, George Walton and Hugh Baillie-Scott were to feature Morris designs in their interiors. Several quotes from Morris's lectures and writings illustrate clearly his belief that even the most modest home could be made beautiful, providing everything in it was well designed and above all useful:

"Nothing can be a work of art which is not useful"

"Have nothing in your homes which you do not know to be useful or believe to be beautiful"

A last development in Morris' huge list of achievements was the realisation of his interest in printing, a craft in which standards had declined drastically. In 1890 he founded the Kelmscott Press. His outstanding talent for calligraphy, combined with his knowledge of block printing of fabrics, contributed substantially to his success as a type designer.

Two years later William Morris decided to become a publisher as well as a printer and from 1892 he published, with few exceptions, the work of the Kelmscott Press. This final achievement in his life coincided with his death in October 1896 of progressive kidney disease. He was buried in Kelmscott Churchyard and later joined by his wife Jane and their daughters, their tombstone being designed by his old friend and colleague Philip Webb. Moving in its simplicity, the tombstone, in traditional Cotswold design, is a fitting tribute to all that William Morris, craftsman and designer par excellence, stood for.

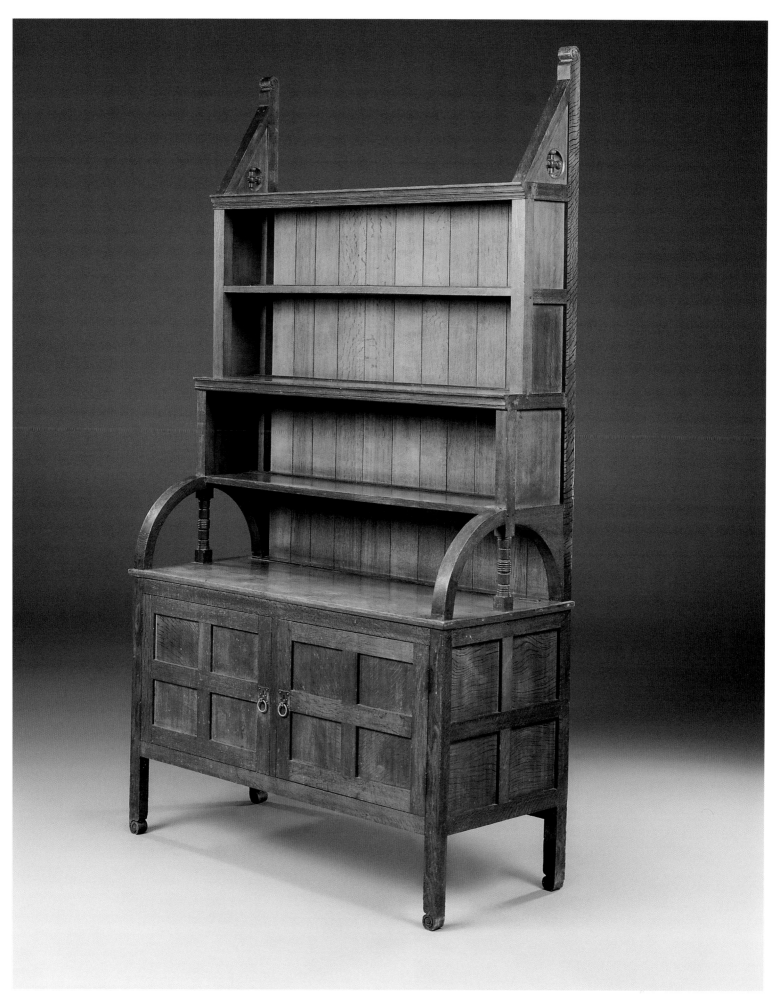

Oak bookcase at Dromore Castle

Biography:

Edward Godwin
(1833-1886)

Japanese style sideboard

Greek chair 1855

Ebonised side table

Oak table for Northampton Guild Hall

Edward William Godwin was born in Bristol on 26 May 1833, the youngest of five children. His father, also William, was a leather merchant or currier. His mother Ann, neé Davies, was Welsh and the daughter of Joseph Davies a tiler, plasterer and painter. Both families were comfortably off, but not particularly wealthy. Both men were small businessmen and acknowledged local parish worthies. William Godwin's leather business flourished and on Joseph Davies's death he bought the building and decorating business, but more as a financial venture than one of involved interest. William bought the Earl's Mead Estate on the edge of Bristol shortly after Edward's birth. The house was the principal dwelling in the neighbourhood, the garden of which contained numerous relics from old churches which were a fascination to young Edward from an early age and he grew up determined to become an architect. William encouraged both his surviving sons (two others had died in infancy) to enter professions and, it seems, he had strong social ambitions for them.

Edward was educated at a private school in Highbury, Bristol and developed a passionate interest in costume, a subject which was to run parallel with his architectural career and at times even to exceed it. On William's death in 1846, while Edward was still at school, the family experienced financial difficulties which were to accompany Edward throughout his life. He became articled to the architect William Armstrong who, fortunately for the family, was in debt to the estate of the late William Godwin to an extent that Armstrong

was obliged to take young Edward into his business as a pupil. In spite of becoming Armstrong's assistant, this turned out not to be a happy time for Edward Godwin, coloured by Armstrong's habit of appending his own name to Edward's designs and taking the credit – an apparently not unusual practice which Edward named "the secret manufacture of architecture". He ended his pupilage with Armstrong in the early 1850s and established his own architectural practice in the city in 1852.

His first commission was the design of a small Gothic school at Easton near Bristol, which was followed by restorations and additions to a number of churches in the West Country, in Devonshire, Cornwall and Wiltshire. He moved to work in Ireland in 1856 and joined his brother Joseph Lucas, a civil engineer, to work on a design for a proposed railway bridge in Londonderry which never came to fruition. Following this, Godwin was involved in more ecclesiastical work, culminating in 1860 with his first completed architectural project, the Church of St Baithen, St Johnstown, Donegal.

It was to his credit that Godwin should have won many of the Irish ecclesiastical projects from the Catholic Church when he himself was an English Protestant and, from what we know of his private life, probably not a particularly committed one. However, Godwin's church work was broadly based across the Church of England, the Irish Catholic, Congregational, the Unitarian and even the Greek Orthodox Churches.

Above:
Edward Godwin 1880

Right:
The Church of St Baithen

In 1858 Godwin returned to Bristol to resume his practice and began a close friendship with the architect William Burges. It is most likely that this friendship influenced Godwin's appreciation of Japanese art, since Burges was a keen follower and collector. The following year saw a number of wide-ranging projects for Godwin, both ecclesiastical and civic in the West Country and in London, and in November he married his first wife Sarah Yonge, the daughter of a cleric in Henley-on-Thames. The couple settled in Brighton Villa, Upper Montpelier, Bristol.

In 1860 he won a design competition for the proposed St Philip and Jacob's Schools in Bristol and for Clifton College. His career at this time was largely related to the increased importance given to civic buildings' symbolic roles over their more functional ones, which allowed large parts of project budgets to be assigned to displays of decoration in the public parts of the buildings. Probably the most significant architectural achievement of his entire career was in 1861, when he won the competition to design Northampton Town Hall after the City Council had turned down another winning classical design in favour of Godwin's gothic entry (see below).

Godwin later said that the building was entirely founded upon John Ruskin's essay on "The Nature of Gothic" in *The Stones of Venice* (1853) which he had read on his return from Ireland. The style of the building is largely French but its structural polychromy is strongly reminiscent of Ruskin in the bands of different colours of stone and brickwork. Godwin's appreciation and respect of Gothic Revivalism so dear to Augustus Pugin who died only eight years earlier, supported by Ruskin's ideal of there being only two fine arts possible for the human race, sculpture and painting, is very evident in the Northampton building.

Interior design took no lesser priority than architecture in Godwin's view of his profession. This was a principle shared by the majority of architects of the Arts and Crafts Movement and formed a large part of the roots of their success. Godwin's respect for the Gothic Revival, together with the sheer size of the architectural projects involved, raised his profile in the public eye beyond those of men like Mackintosh and Walton and, of course, in age he was a great deal nearer to the Gothic Revival's origins, although he did not allow his designs to be entirely driven by them. Also the cost of employing men like Edward Godwin, although high, was more affordable during his working life than it was during those of many who were to follow him, who had to contend with, not only changing style and modernism, but also the economic effects of the Great War. As a follower of John Ruskin, Godwin, like Morris, Burges and Voysey, considered that a unified scheme embracing every aspect of a building, its exterior and interior design and furnishings and fittings, was central to their work. No aspect of detail was too small to attract their attention. He said

Above:
Northampton Town Hall, later named The Guild Hall
designed when he was only 28 years old

Above:
The Great Hall

"in common with a few others in my profession, I look upon all my work as Art Work". Architects and designers of that calling involved themselves in detail down to cutlery and teapots. For those unable to afford the expense of Godwin's services, his furniture, wallpapers and accessories were obtainable from the large furnishing firms such as Gillow & Company who stocked his work. As a researcher of antiquities, Godwin was meticulous without being driven by the discipline. To him the main purpose of such study was to find inspiration and to better his skills of unified design. In just about every project, be it buildings or furniture, one can find evidence of his respect for the enduring disciplines of antiquity. He was a prolific writer in many architectural and art publications for most of his working life and his innovation and artistic skill were ever present in his work in the theatre, be it costume, scenery or acting.

In 1864, Godwin formed a partnership with a former colleague architect Henry Crisp, operating from Bristol. Their joint names appear in projects right across south (particularly Devon and Cornwall, Bristol, Gloucestershire and Kent) central and northern England (Malvern, Preston, Manchester), in London and in County Kerry and Limerick, at Dromore Castle.

From about 1861, Godwin had become involved in furniture design which was to last some 25 years, both as a part of existing architectural and interior design projects and in its own right. Much of his furniture design was executed by William Watt, author of the *Art Furniture* catalogue, who amongst others like Schoolbred, Smee, Collinson & Lock and Jones & Cribb, kept the homes of the middle classes well supplied with fashionably "aesthetic" furniture of good quality. In 1871 the

Godwin-Crisp partnership ended in acrimonious dispute, in common with a number of other associations throughout Godwin's life. This did not, however, seem to affect his output, which can be partly attributed to his habit and indeed ability to de-centralise and ensure that matters of detail were given to staff.

The impact of Japanese culture on Western art and design, or the "Japonisme Movement" as it was called during Godwin's life, was particularly strong in its effect on the decorative arts in Britain. The import of Japanese works of art became prolific and was particularly evident at the International Exhibition in London of 1862 whose most enthusiastic architect-designer visitors included the likes of William Burges and Christopher Dresser. It seems likely that Godwin was also a visitor from Bristol. By the mid-1870s the Japanese were producing objects for a Western clientele, often adapting existing Western designs, while British companies increasingly copied Japanese designs.

When Farmer and Rogers' Oriental Warehouse opened in Regent Street displaying Japanese objects bought at the Exhibition, Godwin, Burges and Rossetti were notable amongst its visitors, although Godwin's enthusiasm had probably been whetted earlier when looking at Burges' collections. In about 1867 Godwin began to integrate Japanese elements into his designs, but with some difficulty in that, so far as printed wallpapers were concerned, manufacturers faced serious problems in replicating some of the faded colours essential to the charm of original Japanese work which Walton insisted be used. He was also hampered by damp conditions in places such as Dromore Castle where some of his colour schemes had to be abandoned.

Sideboard made by William Watt. By courtesy of the Victoria and Albert Museum

There is little doubt that, in spite of Godwin's major and lasting contributions to architecture in the 19th Century, he is held in greater esteem as a designer than as an architect. During a period of some twenty five years he designed at least four hundred pieces of furniture.

Opposite Page: One of the earliest Japanese style pieces and probably the most popular and best recognised of Godwin's furniture designs is this sideboard made by William Watt which appeared in his catalogue of 1877 but this version is often wrongly dated at 10 years earlier.* Here, the wood is ebonised mahogany with silver plated fittings and embossed Japanese leather paper inserts to the door panels.

Below: This four-legged variation of the sideboard made about ten years earlier, is of ebonised deal, and was made by the Art Furniture Company to Godwin's design. This time with stencilled decoration to the door panels and marginally shorter by less than three inches than the first. (Neue Sammlung, Staatliches Museum für angewandte Kunst, Munich 417/93).

Overall it is known that at least ten versions of this design were made and at least six of them are known to survive. A six-legged version in the Bristol Museum is known to have belonged to Godwin's mistress, the actress Ellen Terry with whom he lived between 1868 and 1875.

Continuing with the Japanese style – *shown right:* An ebonised desk c.1875 in Japanese taste and attributed to Godwin. The top is of tooled leather with tapering circular section legs, the drawer pulls silver-plated and below this an ebonised side table with circular section legs and stretchers made by William Watt compared with an almost identical table in the same finish, with the same circular mouldings but with a stretcher just below the top, made this time by Collinson & Lock.

An unusual characteristic of Godwin's furniture designs was his attention to sanitation – dedication to hygiene! The tops of washstands and dressing tables, for instance, would be of plain light woods such as deal, birch or ash bearing the minimum of decoration and were neither oiled nor varnished, so that they could easily be scrubbed clean. His upholstered pieces often have the same precautionary construction with the additional characteristic of not being too inviting because of his abhorrence of the overstuffed seat furniture typically found in mid-Victorian bedrooms which he said "were arrangements of laziness that assumed an almost tyrannical position"! Cane seating was popular with him and his settees and other upholstered pieces are upholstered just enough to be functional without being too inviting.

Japanese style ebonised desk

Sideboard made by The Art Furniture Co.

Ebonised side table by William Watt

Side table by Collinson & Lock

The first cabinets were made in ebonised deal (a cheap wood) in about 1867, but because they were found to be unstable, Godwin changed to ebonised mahogany around ten years later and this is the version which is so well-known.

Another of Godwin's most memorable designs is his oak "Greek" side chair made by William Watt in about 1885 with upholstered seat and back-pad. In contrast, there is a this version of the Greek chair of severely austere design, again made by William Watt, this time in ash with a caned seat and minimal back support.

Much of Godwin's furniture has a thin spindly look, perhaps because of his declared belief that the design of a room should be dominated by its fixed architectural features and not by the furniture. Consequently his furniture was made to the lightest constructional design commensurate with necessary strength. In passing, the early 21st Century minimalistic culture can be said to come from the same belief. A conflicting factor is that users often tend to be overweight, but even this becomes acceptable with the use of metal framed furniture!

Unlike Morris, who abhorred the use of machinery in furniture manufacture – a deeply held conviction by the Movement's earlier founders – Godwin had no qualms about designing for easier manufacture by machine. In appreciation he was paid a monthly retainer between 1872-75 by Collinson & Lock who were fully into mechanised furniture production. and further payments were authorised for special commissions.

An important feature of Godwin's work was his respect, indeed reverence, for Georgian furniture. He furnished his first home in Bristol with antique objects and this preference continued into the 1870s. It was the soberness of execution and beauty of proportion (presumably the "Divine Proportion" or "Golden Rule" of 1:1.618 established as the ideal ratio between height and breadth) together with optimum use of wood-grain that really appealed to Godwin. The mahogany spindle-legged tea table with traditional gates to support falling leaves on either side is typical of his respect for the 18th Century which was also shared by William Walton. The design carried on well into the next century, losing on its way the Arts and Crafts swinging leg modifications favoured by Walton.

Another area for which Edward Godwin designed was what he called his "Cottage Style". This simple furniture was limited in ornament, such embellishment being provided by mouldings and spindle turnings of classic origins, related to the so-called (by Godwin and his biographers) Queen Anne Movement although it has precious little to do with Queen Anne architecture and interiors of the early 18th Century. The "Cottage Cabinet" is an example and is greatly enhanced by its curvilinear panels enclosing strictly linear construction but embellished with 3 and 4-dee mouldings of the door frames,

"Greek" side chair made by William Watt

"Greek" chair in ash with caned seat

Mahogany spindle legged table by William Walton

"Cottage" cabinet

Oak and pine bench used in St Wynwallow
Church, Landewednack, Cornwall

Inlaid Oak Councillor's Chair

The Mayor's Chair

The Chief Magistrate's Chair

traditionally made with a cabinet-maker's scratch-stock but in this case possibly assisted by a spindle-moulder for the side panels at least.

Other designs of Cottage Style-type furniture, although somewhat earlier in his career (1860) are an open construction oak and pine bench used in St Wynwallow Church, Landewednack, Cornwall and an inlaid Oak Councillor's Chair of which a set of twenty-four was made for Northampton Town Hall. The inlay is in the back-rest column supports.

Also for Northampton were the Mayor's Chair (1865) made by Green & King in oak with the same inlaid decoration and upholstered in red leather and the Chief Magistrate's Chair, also by Green & King in oak and deep-buttoned leather.

The upholstery of the Mayor's chair is evidently quite new, the leather rather modern in its tanning and the nails appear to have been "antiqued"!

Below is a Godwin Oak Table also made by Green & King for the Northampton Guildhall and somewhat reminiscent of a similar very simple table design by A.W.N. Pugin.

For Dromore Castle Godwin designed an Oak Bookcase in 1869 which is one of six examples produced by makers Reuben Birkett and William Watt. Particularly interesting features are the two central turned columns supporting the arched brackets between the chest top and the shelves, together with the scrolled feet supporting the four square section legs. See also similar features in the table by Pugin made for The Convent of Our Lady of Mercy, Handsworth in 1841.

The Walnut Music Canterbury with brass tubular tee fittings supporting the shelf between the legs made by William Watt c.1876,

is an example the influence of bamboo furniture on Godwin's designs, well demonstrated in this piece's ring-turned splay legs.

Made by Collinson and Lock c.1878, this Macassar ebony and rosewood veneered octagonal centre table, opposite, with ivory inlay to the top and radiating stretchers is a development of Chinese hardwood wash-stands from the Ming Dynasty and the ebonised cabinet, possibly also made by Collinson and Lock, has a forward-curving arched hood over a glazed cupboard and complimentary lower cupboard supported on six turned legs with a stretcher-shelf. This cabinet echoes the central attraction in Godwin's pencil and watercolour sketch of an interior design he named "Early 15th Century" c.1880. Also shown is an ebonised easel with red leather stamped and tooled with some brass fittings, c.1870.

Oak table by Green & King for Northampton Guildhall. By courtesy of Christie's

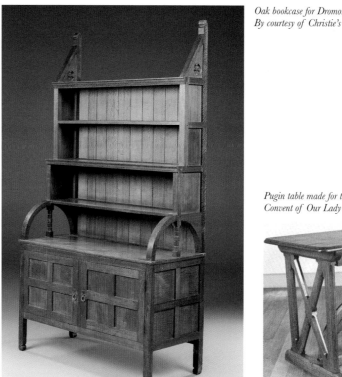

Oak bookcase for Dromore Castle
By courtesy of Christie's

Pugin table made for the
Convent of Our Lady of Mercy

A similar table design by A. W. N. Pugin.
By courtesy of the Victoria and Albert Museum

A walnut music Canterbury
by William Watt

Octagonal table by Collinson & Lock

Ebonised cabinet with arched hood

Ebonised easel c.1870

"Early 15th Century"

Godwin's Butterfly suite painted by James McNeill Whistler caused the greatest attention internationally and is again one of the most popularly recognised examples of their work together. It attracted worldwide press attention. Shown opposite is the cabinet in a furniture suite designed for William Watt's stand at the Paris Exposition Universelle in 1878. It is of mahogany with glass, ceramic tiles and minimal brass fittings. The mahogany panels are painted with a sprinkling of butterflies and chrysanthemum petals in gold while the door panels and central panels above the moulded shelf carry a Japanese cloud motif and butterflies on a primrose ground. But for Whistler's exotic painted decoration the cabinet would arguably be a looming and massive piece of dubious attraction and well outside Godwin's more usual light designs.

The "Lounging chair" with wheel-shaped arms also caused a sensation in the international press with a number of negative comments such as "rather slight for everyday use" and "This 'agony' in yellow". By intent presumably, it does not follow Godwin's principle of "uninviting" design and there is evidence that the originals had a padded headrest. Whatever views of the press, the controversy surrounding the chair contributed a valuable spread of commercial interest in Godwin's designs.

Another version of an upholstered chair, perhaps better described as a club chair was also designed for Watt about four years later in 1880.

Godwin's work attracted much interest in Europe at a time when, as Hermann Muthesius wrote, Godwin's work was much admired in Germany and Austria at a time when English work was not well considered. This was some twenty-five years before both Mackintosh and Walton received European accolades for their work, notably from Muthesius.

Juliet Kinchin wrote in her catalogue essay "E.W.Godwin and Modernism":

"Throughout his entire career, Godwin argued that design resided in the concept rather than the craft of the object executed. He responded with subtle and integrated designs for interiors of his wealthy clients using his scholarly and erudite knowledge of the past. The architect used antiquarian science as merely a way to create a foundation for the exercise of the imagination. With a design philosophy solidly rooted in his belief, Godwin disregarded the architecture of Greece and Rome as unsuitable for the climate needs of Scotland".

Aside from his furniture design and architectural work, throughout his career Godwin was involved in ceramics and textile design, the latter often for theatrical productions in which he often acted as production manager and designer.

Edward Godwin died at the age of fifty-three following surgery for the removal of kidney stones – a massive loss to the three professions he represented so brilliantly as architect, interior and theatrical designer.

M. PAGANO after TITIAN.

TINTORET.

K.S.M.

VERONESE

K.S.M.

Designs for costume and musical instruments for The Merchant of Venice c.1880, by Edward Godwin. By courtesy of the Victoria and Albert Theatre Museum

"Lounging chair" with wheel-shaped arms. Made by William Watt c.1876.

Cabinet shown at the Paris Exposition Universelle

A club chair by Watt

Electroplated letter rack. By courtesy of Christie's

Christopher Dresser
(1834-1904)

Textile and carpet designs

Plated teapot

Wrought and cast iron hall stand

Copper kettle

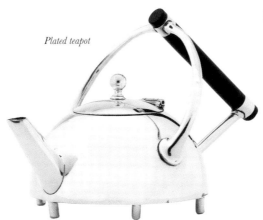

Christopher Dresser, the son of an Excise Officer, was born in Glasgow in 1834, the same year as William Morris. In 1847 he attended the Government School of Design at Somerset House in London at the age of thirteen, where he studied both design and botany, following a system of art education set up to train designers for industry. He later transferred to Marlborough House (Henry Cole's School of Design).

He was seventeen at the time of the Great Exhibition in 1851, which he visited and was particularly impressed by the Indian exhibits which he observed as being a great contrast to the moribund pastiches displayed by British and European industry at that time.

In 1854 Dresser (now 20 years old) married Thirza Perry of Maidley, Shropshire. He lectured in botany at The Department of Science and Art at South Kensington and published a number of works including botanical illustrations and diagrams which are now in the V&A Museum. He continued to explore the relationship between botany and design with a later interest in Japanese art. In consideration of his services to Botanical Science, he was awarded the degree of Doctor of Philosophy by the University of Jena. Subsequently he was elected Fellow of Edinburgh Botanical Society and in the following year a Fellow of the Linnean Society.

In 1860 he decided to concentrate on his design career and set up his own studio in Kensington. He worked as a designer, as a supplier of designs drawn up in his studio and as an advisor to manufacturers. In the late 1860s he included designs for furniture by the architects William Burges and Bruce Talbert.

John Ruskin (1819-1900) had pleaded for individuality in artistic creation at a time when the scale of commercial production was soaring and increasingly isolating designer from maker, this being one of the foundation stones of the Arts and Crafts Movement. As Christopher Dresser had observed when visiting the Great Exhibition in 1851, the standard of British design was at an extremely low ebb and this became a widely held feeling, not least by the Exhibition's Director Henry Cole. Under Cole's guidance, government schemes to create new design museums with historic collections and schools to teach new methods of ornamental instruction were founded.

A move towards stronger colours from the 1830s onwards was largely inspired by the use of polychrome decoration in the ancient world. Through the influence of a group of Franco-German architect designers, this found its way into the programmes of Henry Cole's School of Design.

Right:
Details of cabinet and bookcase doors designed by Burges in which Dresser may have had some influence. By courtesy of the Cecil Higgins Gallery

Owen Jones

A page of Dresser's Contribution to the book

One of the School's lecturers, designer Owen Jones (1809-74), led the English revival in polychromy and his *Grammar of Ornament* (1856) was the culmination of many years of study of the use of colour in early civilisations. The book quickly became a pattern book for British design and taste. Jones favoured a mathematical approach to colour and design instead of the imitations of nature then being offered to the British market.

In his book Jones acknowledges the contribution of: "...Mr C Dresser of Marlborough House of Leaves and Flowers from Nature exhibiting the geometrical arrangement of natural flowers". Owen Jones had been Superintendent of Works at the Great Exhibition of 1851.

No less than five of Dressers' clients were involved with Henry Cole's experiment in design reform. They were Wedgwood and Minton (Ceramics), Elkington and James Dixon (silver plate) and Coalbrookdale (cast iron). These companies were "showcases" for design reform and took part in a succession of international exhibitions, and were also to manufacture very many designs by Dresser.

The fine and the applied arts were segregated by the government's design reform schemes. Ruskin responded vigorously, stating that decorative art was not a degraded or a separate kind of art. In contrast to Jones, Ruskin supported freedom of expression for the designer and the direct study of nature as a source for both artist and designer. Most importantly he reintroduced morality to art and design,

arguing that the way to improve society was to reform its art. He also supported indigenous historical sources for design.

Dresser the Ornamentalist

Christopher Dresser led the counter-attack on Ruskin in 1862 in a book *The Art of Decorative Design*. Dresser wanted design to represent the laws of natural growth, not its appearance and his senior scientific qualification as a botanist gained him great respect, authority and influence in Britain. His own designs, reflecting his theory, were simplified, angular and cheap to manufacture. He was thus at odds with the Arts and Crafts Movement's founders Ruskin and Morris, but not entirely Morris, like Ruskin was revolted by what he saw as a sick society. He took Ruskin's love of the hand-wrought roughness of the crafts and wanted to see it applied to modern commerce. This was a vision shared to a large extent by Dresser with whom Morris also had a close affinity in floral/ornamental design.

Strongly supporting these initiatives were the British manufacturers who, reacting to the recent fashion for French floral textiles and wall papers, were finding the technical aspects of production needed to manufacture these were un-commercial.

Dresser styled himself as an ornamentalist and almost certainly ran the largest practice in ornamental design in the country at that time. He acted as an art adviser and chief designer to several of the largest art-manufacturing firms.

As an example of his design output, in 1869 he supplied 158 designs to Wards alone, as well as other large manufacturers such as Liberty & Co. whose goods were factory-made. Liberty's tended to make no acknowledgement of the designers such as Dresser whom they employed. Not surprisingly, and in common with later designers such as Edward Godwin, Dresser came to realise that he had little real control of manufacturers' use of his designs, and in a bid to establish his individual identity, he exhibited metalwork, carpets and ceramics under his own name at the 1871 London International Exhibition. By 1874 his own name began to appear on products and he established himself as a pioneer of branding. Much of his later work bears his facsimile signature or the words "Designed by Dr C Dresser".

In his book *The Art of Decorative Design*, Dresser stated "...that true ornamentation is of purely mental origin, and consists of symbolised imagination or emotion only. I therefore argue that ornamentation is not only fine art, but that it is high art... even a higher art than that practised by the pictorial artist, as it is wholly of mental origin..."

Many of his most celebrated works concentrate on his metal and electroplate creations, from cast iron furniture to teapots, cups and cutlery.

Dresser made his first designs for ironfounders The Coalbrookdale Co. in Shropshire in 1867. He ardently advocated the use of cast iron in the creation of functional yet decorative pieces of household furniture, added to which he was attracted by the creative potential of the company. By the end of the 1860s Dresser had become

Coalbrookdale's principal designer. This was a fitting union which helped him in his pursuit to reform design and industry in Britain.

He borrowed forms of natural beauty, inspired by his botanical studies, the forms blending suitably into the decorative capacity of the cast iron medium. In this seat, only the seat area is of wood and it is flat. An unusual embellishment is the spiral tie rods from under the seat centre to the stretchers of the two sets of legs, which lend strength to the design. The same cap nuts are circled.

Even greater problems arise today when attempting to weld broken areas of cast iron because of accompanying localised expansion and shrinkage which can cause fractures. A method of dealing with this is to heat up the whole cast iron panel in a bonfire before welding, carry out stick or inert gas welding and allow it to cool as the fire dies down, thus imitating the conditions undergone during the frame's original casting.

The hall stand opposite is composed of a mixture of wrought iron produced by the blacksmith and cast iron, the medium of the iron founder. Cast iron, as Dresser observed, lends itself well to accurate reproduction of natural forms such as foliage, whilst wrought iron, forged from billets or, by the 19th Century, from varying hot-rolled sections produced in iron and steel rolling mills. The employment of the two materials together is particularly relevant to the making of gates, fencing and grilles.

This pair of iron seats consists of hardwood (almost certainly teak) slats for the seat and back, enclosed within the stylised cast iron ends of water-plant design. By courtesy of Christie's

The cast iron seat frame is bolted to the two end frames with steel studs and brass, or more probably gun-metal, cap nuts which can be seen as parts of the overall cast form By courtesy of Christie's

A single version of the same sort of seat as the above but with contoured seat and cast iron back. The manufacture of the cast iron panels is hazardous in that, while the iron castings are cooling, if this is not carefully controlled, fractures in the iron can occur because of stresses in the cooling and shrinking iron. By courtesy of the Bridgeman Art Library

The Post Japanese Reappraisal

The reopening of trade with Japan in the 1860s had a tremendous impact in Europe and America, affecting particularly the development of "aesthetic" furniture in the 1870s and later. Dresser was one of a group, including Edward Godwin, who inspired a whole generation of mass-produced furniture embellished with sunflowers, chrysanthemums, peacocks, sunbursts and other "Japanese" motifs. In 1877 he visited Japan for about four months. As an agent of the South Kensington Museum, the Japanese Government invited him to tour the country and advise on the future of their art manufacturers. He visited sixty-eight potteries and many manufacturers. He bought thousands of Japanese art objects for Tiffany and Co. in New York and for Londos,

the wholesale oriental merchant in London of which he was the Art Director. On his return he wrote *Japan: Its Architecture, Art and Art Manufacturers* (published 1882).

The visit to Japan changed Dresser's perceptions of his involvement in decorative art considerably. Having considered himself principally as an ornamentalist, he virtually rejected ornament. Japan had taught him that "form" was enough to entertain and please the eye and that ornament can distract from, rather than enhance, form. This change in design direction entirely suited machine production but must have been somewhat of an anathema to the followers of Morris. Moreover, in the market place Dresser's designs must have been competing with Morris and Company's.

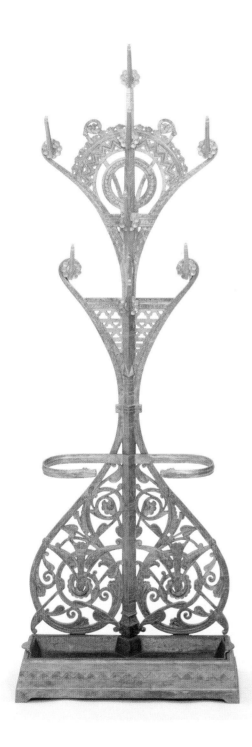

The Victorian hall stand was a popular item and is found in several different patterns – again made by The Coalbrookdale Company. By courtesy of the Victoria and Albert Museum

Dresser stamped Metalware – Plated and Raw

As a part of his rejection of Victorian historicism, Dresser concentrated on simplicity of form appropriate to the function of the object and this electroplated teapot is typical of his work and was made by James Dixon and Sons of Sheffield, with a facsimile Dresser signature.

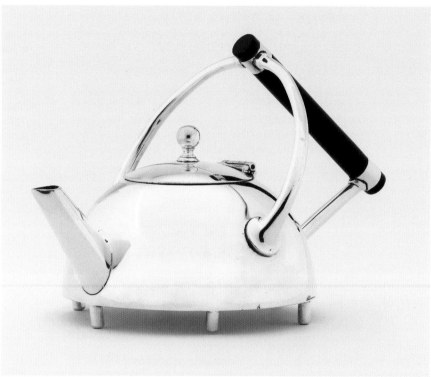

Above:
A plated sugar basket by Hukin & Heath stamped "By Dr C Dresser". By courtesy of Christie's

Above:
This teapot sold for £94,850 at auction in the summer of 2004

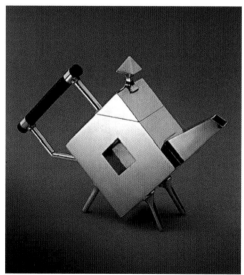

Above:
Probably better known is this plated Dresser polyhedral teapot c. 1880 which featured at the summer 2004 Exhibition of his work at the V&A Museum. By courtesy of Christie's

Above Left & Right:
A copper coffee pot and a copper kettle, both by Benham & Froud and both with stamp marks. By courtesy of Christie's

Above:
A silver egg steamer or boiler made
by H. Stratford, Sheffield, 1884-85

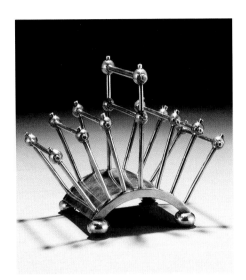

Above:
Electroplated Letter Rack by
Hukin & Heath

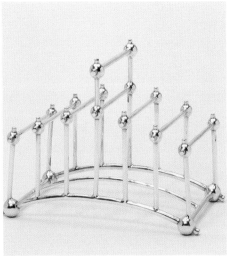

Above:
Toast Rack

Left:
A pair of Gothic
Revival Candlesticks,
brass with paintwork
- 7 inches high

Right:
A Christopher Dresser
Watering Can of 1876
made by Richard Perry &
Son. In painted tinned-iron.
The tinning was applied hot
to make the object rust-proof
before painting

Left:
A Picnic Set, maker not
known, but in the line of
goods sold by Liberty in the
early 20th Century, the kettle
standing on a spirit burner

Left:
A soup tureen and ladle,
electroplate with ebony
handles manufactured
by Hukin and Heath,
Birmingham, 1880

Left:
A silver sugar boat and sifter,
manufactured by Hukin and
Heath, Birmingham, 1884

Dresser Furniture

In 1880 Dresser was appointed Art Editor of the *Furniture Gazette*, a position which he held for a year before being appointed "Art Manager" of the Art Furnishers' Alliance, established to "carry on the business of manufacturing, buying and selling high class goods of artistic design". Unfortunately and despite strong support from many influential manufacturers, the Art Furnishers' Alliance went into liquidation in 1883.

He believed that people's surroundings had a marked psychological influence on how they felt. He was working at a time when there was a noticeable increase in the population and Britain ruled a vast colonial empire. The wealthy could afford whatever style of furniture appealed to them and there were plenty of firms to supply cheap copies to less well-off buyers. The Victorians were seeking comfort and elaborate decoration as a reflection of their collective feelings about their powerful place in world affairs.

Dresser's approach to furniture design was based on the same functionalist principles as all his other work – objects must fulfil the purpose for which they are made, they must be made of the most appropriate material and must be pleasing in shape and well-proportioned. He did not like the contemporary Victorian furniture which normally featured intricate carving and inlaid decoration. He saw the use of padding to fulfil the need for comfort as concealing the essential form which he considered ought to be seen. His own designs display the simplicity which was a hallmark of his approach to all his work. Early English, Egyptian, Greek and Japanese influences are reflected in his pieces, of which the chair below is an example.

Dresser not only designed furniture made of wood, he also produced designs for pieces such as chairs, hat stands and hall tables to be made of cast iron. The term "furniture" in Victorian times also included such items as hot air stoves, grates, fireplace fittings and coal boxes. His holistic approach to interiors meant that every single object in a room was worthy of careful design.

Dresser's work in the area of furniture design is not as well documented as that of his other media. It has been suggested that this is because he worked directly with industrial manufacturers and not through architects and builders which was the normal practice at the time, and that, in fact, he operated in much the same way as design studios do today.

Coal Box/Scuttle. By courtesy of Christie's

This demi-lune (nearly a semicircle) seat is ebonised and has decorated front legs and backsplat with a triangular stretcher below the seat. The chair was made by the short-lived Art Furnishers' Alliance c.1880 and was sold at auction in 2000 for £25,850. By courtesy of Christie's

Left:
A pair of cast iron fire andirons.
By courtesy of Christie's

Above:
Ebonised and gilded chair. By courtesy of the Victoria and Albert Museum

The Arts & Crafts Movement   229

Carpets and Textiles

Dresser said that to be effective, a carpet should be neutral and act as a background to the contents of the room. Many of his designs were based on geometric principles with a continuous radiating pattern featuring flowers and foliage. He also often used scrolls or banded borders to frame the design.

The introduction of power driven looms in the 1850s led to an expansion of the machine-made carpet industry. Axminster Carpets, founded in 1755, took inspiration from the Renaissance and Arts and Crafts Movements and was one of the manufacturers of designs by Dresser. As in other areas of Dresser's work, Japanese influence can be traced in his carpet designs. Unfortunately very few examples of his work in this area have been found and it is only in articles written at the time that any information on the colours used can be found.

His influence spread to America along with that of William Morris. In 1873 the American Government asked Dresser to produce a report on the current state of design there and this led to an attempt by some manufacturers to improve their standards. The possibility of mass production enabled Dresser to realise his wish that good design be brought within reach of everyone. But by the end of 19th Century the desire for ever-changing patterns saw his ideas and principles disregarded with ever more elaborate and convoluted designs being produced.

By courtesy of the Victoria and Albert Museum

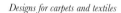

Designs for carpets and textiles

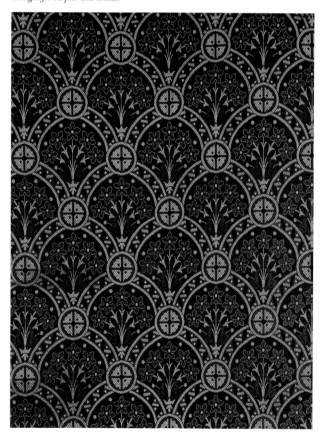

By courtesy of the Victoria and Albert Museum

By courtesy of the Victoria and Albert Museum

Opposite Page: *By courtesy of the Victoria and Albert Museum*

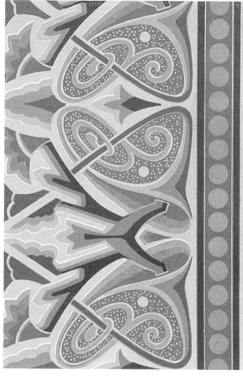

Some of Dresser's textile designs were based on geometrical units formed by curves and squares and others on flower and plant forms (vide: His contribution to Owen Jones's *The Grammar of Ornament*). One of his principles was that design should be in keeping with the quality of material used. This meant, for textiles, that cheaper materials had the simpler designs, while the more expensive materials could be more elaborately decorated.

One feature which distinguished his work from that of his contemporaries was composition and balance, displayed in his Egyptian and Oriental patterns. One innovation introduced by him was the Japanese technique of shading the background from one colour to another. He used fish, bats, dragons, insects, birds, and butterflies as motifs. He also produced designs for lace, quilts, tablecloths, bedspreads and towels.

Christopher Dresser was one of the most remarkable designers Britain has produced. His influence was worldwide and his designs world related. He is quoted by many as the father of Art Deco. A fitting tribute to him appeared in his obituary in *The Builder* of 10th December 1904 :

"...he spent most of his time in preparing designs for manufacturers and in the enjoyment of his garden and flowers. He was a most genial companion and interesting talker, and never tired of discussion on Art and the habits of the Nations of the East, trying to trace their histories by their ornamental forms as a philologist does by their language...".

Christopher Dresser died in his sleep aged 70 years at The Hotel Central, Mulhouse (Alsace) whilst on a business trip accompanied by his son Louis.

This Page and Opposite: *Various pattern designs*

One of several white painted chairs in the Glasgow style, made for a private customer in 1902 and which led to more decorative examples exhibited in Italy in the same year

Biography:

Charles Rennie Mackintosh (1869-1928)

High-backed oak chair first used at the Argyle Street tea rooms

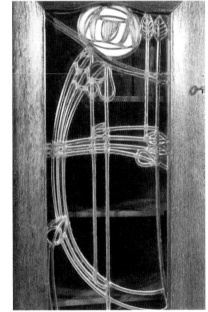

Leaded glass panel from a stained oak cabinet

Dressing table in geometric style with cubic motifs

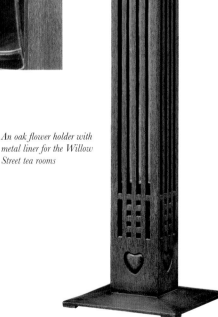

An oak flower holder with metal liner for the Willow Street tea rooms

Of all the designers of the Arts and Crafts Movement, Mackintosh, in terms of furniture, is possibly the most instantly recognisable. Although his training was as an architect, his reputation is founded equally on his interiors, which demonstrate very clearly his innate ability to integrate furniture and decoration with its setting, which principle was fundamental to the Movement and one which all its leaders strove to achieve. Also central to his architectural philosophy was the belief that a building should fulfil the purpose for which is was designed. Mackintosh would not prepare any designs for the elevations of a house until the internal arrangements had been submitted and approved. The characteristically random positioning of windows in an elevation reflects not only the priority of the internal layout over external appearance, but is also part of an abstract composition resulting in a perfectly balanced mixture of solid and void.

He was undoubtedly one of Glasgow's greatest exports and his work in furniture design dwarfs most furniture made by his Arts and Crafts contemporaries. It is, however, ironic that during his lifetime he received scant recognition at home, finding greater popularity for his designs in Europe than in his own country. To him his role as an architect encompassed fine art and craft as well, the relationship between the three being inextricable, a tenet which William Morris, the Movement's "founder" both approved and practised. In 1901

Mackintosh, who was as much an artist as an architect, said "The craftsman of the future must be an artist", a statement which still rings true today but seems to be conveniently ignored by many educationalists. That view was also valid at the very start of the Arts and Crafts Movement in the 1850s and 60s, when craftsman and designer were seen to be losing touch as a result of modern manufacturing methods.

Mackintosh was the fourth of eleven children born to William who was a police clerk and Margaret Rennie Mackintosh. William had a passion for gardening which he encouraged in his son with the result that he sketched flowers throughout his life. Charles was to become an accomplished water-colour artist. Glasgow was a booming city both industrially and in the arts world. A group of local artists known as The Glasgow Boys was rising to prominence at home and abroad and Mackintosh, as well as George Walton, a fellow Glaswegian architect, joined them. In 1883, at the age of fourteen, Mackintosh began attending classes at The Glasgow School of Art. The Director, an Englishman called Francis Newbery, was acutely aware of the school's loyalty to traditional neoclassical design and was determined that the school should move away from its political origins and encourage individual contemporary talent. Newbery was very supportive of Mackintosh from the start and became a lifelong friend.

Above:
Charles Rennie Mackintosh in about 1900 by which time he regarded himself as an artist-architect

Right:
Glasgow Institute Poster by "The Spook School" c.1896. Courtesy Glasgow School of Art

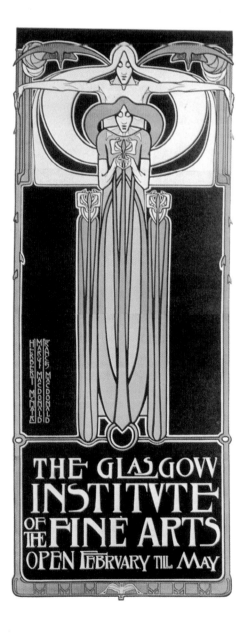

In 1889 Mackintosh joined the firm of Honeyman and Keppie as a young architect. Keppie was a young progressive import, brought in to breathe new life into the firm. In 1891 Mackintosh delivered a lecture to the Glasgow Architectural Association entitled "Scottish Baronial Architecture" in which he made a forceful case for a vernacular style but adapting it to modern needs. He had already won the prestigious Alexander Thomson Travelling Scholarship for the design of a public hall and went to Italy where he travelled, sketching and painting the buildings he liked. Whilst this experience apparently did not influence his own work, it must have enhanced his status in local architectural circles on his return home.

Mackintosh became involved with the interior refurbishment of Craigie Hall and the Glasgow Art Club and his hand can be seen distinctly in the details of their wooden carvings. He had a close relationship with Keppie's sister Jessie and through her, both he and a fellow draughtsman Herbert McNair were introduced to a group of women art students calling themselves "The Immortals". Two of the women were Frances and Margaret Macdonald with whom Charles and Herbert worked closely and they became known as "The Four", and later as "The Spook School", because of their

distinctive style of painting, their work frequently featuring long-haired women with sickly pale complexions and ghoul-like appearance. Mackintosh developed this style to produce huge arresting posters designed to shock – and shock they did. In 1896 "The Four" exhibited their paintings at the London Arts and Crafts Exhibition where their work was met with a mixed reception from approval, through indifference to outright scorn. They were never invited to exhibit as a foursome in England again!

In the same year Mackintosh was invited to work with George Walton in producing stencilled murals for Miss Cranston's Buchanan Street Tea Rooms. This was the beginning of a long and very successful business relationship in which Mackintosh created a series of spectacular interiors for the growing number of Cranston establishments. It was in this environment that the high-backed chairs which typify his work were created.

Glasgow School of Art
Their employers, Honeyman and Keppie, won the commission for the building of the Glasgow School of Art and although Keppie ran the project, the design was undoubtedly Mackintosh's and was to prove his masterwork.

Above Left:
Main Entrance

Above Middle:
This stone relief over the front door depicts two female guardians on either side of a stylised tree, clearly linked to the work of the "Spook School"

Above Right:
The West Façade

Courtesy Glasgow School of Art

Left:
The Mackintosh Room at The Glasgow School of Art as it is today. Originally designed as a boardroom it became a studio partly because of the Governors' dislike of the room and partly because space was at a premium. It is now a showpiece of Mackintosh interior architectural and furniture design. Courtesy Glasgow School of Art

In 1900 Mackintosh and Margaret Macdonald were married and Margaret worked almost entirely with her husband, probably creating little on her own. but from this point it is often difficult to know how much of her husband's designs should in fact be credited to her. Two large building projects of Queen's Cross Church and the Daily Record Building followed, leading to his first commission to design detached houses. One of the first was Hill House for the publisher William Blackie. This gave Mackintosh the chance to put his design theories into practice, creating bold new buildings with their roots in Scottish traditional architecture. Meanwhile, he and Margaret had moved into a new flat in 120 Mains Street where they could design exactly as they pleased – spacious and light interiors in complete contrast to most interiors of the time. Below and on the opposite page are examples of their own private furniture:

They were able to incorporate these themes successfully into more interior work for Catherine Cranston's expanding tea room empire and for private houses he designed. Moreover, George Walton had moved out of Glasgow, giving the Mackintoshes yet more freedom and sole involvement in Miss Cranston's commissions as well as the refurbishment of her own home "Hous'hill".

Above:
Margaret Macdonald

Right:
A white painted oak bedroom table. The front legs have a raised linear moulding curled over petal-shaped piercing at their upper ends. The white paintwork complimented the white decoration of their bedroom and signified a breakaway from his natural wood finishes and bears a strong relationship with his later work in Austria and Germany.

For the Tea Rooms

Firstly his work in Miss Cranston's tea rooms in Argyle Street.
Ingram Street, Willow Street and at Hous'hill :

A dark stained oak high-back side chair with an oval back and rushed seat*. The best known and most characteristic of Mackintosh's designs whose plain unadorned wood surfaces link it firmly to the Arts and Crafts Movement. He was more concerned with looks than comfort and indeed the craftsmanship. By courtesy of Christie's

A similar but plainer version for Willow Street

*Hair Cloth was also used for seat coverings. This is a mixture of dyed horse hair with a cotton, linen or silk warp. Invented in 1837 by John Boyd, a travelling textile merchant from Scotland who died in 1890. Hair cloth is still made in the same factory, John Boyd Textiles at Castle Cary, Somerset who are the only hair cloth weavers in Britain and one of very few worldwide.

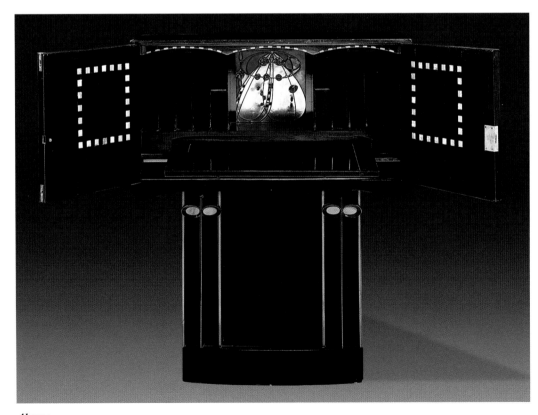

Above:
Mackintosh had two of these cabinets made, one for Walter Blackie at Hill House and a duplicate for himself, 1904

Above:
A dark stained oak table of 1898, square top over angled legs pierced and carved with stylised heart and teardrop motifs with a single stretcher shelf. Height 27 ³/8". This table realised £83,650 at auction in 2002. By courtesy of Christie's

Above:
A Domino table in oak on four plank supports with four stretchers in a square. 30 ³/8" high, which is writing height

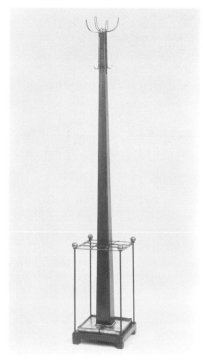

Above:
An oak and wrought iron hat, coat and umbrella stand made c.1900 for Ingram Street with twin brass drip trays. By courtesy of the Bridgeman Art Gallery

Above:
Oak arm and single chairs with drop-in seats. The pierced side panels compliment those of his high-back chairs illustrated on previous page. By courtesy of Christie's

Above:
An oak flower holder with metal liner made for the Salon de Luxe at The Willow Tea Rooms. This marked another change from the harshness of his earlier designs. By courtesy of Christie's

Above:
An oak card table for Miss Cranston's
Hous'hill. Left shows the drawer pull
of typical "foliage" shape.
By courtesy of Christie's

Above:
A sycamore chair with inset oval lilac
glass panel. By courtesy of Christie's

For Private Houses

Above:
A washstand for Hill House using
geometric shapes which dominate
the furnishings throughout

Above:
A dressing table for W J Bassett-Lowke of
Derngate, Northampton

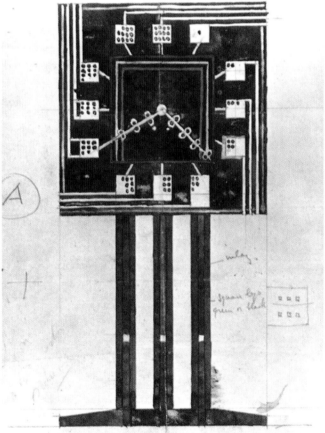

Mackintosh's output in furniture design was enormous – he designed well over 400 pieces which can be viewed as falling into phases. At the start in the 1890s, his work had close affinity to that of his English contemporaries Voysey and Baillie-Scott, but are nevertheless instantly recognisable and identify with the popular conception of his furniture design work. As time went on, and particularly from the time he married and started to design his own house, his furniture became more decorative. When working for Catherine Cranston later in 1917, he designed the yellow-painted settle below for the "Dug Out" (basement) of the Willow Tea Rooms which although incorporating the simple vernacular and geometric features already in place in the building, shows a breakthrough in decorative taste probably influenced by Margaret his wife. It was almost certainly with her support that Mackintosh was able to make metalwork a key part of his output. From the start he had designed simple metal locks, hinges and handles for his furniture, the latter usually broad and tapering into leaf shapes. Then came the introduction of repoussé panels in door and drawer fronts of both carved gesso and engraved and beaten metals, and it is here that Margaret made important contributions *(see opposite page)*. Cutlery and cruets also became part of his repertoire for Miss Cranston's tearooms, although he was not alone amongst the Movement's designers to incorporate cutlery. Light fittings, such as that shown below, also received his attention.

Glass too was a medium in which Mackintosh applied his genius in the form of panels in furniture, fire-surrounds and doorways, examples of which are shown opposite.

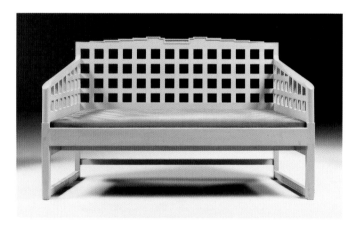

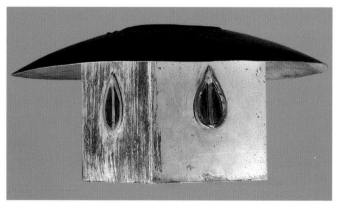

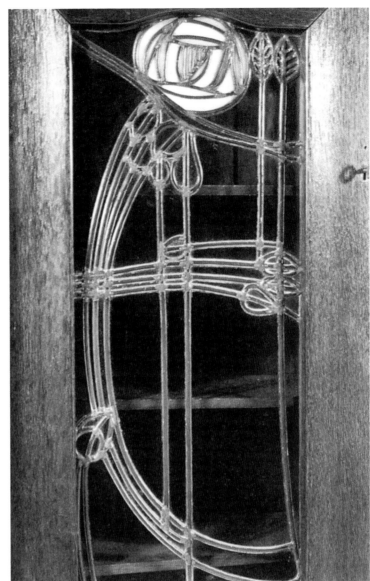

Above Left:
An ornamental repouss copper panel from a stained oak cabinet

Above Right:
Leaded glass panel of stylized roses in a stained oak cabinet. The glass coloured to compliment the room's décor

Right:
The leaded coloured glass panels in the doors of these bookcases for Mackintosh's own home represent some of the best designs in glass that he was to produce

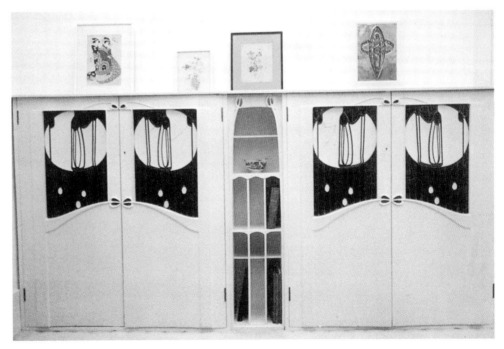

Whilst Art Deco faced considerable opposition in Britain at the start of the 20th Century from the Arts and Crafts Movement, the opposite was true in Europe. Brussels and Paris were the centres of the new style and Art Deco made its mark at the turn of the century. Whilst, apart from his scholarship tour in 1891, Mackintosh does not appear to have even visited Europe before 1900, he and the "Four" were undoubtedly attracted by the new (to them) Art Deco fashion. They eagerly accepted an invitation to design a room for the Successionist Exhibition in Vienna. In 1901 Mackintosh submitted a scheme for the, by now, famous "Haus eines Kunstfreundes" (House of an Art Lover) competition and designed a music salon in Vienna for one Fritz Wärendorfer. In the following year the Mackintoshes exhibited in Turin and soon gained widespread acclaim as leaders of the new movement. Mackintosh's fame in Europe was now launched and it sadly exceeded his achievement in Britain. Curiously, much if not all the furniture used in these European exhibitions came from Glasgow and principally 120 Mains Street!

After the successes of Vienna and Turin, Mackintosh returned to Glasgow, bent on bringing about a revival in the applied arts and architecture – a Scottish Succession. Indifference to and ignorance of the new art were stronger than he had realised. His relentless pursuit of perfection affected his working relationships with both craftsmen and clients. At the same time he was aware of the success in Europe of his Austrian friends. He began turning to alcohol for consolation and became moody. His relationships at work worsened and clients began to object to the treatment received.

In 1913 he finally resigned from Honeyman and Keppie and a year later he and Margaret left Glasgow and moved to the village of Walberswick on the Suffolk coast. Local suspicion of new arrivals just prior to the start of the Great War was directed at the couple. In a police search, reference to the Vienna Succession was found in their house and he had the greatest difficulty in persuading the War Office that he was not a spy. They then moved to Glebe Place in Chelsea.

Mackintosh was unable to practise architectural work in London where he was largely unknown. However, he was introduced to W.J. Bassett-Lowke, owner of the well-known engineering and model engineers' supplier of the same name in Northampton. Mackintosh was engaged by Bassett-Lowke to alter, and decorate and furnish his red brick Victorian terrace house in Derngate Street. The guest bedroom is one of the best known of Mackintosh's designs and the remainder of his work there was extremely successful but did not lead to more. Sadly the interiors of the house were not illustrated in the press until three years later in 1920.

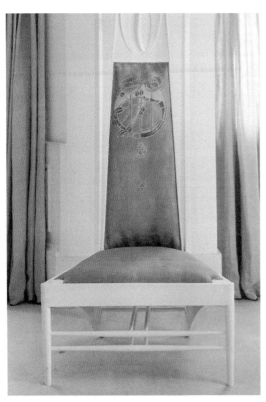

This white-painted chair, which was exhibited in Turin in 1902 and bought by Fritz Wärendorfer, echoes the Glasgow style of Fig (a) made in the same year for Mrs Rowat, mother-in-law to Francis Newbery, headmaster of the Glasgow School of Art, and Mackintosh's earlier work in Argyle Street at Fig (b). The high-back chairs can be seen as symbols expressive of the upward surging vitality of so much of Mackintosh's work. In the smart Willow Tea Rooms the spindly backs of the chairs were supposed to convey the idea of a forest of young willows.
By courtesy of Christie's

Fig (b) By courtesy of the Glasgow School of Art

Fig (a)

The following years in Chelsea saw Mackintosh devoted to a number of projects involving studios and a theatre for Margaret Morris. By this time his architectural work had become, if anything, more powerful and certainly less pretty, and it failed to attract the approval of conservative local authorities.

He became very dispirited, morose and apathetic and they moved abroad, settling in Port Vendres on the Mediterranean side of the Franco-Spanish border. He then engaged himself entirely in perfecting his watercolour painting, with extraordinary results, quite different from anything he had produced before. He preferred landscapes and flowers and his paintings were exuberant and full of colour and life.

In 1927 he fell ill complaining of a sore throat and on medical advice returned to London where he was diagnosed with cancer of the tongue and throat and he died at the age of 60 on 18 December 1928. Margaret survived him by four years and died in London in January 1933.

So ended the lives of two of the most remarkable and, very sadly largely under-appreciated, pioneers of the applied arts in 19th and 20th centuries. A collection of his sketches and drawings left behind in Chelsea was valued at "no more than £88 16s 2d" and incredibly four of his chairs were valued at £1. At auction in 2002 one high-backed chair sold for £380,650 !

It was not until the 1950s that Mackintosh's name became recognised as a pioneer of modern architecture, with the result that there is now a large following of his work across all the fields of his interests and the Ingram Street Tea Rooms, Glasgow School of Art and other sites stand preserved as monuments to his many achievements. The Charles Rennie Mackintosh Society was established at Queen's Cross Church, Maryhill, Glasgow in the late 1970s.

Above:

Derngate Street, guest bedroom. The colour scheme was based on black and ultramarine. The ceiling and walls were painted white and the carpet was grey. The furniture was decorated with narrow bands of black with stencilled squares of ultramarine. The beds were simple and undecorated except for six squares pierced in each foot board and a checked border. Black stripe patterned wall-paper edged with ultramarine harness braid suggested a canopy linking the beds, secured by black-headed drawing pins. The chairs and lamp fittings and bedside table all followed typical Mackintosh fervour for completeness

A caned Sheraton style armchair, also produced without arms, used in the Buchanan Street tea rooms, Glasgow

Biography:

George Walton
(1867-1933)

Leather seated Sheraton
style chairs 1896

A mahogany Pembroke style
table on a stand echoing a nest
of quartetto tables

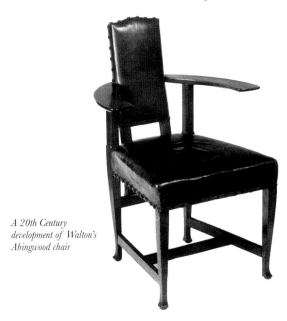

A 20th Century
development of Walton's
Abingwood chair

Caned black chairs for the
Buchanan Street tea rooms
in Glasgow

Jackson Walton

Born in Glasgow, five years after his parents' move from Manchester, George Walton was one of twelve children. His father Jackson Walton, a somewhat flamboyant character pictured here, had inherited a flourishing cotton commission agency, but his indifference to business and belief that as a gentleman he had a right not to work, evidently had an adverse effect on the business. The attraction of Glasgow as a prosperous manufacturing city, in which the textile industry was gaining importance, was apparently not lost on Jackson Walton (albeit temporarily) and was probably the principle reason for the family's move to the city in 1862. However, his efforts to re-establish himself as a commission agent failed and he became a manufacturer of patented steam boiler coverings (lagging), and five years after that, a manufacturing chemist. Jackson was an artistic and creative man and Glasgow, despite its industrial bias, was an ideal habitat for the artistically inclined. He loved painting and photography and immersed himself in these activities in a fast-growing artistic environment.

No doubt he was most content to see some of his large family showing signs of artistic flair, the first of whom was Helen, a child of his first marriage. She was twelve years old when the family came to the city and was sent to the burgeoning Glasgow School of Design three years later, where despite its rigidly traditional focus on the training of working-class men and women in the textile industry, she excelled in her own right, particularly in plant drawing and winning a coveted award, the Haldane Prize, in her final year 1871. Helen was to have a significant and important influence on her brother George seventeen years her junior, Jackson's dwindling enthusiasm for his boiler-lagging manufacturing business was accompanied by increasing ill health and he died of tuberculosis in 1873 having fathered a further three children, the youngest of whom was George Henry.

George grew up principally with five unmarried sisters and his brother Edward in reduced financial circumstances, but evidently in a caring, happy environment, led by his mother Eliza, seventeen year's her late husband's junior and ably assisted by his sister Helen.

Jackson Walton's legacy to his family may be seen as that of Helen and the four children of his later years, Edward, Hannah, Connie and George, all of whom showed remarkable abilities in creative work. The Walton house became a veritable art club on its own, with Helen taking a leading part. In 1876 Edward had attended for one year the Staatliche Kunstakademie in Düsseldorf, which gave him a good grounding and put him in the position of being the bright hope of the family. Helen was taking students for private drawing and painting classes which, together with the sale of floral-decorated pottery, provided a living income but little more. Young George, aged thirteen, had to be withdrawn from school at Patrick Academy because of a lack of funds, and in 1881 was found a job at The British Linen Bank.

Edward, having tried unsuccessfully to enter the Glasgow Art Club, started to associate with a number of young men, all painters, of similar backgrounds and aspiration. Together these young painters formed a disparate group with the focused aim of finding alternative means of expression to those of their elders in the Art Club, whom they viewed as entrenched and dull Impressionists and referred to as "Gluepots", wishing to learn nothing from them! Instead they looked abroad in London, Holland and France seeking fresher subjects, means of expression and a brighter palette. The group came to be known as "The Glasgow Boys" and it was not long before young George joined them.

George's life in the 1880s was very much centred round the artistic interests of his family and the Linen Bank had little attraction for him, although he had to struggle on. Whenever he could, he would join Edward in his Bath Street studio and on sketching trips. George delighted in the company, the talk and views on artistic subjects of the artists in the group and also their successes. In 1884 George visited London, probably with Edward, for a fortnight's exploring the sights and exhibitions, and it is likely that Morris and Co.'s showroom in Oxford Street featured in his programme, as did a generous amount of time with a young lady called Kate Gall, to whom he became engaged.

An important turning point in George Walton's career came in 1888 when Catherine Cranston, the owner of a burgeoning restaurant empire in Glasgow, invited twenty-one year old George to work on the redecoration of her Argyle Street Tea Rooms. which he accepted avidly and abandoned his career at the Linen Bank, never to return. Miss Cranston, as she was universally known, was a lady of considerable character who had set up her own business at 114 Argyle Street in

1878 and was pioneer of the "essential Glasgow tea-room", a claim she wrested from her tea-dealer brother Stuart, through her emphasis on the best quality in catering and décor. The enviable position of Glasgow as a manufacturing and international trade centre, together with its burgeoning civic pride, second only if not equal to London, encouraged such entrepreneurial opportunists. George Walton & Co., Ecclesiastical and House Decorators, was formed, which was to be a significant part of the city's recognition of the "Glasgow Boys".

So far as George was concerned, it was largely because of Miss Cranston's ability to combine caution and nerve in her business planning, that he was her choice for work at Argyle Street, for which she envisaged a significant departure from more traditional styles in her other premises. At the same time, the Glasgow Exhibition provided incentives for George which, together with his admiration for William Morris & Co, the aspirations and work of the Art Workers' Guild in London and Charles Robert Ashbee's Guild and School of Handicraft, combined to establish the influence of the southern Arts and Crafts

Movement in Glasgow. Five years later, Charles Mackintosh was also to benefit from the same Cranston-inspired opportunities, as the Glasgow-based "Spook School" gained recognition, of which he was one of the four originators.

Although Walton, in common with many of the designers of furniture of the period, had never learned a skilled craft, he was practical in his approach to decorative painting and could often be found up a ladder with a brush doing it himself. His innate interest in, and recognition of, the skills required to execute his designs in whatever medium, inspired him to seek the expertise of others. To begin with, Walton ordered in furniture, but in 1892 he took on his own cabinet-makers and announced the services of cabinet-making and furniture warehousing in local directories. It is not clear whether, at the outset, Walton's designs were part of the furniture service.

Evidence suggests that this rush-seated arm chair of 1895 from the company was in production earlier in other regional forms, closely resembling designs produced by William Morris of some thirty years earlier. Similarly, its armless sister was designed by Walton for the John Rowntree Café.

A later design known as the "Abingwood" designed in oak by Walton in 1897 on essentially traditional country lines, carried on into the 20th Century with marked changes in design: the double-tapered legs which, unlike 18th Century chairs, are tapered on the outside as well as the inside; producing a slightly "perched" effect; also the framed and padded back support and the nailed leather upholstery.

It is interesting that Mackintosh was hired in 1896 to work with George Walton, the principal contractor at Miss Cranston's Buchanan Street Tea Rooms. Catherine Cranston helped propel the careers of both men. Both were astonishingly able in their ability to design subtle colour palettes and harmonise the various aspects of a room's overall design. Both painted and designed glass and metalwork.

Rush-seated arm chair of 1895
By courtesy of Christie's

Armless version designed by Walton
for the John Rowntree Café
By courtesy of Christie's

"Abingwood" chair
By courtesy of
Christie's

The 20th Century
version of the
Abingwood chair

As Walton's confidence increased, he moved away from country styles and started to replace them with his own interpretation of earlier furniture with distinct classical elements. The fitted cabinet of c.1893 for Drumalis, a grand mansion in Larne, Northern Ireland and commissioned by Sir Hugh Smiley, is a fine example with its classically moulded pediment with central swan-neck and turned wood finial; similarly the layout of the drawers and the cloister effect reminiscent of chiffonier designs some seventy years earlier.

The caned-seated chair, made for the Luncheon room of Miss Cranston's Buchanan Street premises, relates closely to the Aesthetic Movement and early Regency designs with Sheraton style and turned splayed front legs, four turned bobbins above and below the caned back panel and the gently flowing arms. George and Kate also used this chair in their own drawing room in Holland St, London in 1901. A variation on this chair was produced without arms and with a high back, reminiscent of the popular high-back country chairs favoured by Mackintosh in Argyle Street, as the picture of the luncheon room in Buchanan Street shows.

In August 1897, drawn by his brother Edward's success in London and the wealth of possible new work in the city, George and his family moved there to a rented house in Westbourne Park Road. Probably an added incentive was the attraction of a group of well known artists, architects and designers with whom Edward associated and often mentioned. Amongst them were C R Ashbee, Burges, Godwin, Rossetti, Philip Webb and James Whistler to mention just a few. Rossetti and Webb were close friends of William Morris. Although there is no record of a personal friendship between him and Ashbee, George would almost certainly have been interested in Ashbee's Guild of Handicraft, set up in the same year as his own company. Also, because of the high standing of artists in London, one of their leaders James Whistler, had made it acceptable, respectable and even fashionable to take up a career in decoration.

Cane-seated chair for The Luncheon Room. By courtesy of Christie's

Cabinet for Drumalis

The Buchanan Street Luncheon Room

Brussels chair

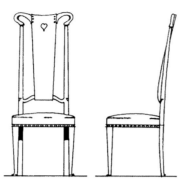

The Cholmondeley chair – Walton's drawing

Kodak Company boardroom showing the Cholmondeley chair

Mahogany drop-leaf table

Sheraton nest of quartetto of tables

In London George was virtually unknown, but his position was far from insecure. He had maintained links with his company in Glasgow and was committed to the active role of Managing Director. Moreover he was obliged to pass newly acquired work to the company workshops.

It was at this time George became engaged in work for the photographic industry and his first foray in this area was the interior of the Dudley Gallery, followed a year later by the company's showroom at 59 Montagne de la Cours in Brussels, for which the Brussels chair was designed. The chair is a clever development of a traditional early 18th Century Queen Anne swept-back chair so well known in England, together with the country backstool or stick-back chair with its wooden seat on legs that belong to neither but are eminently compatible with both.

A variation of this design was made for the Kodak Company Boardroom in Clerkenwell Road. This chair was known as the Cholmondeley chair, with its high, slightly swept back with the panel in nailed leather and a nailed padded seat. The turned-out toes or pad feet on the front legs conform more to the Queen Anne period than the Brussels chair. Also shown is Walton's drawing of the Cholmondeley chair c.1898.

The mahogany drop-leaf table by Walton is another example of his respect for, and attachment to, the 18th Century. It is reminiscent, in the design of its legs, of a Sheraton nest of quartetto tables, with a top from the ever popular and very practical Pembroke table, but with a quintessential perpendicular Arts and Crafts layout of the swinging groups of legs and the one turned stretcher. To cap it, the table top is of "piecrust" design – the piecrust being an applied moulding around the circumference. This design was copied in simpler forms during the Edwardian period and must be found in many homes today, possibly marketed by Liberty and/or Heals. In its earliest forms in the 18th Century, the piecrust was part of the table top material, the centre having been carved out of the solid wood.

The Sheraton-style chairs of 1896, opposite, upholstered in close-nailed leather, are imitations of bentwood design, but are made out of the solid as opposed to being steam bent or bent in hot sand – an 18th Century practice.

George Walton's involvement with the American Eastman Photographic Materials Co. (later to become the Kodak Company) in Clerkenwell, was an important addition to his portfolio of work for them in several parts of London, Dublin, Brussels, Milan, Vienna and Moscow. In London he was involved with exterior decoration, such as this hoarding in the Strand (see opposite page top left) and with the wide range of interior decoration and furniture for which he was so well respected in his home city. The new showrooms he designed had special fitted cabinets for storage and display, often with stained glass panels and copper details in the doors.

There were similarities to Mackintosh designs of the same period, but without the carved details. Of the furniture, most common was Walton's black caned-back chair with tapering legs, first used for John Rowntree's Café and Miss Cranston's Buchanan Street Tea Rooms. A white-painted version was also used in a bedroom at Elmbank, York, together with the white fitted cupboards, panelling and light stencilling of the frieze above the panelling.

Sheraton style chairs

Black caned-backed chairs

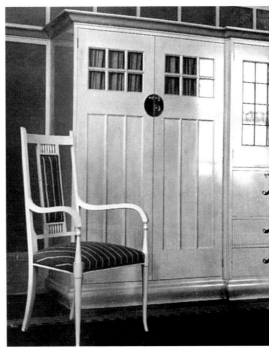

Far Left:
A mahogany vitrine c.1900 of
the same design as one in his own
drawing room. The cabinet recalls
the work of C.F.A Voysey, of whom
Walton was an admirer and has
curved glazed panelled doors.
By courtesy of Christie's

Left:
A white painted version for Elmbank

Walton benefited greatly from an association with another photographic materials company, Wellington & Ward, when in 1898 they asked him to design their display at the annual exhibition of the Royal Photographic Society, which was followed in 1900 by a further commission. Photography was by this time becoming big business, particularly with the introduction of snap-shot photography, to which Walton himself was very much attracted. His successful connection with this company resulted in an even more successful relationship with its owner James Brooker Blakemoor Wellington, himself a photographic enthusiast. Wellington was trained initially as an architectural draughtsman and never lost the architect's dream of building his own house, a responsibility he passed to Walton and one which the latter accepted with great enthusiasm. Walton was becoming increasingly aware of the impermanence of his interior designs which would not last or claim permanent places in the annals of art, unlike for instance the work of his artist colleague James McNeill Whistler. Consequently he was drawn towards establishing himself as an architect rather than a designer, which, when viewed in the context of the Movement, was the reverse of just about all his contemporaries who had started as architects. J.B.B. Wellington's commission of the house in Elstree (The Leys), was an opening for Walton even more startling and with greater potential than Miss Cranston's commission which had launched his career. Wellington saw in Walton the creator of his own greatest architectural dream. He wanted a homely building of distinction to enjoy with his family and friends. The Leys was set in large grounds in which the gardens were to play a prominent part and would be much used. Indeed Walton was asked to add details to the gardens for the next twenty-three years until Wellington died.

The Leys, like its architect, is quite individual. The frontage is symmetrical, almost to the point of severity, but it is surmounted by an enormous hipped roof which, from the front, conceals high chimneys which give the building a soaring quality. In this house Walton's special talent is revealed by his achievement of continuity throughout the house between interior design, fittings, and furniture. Despite Walton's inexperience as an architect, it is said that The Leys was a feat of supreme control throughout.

On the left above is Walton and Co.'s headed paper for their London and Glasgow establishments and, on the right, their furniture label of 1898-1901.

Walton's sketch of The Leys in 1901. The front elevation entirely conceals the surprises of very different styles to the rear

Rear view of The Leys

Shown opposite, this view from the rear shows the high chimneys and hints at Walton's Glasgow origins in the elongated windows and Scottish baronial feature in the tower-house turret behind the frontal block. However, the differences in design between the horizontal front and the verticality of the rear have no satisfactory link and this has been observed as an architectural failing, but so dramatic is the difference in concept that it would take an exceptionally talented and experienced architect to bridge that gap!

Following The Leys, Walton's circumstances became altogether more comfortable. The Glasgow premises of George Walton and Company now had sizeable premises including show-rooms and workshops in Buccleuch Street. The services offered by the company were wide and diverse, covering almost every aspect of design and its implementation. Stained glass was a major part of the services provided, but cabinet-making occupied the largest space.

In 1901 the Walton family moved from their house in Westbourne Park Road to Holland Street in Holland Park and this picture of their drawing room in the new house shows a wide collection of George's furniture work:

White-painted Regency style caned chairs and a high-backed eight-legged three-panel caned settee reminiscent of George III style, two drop-leaf tables and a pair of Brussels chairs on either side of the Walton-designed fireplace with his fireirons.

Walton's bookplate, shown here, from the Holland Park years, showing artist tools (squares interlinked & brushes). Walton hardly ever read, which may account for the mis-spelling of the Latin "Ex Lebris" at the head!

The move to London and a new environment four years earlier had started a considerable change in Walton's life. His circle of friends, and particularly those he met in the art world, grew with his increasing reputation. In 1901 he was elected to membership of The Art Workers' Guild in Queen Square, which further increased his circle of artistic friends and his reputation in interior design and furniture. Increasing interest was being taken in Walton's work in the art press and his Guild membership enabled him to rub shoulders with many of the great men of the day. He was younger than most of them but regarded them as models, and his empathy with English classicism which he had so ably demonstrated in his work at The Leys, attracted their encouragement.

This magnificent stand for the Kodak Company incorporating Voysey's buttressed effect, was designed by Walton for the American Exhibition at The Crystal Palace in 1902. Walton's continental connections increased as the Arts and Crafts Movement, inspired earlier in Central Europe by Ruskin and William Morris, took hold and there was a sudden surge of interest in his work. This interest was also focussed on the work of Charles Mackintosh who was better known and recognised in Europe than in Britain. An influential character in support of both men was the German cultural attaché in London, Hermann Muthesius, who wrote *Das Englisches Haus (The English House)*, which was his passion, following a German fascination for English architecture at the time. Walton's furniture and interiors were almost as well illustrated in Continental periodicals as they were at home.

Holland Street drawing room

Holland Park book plate

Stand for the Kodak Company

George Walton resigned from his company in 1903 as the culmination of his longing to be free of the company designs to which he was committed. He was consequently relieved of responsibilities which he had outgrown and became free to follow his own artistic ideals. Also his prosperity now enabled new freedom. He was only thirty-six years old. It was at this point in his career that George really became Walton the Architect, albeit still formally unqualified! This transition away from his artistic upbringing did not restrict him from involvement with his buildings' interiors down to the last detail, but it signalled more of a change in emphasis and consequently new designs of furniture lessened, which in any case was in harmony with his withdrawal from George Walton and Co. as a company.

One very wealthy client, George Davison (known as G.D.), of Molesey-on-Thames, who advanced from being a civil servant in the Exchequer and Audit Office at Somerset House, to becoming assistant Manager of Kodak and amassed a large fortune, also became a close friend of George and Kate. G.D. was fascinated by boating and in fact any form of river pleasure. On leaving the civil service he moved to a house called Beechcroft at Molesey and it was here that Walton started a large portfolio of commissions on G.D.'s behalf. Probably the earliest piece of furniture for Davis was the Beechcroft buttoned leather chair, of which there were several, probably for the hall.

Then came the most unusual project of Walton's career. There were not many fields within architecture and interior design in which he had not worked and created a very favourable reputation for himself, but marine engineering, or boat building in this case, was an exception.

G.D. was an avid water enthusiast and loved the river environment. The Davisons usually rented their houseboats for August and September each year, until about 1902/3 when G.D. had a bright idea of building his own and he turned to George Walton for help. With absolutely no previous training in marine work, this was quite some task; but to Walton, whose expertise and flair across a very wide spectrum was already well known and respected, it appeared to be of minor concern. He probably saw it as an interesting challenge in much the same way as he entered the exhibition environment and designed for a number of different art forms such as glass-making, decoration and blacksmithing. However, he did share these diverse interests with most of the names at the head of the Arts and Crafts Movement, but in marine work he was unique. It is probable that in his canny way he saw a long line of commissions ahead in working for G.D. – if so, he was quite correct and Davison proved to be a patron as loyal and admiring as J.B.B. Wellington. Both Wellington and Davison were close friends of the Waltons.

The project presented to Walton was for a houseboat , for which he must have taken at least some marine expert's advice, but for the most part the design throughout was his. The houseboat was built on two floors and, at the continuing behest of G.D., Walton involved himself in every aspect of its design and fitting down to carpets, wall tiles and coverings, cutlery and even this notepaper heading with the American Indian motif used throughout the houseboat, which as this logo confirms, G.D. named "The Log Cabin".

The Log Cabin

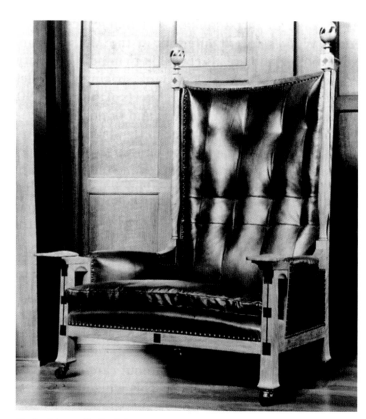

Beechcroft buttoned leather chair

Notepaper heading

Kate died in 1915 after severe illness and this tragedy, compounded by the effects of the Great War, took its toll on George, then only 48 years old. The War did not affect the ambitions nor indeed the wealth of Wellington and Davison, and more commissions for George followed. In 1916, he was employed as an assistant architect by the C.C.B. (Central Control Board (Liquor Traffic)) set up by Minister of Munitions Lloyd George in a desperate attempt to deal with the worsening drink problem of immigrant Irish workers in the munitions factories across the country. Walton's involvement was with the closing down of the worst drinking venues and the upgrading of the better. Walton became depressed because of the downturn of interest in the arts and indeed the gradual side-lining of the Arts and Crafts Movement which "'was losing its way", both in the artistic sense and practically, as being "for the rich only" – an altogether not surprising development when one remembers the same epithet being used during the early years some sixty years before.

He married the daughter of a doctor, Dorothy Anne Jeram (always known as Daphne), in August 1918 and his old friend C. F. A. Voysey was their best man. Daphne had worked in the C.C.B herself. Walton was 23 years her senior. They had a son Edward in 1920.

Various intermittent commissions followed from both old friends like Davison and Wellington and new clients with work on private houses, but the trend did not last. During the earlier years of his working life Walton had been employed by wealthy clients with expansive ideas who were drawn to his exceptional talents. He failed fully to appreciate the possible long-term success of Walton & Co,

ignored offers of shares in the photographic industry and was generally disinterested in making money – he lived more for the moment. British taste after the end of the Great War was conservative and interest in many of the finer aspects of living declined. Men like Walton were quite unprepared and unready for the "slump". In the summer of 1926, Walton saw some relief, albeit temporary, when weavers Alexander Morton & Co employed him in textile design and the range of his designs was remarkable but sadly short-lived.

His last years saw a most surprising piece of architectural work. Davison died and Walton was commissioned by G.D.'s widow Joan to design a memorial chapel in his name (G.D. was both an anarchist and an atheist) at their home in Cap d'Antibes.

Walton's preliminary design in 1931 suggested an eye towards Edwin Lutyen's work in New Dehli but he changed this entirely in favour of a more simple building with accentuated form effecting a quiet splendour, a peacefulness embracing marvellous woodwork, decorative metalwork and perforated, symbolic carving. The effect was one of reaching forward to new experience and never backwards.

By this time the family had moved, because of reduced financial circumstances, to Hythe in Kent where in 1933 he died quietly, a sad and disappointed man. His son Edward's memories of his father are testimony to an outstandingly kind, courteous but reticent and gentle man with huge creativity. To quote from Edward's memoir: "Although George Walton was a quiet, modest man, he started work in an atmosphere where anything might be tried, and almost anything was possible. It was in this context that he worked his artistic revolution."

"Designer then Architect"

Textile designs. Peony & Lily, 1927

"The Thistle" 1927-8

"The Dove"1929

George Walton in c.1930 with son Edward aged 10

"Birds & Blossom"1929

Design for a memorial chapel

A more simple design

Clock case design of 1895 for Charles Voycey's own use

Biography:

Charles Voysey
(1857-1941)

Wallpaper design

Oak desk with fold-over writing surface

The Chaucer cabinet

The "Swan" chair

Charles Voysey was born at Hessle, near Hull in Yorkshire, the son of a schoolmaster, also named Charles, who became vicar of Healaugh and was the founder of the Theistic Church. He was later tried by the Anglican Church as a heretic for denying the doctrine of everlasting hell and deprived of his living. The Reverend Voysey was friend to some of the most respected figures of the 19th Century – including Darwin, Ruskin and Huxley, all of whom had some influence in forming the character of young Charles who was educated firstly by his father and then briefly at Dulwich College.

Charles's grandfather was an architect with roots in the Gothic Revival, so he looked naturally towards architecture for his future. This led to his studies with the prolific London architect J. P. Seddon to whom he was articled. He worked firstly as a student and then as an assistant. Seddon worked with Edward Godwin on a number of architectural projects, in London in particular. Voysey remained with Seddon until 1879 and then moved to work in the office of architect Saxon Snell before accepting an offer to join the staff of the highly respected, but underestimated, traditionalist architect George Devey as assistant. This experience was to add considerably to Voysey's architectural vocabulary.

Voysey set up his own practice in Westminster in 1882 and, while he was building this up, he produced patterns for several companies. He had a great talent for pattern-making and designed wallpapers for Jeffrey & Co, and Essex & Co; textiles for Alexander Morton; tiles for Pilkington's and later Minton's; and carpets sold through Liberty's. It was amongst his peers, Mackmurdo, Norman Shaw, Morris, Godwin, Lethaby and Baille-Scott, that Voysey began to distinguish himself, enthusiastically promoted by the magazine *The Studio*.

Voysey joined The Art Workers' Guild in 1884 and was a founder member. The Guild was soon to become the hub of the Arts and Crafts Movement. The Guild building is still at No. 6 Queen Square in London and is used by a number of professional bodies in the art and heritage worlds today. At the time Voysey joined, membership of the Guild was restricted to men only and most were architects, designers and artists. The goal of the Guild was to establish a proper status for the artist-craftworker and the designer and to put these in touch with industry and the users of their products. To begin with, annual public exhibitions of "Combined Arts" were staged in London, but after 1890 exhibitions were held every three or four years. Voysey designed the cover for the first volume of *The Studio* magazine in 1896.

Charles Voysey

The Reverend Charles Voysey
Vanity Fair Cartoon

His design output was typified by the complete integration of interior with exterior, and in this he was a direct influence on Charles Rennie Mackintosh and therefore a critical link between the Arts and Crafts and Modernist Movements. Voysey's almost ruthless simplicity and emphasis on craft and nature had a considerable affect on Mackintosh's work in the design of Hill House, Helensburgh, Dunbartonshire. It was through the influence of men such as Morris, Ashbee and Philip Webb that a tradition of simple domestic building evolved, exemplified by Webb's Red House for William Morris in Kent and Baillie-Scott's and Voysey's cheerful and cosy houses in Cumbria. In 1888, Voysey won his first architectural commission of a house at Bishops' Itchington, near Stratford-on-Avon for M.H.Lakin which was the catalyst for further offers of architectural work.

From the mid-1880s, Voysey experimented with furniture, much of which was made by F.C.Nielson. Like many of his contemporaries, Voysey was fastidious about the use of plain good-quality materials, made to the highest standards. Simplicity of form and subtlety of proportion were fundamental to his design work. When made, his furniture tended to be very pale in colour and he preferred the use of oak and, for reasons of its more even grain, he often specified Austrian oak rather than English. He also preferred that brass fittings be left unpolished and allowed to mellow through natural patination. He would repeat design features which he deemed to be successful in future pieces of furniture, perhaps with small modifications in proportions. With the influences of rectilinearity from MacMurdo and elegance reminiscent of Godwin, Voysey's furniture is slender and poised, employing simple and beautifully-proportioned forms.

"Swan Chair". By courtesy of Cheltenham Art Gallery

An early Voysey design, and maybe his first in furniture, is this "Oak Armchair for use in Reading Room, Writing Room or Hall" known now as the "Swan Chair". The chair was made for London solicitor client William Ward-Higgs who leased a large house at 23 Queensborough Terrace, Bayswater and entrusted the furnishing of the house to Voysey. The chair is made of flat boards joined with dowels and tenons. The curve of the leg has been carefully cut with the grain running downwards, though the overall shape is problematic and may account for the back support of one arm breaking at a weak point (since repaired). Holes under the top rail and the seat indicate that there was a covering at one time but whether this was close-nailed leather as the design specified, or an instruction, initialled by Voysey "omit this cushion" was followed, is unclear. In any event the chair, as presented today, is extremely uncomfortable. There is a good chance that, when made, it had a slung seat like a deck-chair, between the top-rail and the seat-board and that the original concept of padding the seat board (a cushion?) was abandoned in Voysey's note. The picture overleaf of daughter Haydee Ward-Higgs seated in the chair appears to confirm this. There is no note as to the maker.

This tall-backed chair with a rushed seat was probably made as a part of a set of at least six by C.H.B.Quennell, also a designer, for either the Ward-Higgs' in London or their house The Briars at Bognor Regis in Sussex.

Voysey, like Baillie Scott, claimed the whole range of decorative media as his territory, designing houses and nearly everything in them. Unlike many designers of the time, both men had few inhibitions about designing good furniture for manufacture (mass production) as long as it was well-produced. Although the poor quality of mass-produced goods was one of the catalysts of the Arts and Crafts Movement, many other leading designers such as Godwin and Dresser followed suit and designed for manufacture. Liberty & Co and Heal and Son also sold factory-produced furniture of the period

Tall-backed rush seated chair. By courtesy of Cheltenham Art Gallery

and Edward Godwin's contribution to the hall-marking of goods to establish designer's provenance was a most important aspect in the fight for maintenance of quality.

The flat-topped finial, borrowed from A.H. MacMurdo, was a trade-mark of Voysey, as the two examples of a sideboard and card table show.

The finials are also incorporated in the oak bookcase, below, and desk designed for Haydee Ward-Higgs in 1899. She is pictured seated on the Swan Chair with evidence of the slung deck-chair type of seat mentioned above.

Liberty's openly imitated Voysey's, and indeed other designers' styles and the writing desk on the opposite page is an example. More often than not the furniture was stamped "Liberty's" without reference to the designer – it made sound business sense.

The strong vertical aspects of Voysey design, capped off, albeit in miniature, and with striking metalwork in the drawer pulls are all characteristic.

Also shown is an oak desk of 1895 with a fold-over writing surface whose "card table" brass hinges can be seen along the front. It is plain but well-made with the legs and pillar supports only as large in section as they need to be to fulfil their purpose. The pronounced vertical elements of the piece are skilfully balanced by the horizontal overhang of the top and by the wide stretcher between the rear legs – examples of Voysey's superb sense of proportion. Designed for William Ward-Higgs.

Example of the flat-topped finial

Sideboard

Card table

Haydee Ward-Higgs. By courtesy of Cheltenham Art Gallery

Oak bookcase

Liberty's writing desk

Typical of Voysey's furniture, decoration is limited to the pierced brass strap hinges, indicating the designer's skill in metalwork design as well as wood.

One of the best known and most easily recognisable of Voysey's pieces is the Kelmscott Chaucer Cabinet in oak with brass fittings the lettering of which is backed with red suede. The inside of the cabinet is painted red. The woodwork is by F.C.Coote and the brasswork probably by Thomas Elsley & Company.

We know that the cabinet was made specifically to hold a copy of William Morris's Kelmscott Press masterpiece *The Kelmscott Chaucer* published in 1898, just two years after Morris's death. The interior of the cabinet is rather too large for the book – an indication that either Voysey had additional ideas for the contents of the cabinet, or that its overall size was designed to suit the room for which the cabinet was destined (the more likely explanation).

This piece was displayed at the 1899 Arts and Crafts Exhibition and also illustrated in *The Studio*, Volume 18, page 42.

Oak desk with fold-over writing table

Kelmscott Chaucer cabinet

Pianos

Like several other designers of the period, Voysey designed piano cases. The piano makers were typically Broadwood and Collard.

Below: Voysey case for a piano by Collard in dark-stained oak with pierced panels above the keyboard lined with fabric.

Voysey's contemporary, Mackay Hugh Baillie Scott's "Manxman" piano of 1903. The design is very plain and typically cuboid. It was so-called "Manxman" because he lived on the Isle of Man. He and Ashbee worked together for the Grand Duke of Darmstadt.

The Broadwood Piano, with the case designed and painted by Charles Robert Ashbee between 1898 and 1890, is a masterpiece of decorative art. It is made in oak and holly with wrought-iron hinges featuring ash and bee motifs laid in parchment. The paintwork was carried out to Ashbee's design by Walter Taylor, a former Guild of Handicraft apprentice who also worked for Morris & Co. The words and images were taken from a poem by Ashbee "Beethoven in Olympus"; he had a particular fondness for Beethoven's work.

This piano was a wedding present to Ashbee's wife, Janet who was a keen pianist. The words start inside the left-hand door of the keyboard, across its front and on to the inside of the right-hand doors, and continue round the inside of the painted lid. The poem ends where a figure wrapped in a blue cloak lies sleeping.

Beethoven in Olympus

I dreamed that in a garden once I lay,
Where three strange women garlanded with vine,
Rose and woodbine, and trellised from the sun,
On pipe and lute and viol played to me,
And as they played, the music of all time,
Woke in my soul, and great grey poppies flung
Their spell about me, and the gates stood clear
Of ivory cities such as men pass through
Who seek the infinite, their domes of glass
Translucent, purple, and their gilded vanes
Reflecting light from light. Then at the call
Of one deep chord the dreaming whole awoke;
Voices, and strings, and wind made melody,
And sound there was of myriad instruments
Cunningly fingered, moving to some law
In one triumphant expectation, till
Unto the measure of all form, the old
Deaf master called, when all once more was mute.

The Morris (Faulkner) Broadwood piano – the case is decorated with birds, fruit and flowers in relief in silvered and gilt gesso. Designed by Edward Burne-Jones and commissioned by Mr S. Ionides of Holland Park. Exhibited at the Arts and Crafts Exhibition 1888. The decoration is by Kate Faulkner for Morris Faulkner.

Voysey case for a piano by Callard

Broadwood piano by Charles Robert Ashbee

"Manxman" piano

Morris (Faulkner) broadwood piano

This design for a clock, shown right, was completed by Voysey in 1895 for his own use.

An oak sideboard, below, by Voysey with brass pierced strap hinges, drawer pulls and key plate escutcheons designed for W.Ward-Higgs' house in Bayswater. Note again the characteristic flat-top finials.

The chair, below right, represents Voysey's essentially conservative design philosophy; he saw the traditional style as the only proper style for English design and this, despite his father having suffered expulsion from the Anglican Church for denying established doctrine! This chair is completely unpretentious and looks functional and elegant, having only the one decorative element of the pierced heart in the back-splat. Unlike some of his contemporaries, such as Edward Godwin, he vigorously opposed reliance on foreign sources. He preferred to rely on established precedents, specifically the vernacular rural cottage tradition. Also he eschewed the use of superficial decoration simply for decoration's sake. Four years before the execution of this chair, Voysey complained:

"The intemperate indulgence in display and elaboration, in gilding and veneer, and the feverish thirst for artificial excitement are all part and parcel of our proverbial restlessness. Too much luxury is death to the artistic soul. So there is no desire for simplicity, repose, harmony, dignity, or breadth. The poor architect, who labours to attain these virtues in his interiors, is exposed to the insult and indignity of having all his work spoiled by the upholsterer."

Design for Voysey's own clock

Oak sideboard

The "traditional" style. By courtesy of Cheltenham Art Gallery

His pattern designs employed beautifully elaborate decorative schemes, but he took care to ensure that his decoration derived from simple, natural imagery and that it did not violate the natural limitations associated with pattern design. He stressed "the walls of ordinary living rooms should be treated as backgrounds, subservient to pictures, furniture and people." He intended his designs for wallpapers and fabrics not as self-sufficient art objects, but as backdrops for other objects more worthy of sustained attention. Baillie Scott argued against this principle in trying to promote wallpaper as a decorative device.

This Page & Opposite: Some Voysey Textile and Paper designs

Above: "The Discomfiture of the Philistines". On being presented with artful and crafty Puzzle by Artistic Friend (Query – Is it the right way up? and if so what is it?)

*Sideboard and plate rack by Ernest Gimson in walnut inlaid
with holly and ebony on a Macassar ebony base c.1914*

Biography:

Ernest Gimson, Ernest & Sidney Barnsley

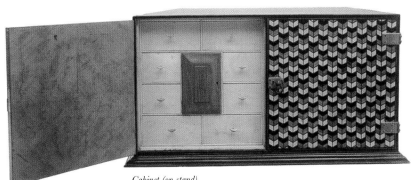

Cabinet (on stand)
by Ernest Gimson

Clergy seat by
Gimson 1914

Oak "Chick" chest by Ernest Barnsley, c.1896

Ladderback chairs by Gimson,
inspired by Hereford chair maker
Philip Clissett

Whilst the life-work of each in the Gimson-Barnsley trio stands proudly in its own right, the combined driving force of this remarkable group also deserves to be recognised and applauded as one of the most important features in the development of interior and furniture design in the 20th Century. I will start with a brief resumé of each character's beginnings to the point at which the trio was established.

Ernest William Gimson was born on 21st December 1864, the son of a prosperous iron founder in Leicester. When he was seventeen years old, he was articled to Leicester architect Isaac Barradale, whilst attending classes in advanced building construction at the Leicester School of Art for which, in 1885, he was awarded first class results. During a visit by William Morris to the city in 1884 to lecture on "Art and Socialism", Morris had dinner with the Gimson family, during which the subject of Ernest's future as an architect was discussed. Ernest asked Morris for a letter of introduction to a London architect and three were immediately written, one of which was to John Dando Sedding, who in 1886 took Ernest into his office where he stayed for two years. The London to which Gimson came as an architectural

student was the centre for new ideas about the arts, and organizations such as the Society for the Protection of Ancient Buildings, The Art Workers' Guild and its offshoot, the Arts and Crafts Exhibition Society, were newly established there. These groups provided a heady mixture of art, handwork, politics, and social economics for the younger generation emerging from the major architectural offices. During his time in London Gimson kept in touch with William Morris through membership of several societies and committees with which Morris had an active association. It was in Sedding's office that Gimson met fellow students Ernest Barnsley and Alfred Powell and also Ernest's brother Sidney who was similarly working in the prestigious office of architect Richard Norman Shaw. Both the Barnsley brothers had graduated from the Royal Academy's Architectural School.

In 1887 Gimson and Ernest Barnsley travelled together in France and Italy studying architectural detail. At the end of that year Sidney Barnsley made a similar trip. In 1888 Gimson started a two-year period of travelling and making competition drawings, for one of which he was awarded a Certificate of Honour. Gimson's enthusiasm for furniture design arose through his involvement with Kenton and

Ernest William Gimson. By courtesy of Cheltenham Art Gallery

Dresser in unpolished oak by Ernest Gimson.
By courtesy of Cheltenham Art Gallery

Company, an influential but short-lived firm set up in 1890 by five young architects of which he was one, together with William Lethaby, Sidney Barnsley, Mervyn Macartney and Reginald Blomfield. They employed a number of trained cabinet-makers to produce well-designed and well-made furniture with each piece individually displaying the designer's and maker's names – in keeping with the spirit of the Arts and Crafts Movement. This experience gave Gimson and Barnsley their first opportunity to tackle seriously the problem of furniture design. Their furniture was well received but the firm did not last. Some examples of their work presented in 1891 in the name of Kenton and Co, are a dresser by Gimson in unpolished oak, shown opposite, and a collection of furniture exhibited at Barnard's Inn in 1891. The picture, right, shows is a gate-legged table by Sidney Barnsley, inlaid cabinet by Blomfield, hexagonal workbox by Lethaby, revolving bookcase and walnut chair by Macartney.

Barnard's Inn furniture

Gimson's oak dresser, shown on the opposite page, has a succession of chamfered uprights in the panel behind the plate rack and is possibly one of the first times such decoration was used. Bruce Talbert referred to it as "wagon-chamfering" as used as "traditional decoration for drays, vans and fishmongers' barrows and such". Both Gimson and the Barnsleys continued to use chamfering as a decorative technique throughout their careers.

During 1890 Gimson, through an architect friend, went for a few weeks to study chairmaking with Philip Clissett, an old Herefordshire craftsman, who in the 1880s had furnished the Meeting Hall of the Art Workers' Guild in Queen Square, London. Here he learnt the rudiments of ladder-back chair-making and seat rushing. He reported to Edward Gardiner, whom he later employed to make chairs at Sapperton, that "Clissett could turn out his work from cleft ash poles on his pole lathe, steam, bend and all the rest and complete a chair a day at 6/6d having rushed it in his cottage kitchen singing as he worked". Clissett said that if you were not singing you were not happy.

Philip Clissett (1817-1913)

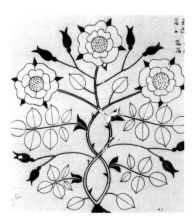

A Gimson drawing of an inlaid design in a bold marquetry surface of palm, cherry and ebony for a fall-front cabinet designed by him for Kenton and Co

Adding to this valuable experience in craft work, Gimson also studied plasterwork with the London firm of plasterworkers Messrs Whitcombe and Priestley, learning and mastering the techniques of moulding and carving plaster. In 1890 he felt able to write "I have taken to furniture designing and plasterwork. I spend four or five hours a day working in a little plasterer's shed modelling friezes and ribbed ceilings. I get on capitally and shall soon be able to undertake work on my own account. I shall have one or two things in the next "Arts and Crafts Exhibition" I hope, and some pieces of furniture as well".

Inspiration for the drawing came from frescoes at Berkeley Church which he had made during a visit there between 1889 and 1890.

An example of Gimson's plasterwork is the ceiling of his "Upper Dorval House" at Sapperton shown over the page. He executed his work by modelling the design with hand-tools and applying it to a prepared plaster background having hand-drawn the designs on to the background. He abhorred much contemporary work because the plaster decoration was cast as a whole before fixing to the wall/ceiling, but conceded that although this method often produced very beautiful results, it is certainly not such a right method as modelling by hand – a remark that epitomises one reason why the Arts and Crafts Movement failed because of the high cost and limited market.

He briefly considered pursuing a conventional architectural career before embarking on a rather more adventurous and romantic course leading him in 1893 to move away from London to the South Cotswolds in Gloucestershire with his friends and fellow architects Ernest and Sidney Barnsley.

... and exhibited in 1891 made it the most favourably received piece in the exhibition.

Gimson's Upper Dorval House showing the plaster ceiling and the unpolished oak dresser. See previous page

Arthur Ernest Barnsley was born in 1863 and his brother Sidney Howard in 1865, two boys in a family of five Barnsley children. The Barnsleys had a very successful building business, John Barnsley and Sons, in Birmingham and lived in Edgebaston, a growing suburb which attracted wealthy middle class inhabitants, many of whom showed artistic inclinations. The Barnsleys were Wesleyans and Ernest and Sidney were regular chapel-goers. On leaving school both boys continued their studies at the Birmingham School of Art. In 1884 and 1885 respectively, Ernest won a third grade prize for historical ornament, having studied drawing, painting, modelling and design and Sidney gained a first class certificate in building construction – interestingly an identical qualification to that received by Ernest Gimson in Leicester in the same year.

Assisted by their healthy financial positions and because they were the younger sons in their respective families, Ernest and Sidney Barnsley, and also Ernest Gimson, were not required to enter their family businesses and so were free to move away from home and to pursue their own chosen careers in architecture, which was a most popular and acceptable choice at the time. The backgrounds of the two Barnsley brothers and that of Ernest Gimson had much in common, which goes some way to explaining both the momentum of their friendship and the similarities in their aspirations throughout their lives. Their partnership started to develop when they met in London, working in the offices of well-known successful architects. Their respective and largely common talents and professional contributions to that profession, together with the experience each gained in working and travelling, cemented their friendships and their bonds as craftsmen and designers at a time when the whole history of design in Britain was in flux and major changes in philosophy were taking place, fired by the originators of the Arts and Crafts Movement Augustus Pugin, John Ruskin, Dante Gabriel Rossetti, William Morris, Philip Webb and James Whistler to mention but a few.

Like Gimson, Sidney Barnsley's involvement in the team of five who founded Kenton and Co. gave him a most valuable insight into the, for him, uncharted waters of furniture design.

Shown opposite is a house at 320 Hagley Road, Edgbaston, Birmingham by Ernest Barnsley and built by John Barnsley & Sons. In 1887 the decision to disband Kenton and Co. in 1892 made Ernest Gimson and Sidney Barnsley seriously consider moving to the country, the Cotswolds in particular. Gimson could have been expected to move back to Leicester, where he had just built a house and taken great pains to decorate it with Morris wallpapers and plasterwork designed and modelled by himself.

Towards the end of the same year they decided to move, probably because of their disenchantment with the professional side of architecture and the belief that to be a successful architect one must live in a town. The lure of quality living in unspoilt countryside also certainly had its attraction. Undoubtedly they would have discussed this with Morris who had already moved with Rossetti to nearby Kelmscott near Lechlade on the Thames in 1871.

Their move out of London was the first step towards the establishment of an ideal "community". According to Sidney, their plan was to get hold of a few trustworthy craftsmen and eventually have workshops in the country where they could join together and around which others would attach themselves. Although this ideal was never fully to be achieved, it continued to play an important part in their philosophy throughout their working lives. After considerable searching between Yorkshire and the South Downs, in 1893 the three, plus Ernest

Barnsley's family, moved to Ewen near Cirencester and concentrated their search which eventually ended at Pinbury Park on the Bathurst Estate. They all moved into Pinbury in 1894. Pinbury is substantially a late 16th Century house with fragmentary structures from the medieval period. The house was bought by the Bathurst Estate in 1786 in a state of decay, described as "dilapidated" and requiring major repairs. Ernest Barnsley was commissioned to repair the house and he adapted two adjoining cottages as workshops and houses for his brother Sidney and for Ernest Gimson, and the house was re-rendered externally with a coating of ochre limewash. It seems that these repairs and improvements were so attractive that Lord Bathurst took over Pinbury as a summer residence and gave Gimson and the Barnsleys land in Sapperton village on which they could build their own houses, Upper Dorval House and Beechanger Cottage. (from a Historical Report by Michael Hill, Architectural Historian and Conservation Consultant October 2003).

Ernest Barnsley and family c.1901

320 Hagley Road. By courtesy of Alan Crawford

A wardrobe in Indian Walnut designed by Sidney Barnsley for Kenton and Co. and exhibited at Barnards Inn in 1891. By courtesy of the Victoria and Albert Museum

Inglewood, Ratcliffe Road, Leicester whose design is reminiscent of Gimson's first employer Isaac Barradale. By courtesy of Cheltenham Art Gallery

At Pinbury the three men were able to indulge in their love of the countryside and their desire for a rural life to the full. However, their inexperience of country life must have presented them with practical problems in the early days. At Gimson's suggestion, one of the Misses Morley, his cousins in Lincolnshire, was asked to join the Pinbury settlement to give them the benefit of her country upbringing. Lucy Morley joined them in 1894 or 1895, and shortly after, she and Sidney Barnsley were married.

The early years at Pinbury must have been amongst the happiest of the three men's lives. Many of their London friends and former colleagues visited them, as did the Barnsley's two elder brothers and their families. Such was their affection for Pinbury that in about 1899 William Barnsley renamed his house, no. 324 Hagley Road, Edgbaston (possibly also designed by brother Ernest), "Pinbury" in memory of happy days spent in the Cotswolds.

Looking at the photograph above of the Pinbury workshop, in the left-hand foreground is a music-cabinet and workbox combined in a single convex-topped chest made by Ernest Barnsley and exhibited at the 1896 Arts and Crafts Exhibition. Part of a review in *The Cabinet Maker and Art Furnisher* said: "Mr A. Ernest Barnsley deserves credit for religiously avoiding relationship with the flimsy and wobbly structures which are usually made for music and workbox purposes, and giving us an article which if not – to all – a thing of beauty, is likely to be a joy and a comfort for at least two or three centuries."

Of the undisguised dovetails showing on the front panel, the reviewer also commented that "its very skilfulness raises the question of whether Ernest Barnsley had had any previous experience of woodwork and cabinet-making whilst in Birmingham, comparable to that obtained by Gimson and Sidney Barnsley through their involvement with Kenton and Co". Dovetails and through (tusk) tenons were a popular decorative feature in their furniture and, predictably their execution was faultless.

It should be remembered that the practical experience of woodworking of all three men was very limited. The little experience they had on arrival at Pinbury came from observation of others at work at Kenton and Co. It was Sidney Barnsley in particular who extended this knowledge through his dedicated experimentation in furniture design at Pinbury, laying the foundations, both technically and stylistically, for the later work of all three men.

Top Left:

Pinbury in 1894. Left to Right: Sidney Barnsley, Lucy Morley (later Mrs S Barnsley), Ernest Gimson, Mrs E Barnsley, Ernest Barnsley, Mary Barnsley, Ethel Barnsley. By courtesy of the Edward Barnsley Trust

Top Right:

The same view 110 years later

Bottom Right:

As a part of the "improvements" a somewhat incongruous square building with a flat roof and rendered and limewashed walls was added to the Eastern side of the house in 1904 as a Servants' Room with access from the scullery and kitchen. (Picture from Country Life 1910)

Bottom Left:

This is how the Servants' Room looks 100 years later in 2004 by which time a pyramid lead roof surmounted with a stone ball finial has been added. The rendered limewashed walls of the house survived until the 1950s or 1960s when the rendering was removed from all but the Servant's Room – presumably in deference to the historical importance of the extension

The Pinbury Workshop c.1896 developed by the group from one of the two cottages. By courtesy of the Edward Barnsley Trust

Sidney Barnsley with his wife Lucy and their two children Edward and Grace 1900

This oak "Chick" chest by Ernest Barnsley c.1896 has inlay in fruitwood and stained oak featuring chicks, chickens and sprays of flowers. There are exposed dovetails, three heavy iron hinges and the lower forward edge of the chest and the end-grain faces of the "slot on" feet are decorated by gouging. By courtesy of Cheltenham Art Gallery

In 1900, Ernest Gimson married Emily Ann Thompson, the daughter of the vicar of Skipsea in Yorkshire. They both shared a love of traditional English music and Arnold Dolmetsch the founder of the firm that made early keyboard instruments (Harpsichord, Clavichord and Spinet), was a frequent visitor to Pinbury.

Ernest Barnsley was retained at Pinbury to oversee further improvements which included the demolition of the 19th Century rear wing and its replacement with a library which is pictured below, showing examples of plasterwork and stone carving by Gimson and panelling by Sidney Barnsley. The firedogs in the Pinbury Library are designed by Gimson and were made in the Sapperton smithy by Alfred Bucknall.

Gimson and the Barnsleys worked together at Pinbury until about 1901 when they moved to the nearby village of Sapperton. Here Gimson built himself a house on the land given to the group by Lord Bathurst and set up workshops making furniture, turned chairs and metalwork to his own designs in the outbuildings of nearby Daneway House, a large 14th Century house on the outskirts of the village. The main reception rooms of Daneway were used as showrooms.

Sidney Barnsley built himself a cottage in the village named "Beechanger", while Ernest Barnsley built Upper Dorval House at a cost, all-in with a stable, of £1700.14s.1d. All the materials were of local origin.

A review in the *Builder* of the Arts and Crafts Exhibition at which the bow-front dresser shown opposite was displayed, was most unsympathetic and ran :

"In the reaction which is taking place against display and over-lavish ornamentation, the new school of designers appear to be losing the sense of style, and of dignity of design which accompanies it, altogether. The object now seems to be to make a thing as square, as plain, as devoid of any beauty of line, as is possible, and call this art.

Look at the oak dresser for instance... the semi-circular plan is effective, but the details are absolutely clumsy; the turn buttons to the small top cupboards look like the work of a savage; the wooden handles to the lower doors, with the panels hollowed out just beneath them for fingers, are actually nailed on at one end, the rough nail-heads showing at the top. This is not only not artistic work, it is not even good craftsmanship."

It needs to be remembered that *The Builder* was one of the most conservative periodicals. In fact all the constructional features singled out in the review were regularly used as orthodox methods of construction of Gothic furniture. Gimson and Ernest Barnsley formed a partnership at Daneway House, while Sidney Barnsley decided to remain on his own, independently making and designing furniture and, where his work exceeded capacity, he passed this on to his brother and friend.

Firedogs in the Pinbury Library

Beechanger Cottage. By courtesy of Cheltenham Art Gallery

Peter Van Der Waals.
By courtesy of Leicester Museum

Above:
The interior of Ernest Barnsley's cottage at Sapperton. "Upper Dorval House". By courtesy of the Edward Barnsley Trust

Left:
Against the left-hand wall is the oak bow-fronted dresser which he designed and made in about 1898, enlarged below. By courtesy of the Edward Barnsley Trust

Between 1902 and 1919 the workshop at Daneway produced large quantities of furniture. By 1910 Gimson employed twelve men including skilled cabinet-makers and apprentices who were under the direction of foreman Peter Waals. Most of the furniture made there was undecorated. Their work covered domestic furniture, as well as a large range of furniture for offices, churches and other public buildings.

Peter van der Waals came from Holland and was employed by the Gimson – Ernest Barnsley partnership as foreman/cabinetmaker from 1901. He had worked extensively in Central Europe as a cabinet-maker before coming to London in about 1899. Later Waals was to produce very fine work to his own designs.

Gimson also ran a separate chair-making business in partnership with Edward Gardiner (1885-1958), whilst in his smithy in Sapperton, three blacksmiths worked on his designs for iron architectural fittings as well as polished steel and brass decorative items for furniture, candlesticks, and fire-irons. The master blacksmith was Alfred Bucknell.

Surprisingly, in spite of the rapid development of Gimson's and Edward Barnsley's joint enterprise at Daneway, Sidney Barnsley managed to retain the greatest public interest in their field. At the seventh Arts and Crafts Exhibition at the New Gallery in London at the start of 1903, Sidney displayed as much work by his own hand as did Gimson and his brother together.

The use of chamfering to provide visual relief in the stouter structural members in furniture, demonstrated by Kenton and Co. on their oak dresser at the 1891 Barnards Inn exhibition, was a proven popular feature which Gimson and the Barnsleys continued to use most successfully. The advent of Waals, with more advanced cabinet-making techniques, brought new innovations to both the Daneway and Sidney Barnsley workshops.

From a review of the 1903 exhibition in *The Studio Magazine* it appears that Gimson and the Barnsleys were not considered by their contemporaries to be amongst the foremost designers in the field. This may have been due in part to a lack of publicity together with the disruption of their move to the countryside. Whilst the work of Charles Voysey and Ambrose Heal deserved the greatest praise, certainly Gimson and the Barnsleys merited more than a number of their contemporaries. Nevertheless their entries in the exhibition found great favour with continental visitors and confirmed, in Hermann Muthesius's eyes, Britain's superior position to Europe in terms of design.

Chairmaking at Daneway was prodigious and examples 1 to 5 *(Opposite)* show this. Because of a team of quite excellent cabinet-makers supervised by Peter Waals at Daneway, Gimson was able to expand his designs into areas of much finer quality, whilst retaining the fundamental elements of design from his earliest days. Sidney Barnsley, working on his own, also achieved noteworthy results as illustrated by the three cabinets on stands 6,7,and 8 opposite.

This oak chest of drawers by Gimson and Barnsley features multi-panel work, together with the relief of chamfering and gougework referred to on the previous page. The piece was part of their 1903 exhibition portfolio. By courtesy of Cheltenham Art Gallery

An Oak Writing Cabinet with square panels of burr oak, made by Sidney for his wife in 1902 but without chamfering, was also in the 1903 exhibition.

1. Gimson while at Kenton and Co. 1891
2. Gimson after Clissett 1895
3. Gimson after Clissett 1904.
   Made by Edward Gardiner in 1920s
4. Gimson 1907 Made by Gardiner
5. Gimson Made by Gardiner 1904-10
All by courtesy of Cheltenham Art Gallery

(1)

(2)

(3)

(4)

(5)

(6)

(7)

(8)

Cabinets on Stands: 6.Gimson 1908, 7. Barnsley 1904, 8. Gimson 1891. By courtesy of Cheltenham Art Gallery

The partnership between Ernest Barnsley and Gimson was short-
lived. The reason appears to have been problems in their personal
relationship rather than anything to do with their work. After the
collapse of their partnership, Ernest Barnsley abandoned any serious
interest in furniture. Gimson, at Daneway, was an immensely talented
and determined man and made maximum use of the existence of
Peter Waals and a highly talented and motivated workforce with
whom he is believed to have had excellent relationships. Earlier lifelong
friendships with fellow architects such as Robert Weir Schultz led to
important and demanding commissions, many of them ecclesiastical,
such as the choir stalls, opposite, in St Andrew's Chapel in the
Roman Catholic Westminster Cathedral, a joint Gimson/Schultz
project in about 1914.

The clergy seat was commissioned by the Fourth Marquis of Bute
via Robert Weir Schultz as a prototype for seven seats in St Andrew's

Chapel, Westminster Cathedral to be made in ebony and inlaid with
bone. This prototype seat, however, is of English walnut inlaid with
bleached bone. As are those in Westminster, the seat is hinged and has
a misericord seat underneath (a device to give support to a standing
chorister). The "prototype" seat was kept by Weir Schultz at his house
in Hartley Wintney, Hampshire and after the wedding of Edward
Barnsley and Tania Kellgren in 1925, the bride sat in state in this seat
for the wedding breakfast. The time involved in making the prototype
seat was 502 1/2 hours. The construction cost of £25.2.6 for the
Clergy Seat at an indicated hourly rate of one shilling resulted in a
total cost, inclusive of Gimson's design time and use of his workshops,
of £44.13.0. The time to make the seven Choir stalls for Westminster
was 3218 1/2 hours. Based on today's hourly rate of say £25, the cost
of the Clergy Seat would be multiplied by 500 i.e. over £22,000! The
circular motif at the head of the chair has been used as Cheltenham
Museum's logo since 1982.

Prototype clergy seat for Westminster Cathedral. By courtesy of Cheltenham Art Gallery

Choir Stalls at St Andrew's Chapel, Westminster in brown ebony inlaid with bone. By courtesy of Cheltenham Art Gallery

The greatest proportion of Ernest and Sidney's architectural work was in the Cotswolds and was dominated by Ernest's work at Rodmarton which took place between 1909 and 1929. The owner, The Hon. Claud Biddulph, a London-based banker, commissioned Ernest Barnsley to design a "small residence" for him and his family which he referred to as his 'cottage in the country' on his Rodmarton Estate. The building plan envisaged spending of £5000 a year "for a number of years".

Rodmarton

Barnsley endeavoured to achieve, on a larger scale, all the principles which he and his brother Sidney had worked with their cottages at Sapperton. The completion of Rodmarton was delayed by the War. On Ernest Barnsley's death in January 1926, Sidney took over supervision of building work and the project was finally completed by Norman Jewson in 1929. The house today is almost unaltered from that time.

An example of furniture made for the house
Above:
One of three Day Beds by Sidney Barnsley 1924-6.
By courtesy of Cheltenham Art Gallery

An example of furniture made for the house

Above:
Walnut Fall-front Writing Table by Waals 1923.
By courtesy of Cheltenham Art Gallery

Above:
A daybed made by Edward Barnsley

The Edward Barnsley Trust

This very brief biography of the Barnsley brothers and Gimson would not be complete without mention of Edward Barnsley and the Barnsley Trust.

Edward, was the son of Sidney and Lucy Barnsley born in 1900, when the Arts and Crafts Movement was at its height. Very much at the head of the movement, as architects and designers, were Edward's father, his uncle Edward Barnsley and Ernest Gimson. Few people today would disagree that the trio were the most significant and influential furniture designers in the Movement. Their output was enormous and would probably not have been achievable but for tremendous personal drive on the part of each of them. With his background and parentage, it is therefore not that surprising that Sidney's son Edward should have chosen a career as a furniture designer and maker in the 20th Century when, economically and politically, conditions were far from favourable. Moreover, fashion was changing fast with Modernism as its catalyst and two World Wars in close succession had an adverse effect on pursuit of luxury in the home and the acquisition of things handmade and therefore more expensive than factory-made.

It is very relevant to remember that, from the time the trio left Pinbury in 1903, Sidney Barnsley chose to "go it alone" rather than go into business at nearby Sapperton village, just down the valley from Pinbury, with his brother and Ernest Gimson. It was no mean feat that Sidney managed not only to keep his head above water as a furniture designer and maker but also as an architect, with a rival business employing a number of very skilled craftsmen, in the very same village. It is touching to read of Sidney declaring that should he have too much work on his hands he would pass it to his brother and Gimson. In fact, the two enterprises continued to share ideas and aspirations of design to the great benefit of both. Whatever genes drove Sidney's determination, seem certainly to have been inherited by his son.

During his childhood, Edward absorbed the principles of the Arts and Crafts work and learned to use woodworking tools, making a small table or stool with his father's help when he was only five. It is not out of place here to add that, unless you have the necessary natural dexterity, you will never achieve high standards in the use of tools – a fact that some of today's educationalists tend to ignore or perhaps are ignorant of. This dexterity is some form of co-ordination, possibly not unlike that needed to hit a ball well. So, undoubtedly, young Edward inherited "the gift".

For a time he was tutored at home by a live-in governess, Hilda Eames, up to the age of nine when he went to school at Cirencester Grammar. Sidney rented a house in the town to enable this and cycled over to Sapperton daily to work. The school did not suit Edward and in 1910 he and Grace were both sent to Bedales School, at Steep, near Petersfield, Hampshire.

Several members of the Gimson family were also educated there but one of the main reasons for choosing Bedales must have been that the school was founded by Oswald Powell, brother of Alfred and very close friend of both the Gimson and Barnsley families. Bedales suited Edward very well. He enjoyed and benefited greatly from the its wide range of activities in which an understanding of basic crafts and recognition of the interdependence of the human community were established principles of the school's philosophy. Edward was made head boy in his last term and in December 1917, having been given an extension to enable him to take over the woodwork classes because the teacher was called up for military service, he received his own call-up. He joined the Inns of Court Officers' Training Battalion and just missed being sent to France as the War ended in September 1918.

He spent the spring and summer of 1919 working in his father's workshop. Sidney advised Edward against becoming a furniture maker on the grounds that he would never make a living at it. Edward accepted the offer of a teaching post at his old school Bedales and, again with the advice and help of Alfred Powell who felt Edward needed some "real experience" of woodworking, he went to train with Geoffrey Lupton, an Old Bedalian himself, who had started a construction business in nearby Froxfield. Edward joined as a student-apprentice. A memorable commission for the Lupton business was the construction of Bedales school library, designed by Ernest Gimson just before he died in 1919.

In 1922 Edward, in a plan to widen his knowledge and experience, attended the Central School of Arts and Crafts in London at which the cabinet-making teacher was Charles Spooner who was a contemporary of Gimson and the Barnsleys.

In 1923 Geoffrey Lupton offered Edward a tenancy of his workshop. This was accepted and, at the age of 23, Edward started taking responsibility for Lupton's team of craftsmen. Edward became the owner of the workshop in 1925 and moved into the workshop cottage with his newly-wedded wife, Tania (neé Kellgren).

The work and output of Edward Barnsley, like his father, merits separate coverage in its own right and this is very well documented by Annette Carruther's book *Edward Barnsley and his Workshop, Arts and Crafts in the Twentieth Century*, White Cockade Publishing 1992 (ISBN 1 873487 03 7 paperback). He died in 1987 after a career which established a permanent and living memorial to the art of furniture design and manufacture to the very highest standards. To mark this achievement, in 1980 the Edward Barnsley Educational Trust was formed as a registered charity with the objects of:

• Assisting persons who are in need of financial assistance and who are preparing for, entering upon or engaged in the craft of hand made furniture-making, by providing them with tools, outfits, or by paying fees, travelling or maintenance expenses or by such other means for their advancement in life or to enable them to earn their living as the trustees think fit.

• In otherwise promoting the education and training of such persons.

The enormously high standard of work produced by the "students" at the Trust's workshops and showroom is testament to both the legacy of Edward Barnsley and the dedication and expertise of the Trust and its team who run the day to day affairs of The Edward Barnsley Workshop in Cockshott Lane, Froxfield, Petersfield, Hampshire GU32 1BB.

Achievement of the objects of the Trust is very largely assisted by the workshop's service to private clients of the design and construction of furniture to the very highest standards.

This picture, taken in 1933, is of Edward "The Young Guvnor", in the centre, and two of the workshop team Charlie Bray (Foreman) and Bob Etherington

Young Edward, aged 20, on the roof beams of the library

Edward Barnsley 1975 in the Lake District

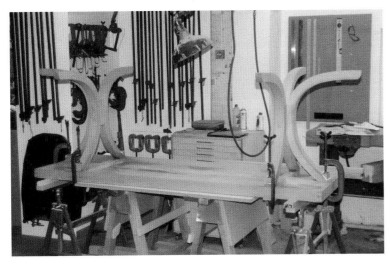

Views of the Edward Barnsley Trust Workshop in 2004 James Ryan, Foreman and Designer, is pictured bottom right. By courtesy of the Edward Barnsley Trust

Further Reading

The Arts and Crafts Movement by Elizabeth Cumming & Wendy Kaplan, Thames & Hudson world of art.

Charles Rennie Mackintosh by Fiona and Isla Hackney, Quantum Books Ltd, 6 Blundell St, London N7 9BH. ©1989 Quintet Publishing Ltd ISBN 1-85627-880-8

The Arts & Crafts Movement by Stephen Adams Page 97, Tiger Books International. ©Quintet Publishing Ltd 1987, ISBN 1-85501-275-8

"Pugin" by Paul Atterbury and Clive Wainwright, plates 1, 220, 241, 244 respectively. ©Victoria and Albert Museum and Authors 1994

"William Morris" by Helen Dore, opposite page 42. ©Reed International Books Ltd, 1990, ISBN 0 600 59073 9

Essential Charles Rennie Mackintosh, by Fanny Blake, published by Parragon, Queen Street House, Bath BA1 1HE. ©Parragon 2001, ISBN 0-75255-351-8

Charles Rennie Mackintosh, by Fiona and Islay Hackney, Quintet Publishing Limited ©1989 Quintet Publishing Limited, ISBN 1-85267-880-8

Mackintosh Furniture by Roger Billcliffe, Cameron Books, 2a Roman Way, London N7 8XG. ©Cameron Books 1984, ISBN 0-7188-2564-0

Arts and Crafts Furniture, Kevin P Rodel & Jonathan Binzen, page 68. ©2003 by The Taunton Press. Inc, 63 South Main St, PO Box 5506, e-mail: tp@taunton.com

E W Godwin Aesthetic Movement Architect and Designer, The Bard Graduate Centre for Studies in the Decorative Arts, New York by Yale University Press. Editor: Susan Weber Soros. ©1999 The Bard Graduate Centre for Studies in the Decorative Arts, ISBN 0-300-08008-5

George Walton, Designer and Architect by Karen Moon, published by White Cockade Publishing, 71 Lonsdale Road, Oxford OX2 7ES. ©Karen Moon 1993. ISBN 1 873487 01 0

Gimson and The Barnsleys "Wonderful Furniture of a Commonplace Kind" by Mary Greensted Curator, Cheltenham Art Gallery, Evans Brothers 1980. ©Mary Greensted, 1980

Good Citizen's Furniture by Annette Carruthers and Mary Greensted, Lund Humphries Publishers Limited, Park House, 1 Russell Gardens, London NW11 9NN ISBN 0 85331 650 3. ©1994 and 1999 Cheltenham Art Gallery and Museums and the authors Victorian Design Source Book by Noël Riley, ISBN 1-84013-044-X. ©Quantum Books LTD, 6 Blundell St, London N7 9BH

The Grammar of Ornament by Owen Jones (1856) re-published in GB 1997 by Parkgate Books Ltd, ISBN 1-85585-378-7. ©1997 Parkgate Books Ltd, London House, Great Eastern Wharf, London SW11 4NQ

VI
The Twentieth Century

Christopher Claxton Stevens

Christopher Claxton Stevens was born in 1952 and received an M.A. in History at Christ Church, Oxford. He joined Norman Adams Ltd, the specialist dealers in 18th Century English furniture in Knightsbridge, London in 1981 and became a Director in 1986. He was author of *18th Century English Furniture – The Norman Adams Collection, published in 1983.*

His interest in modern furniture began when he joined the Worshipful Company of Furniture Makers in 1977 and he became the second youngest Master in the Company's history in 2002. His work as Chairman of the Guild Mark Committee, aiding designer-craftsmen, is commemorated by the annual Claxton Stevens Prize, founded in 1989.

He has served on the Council of the Furniture History Society and was Chairman of the Regional Furniture Society for seven years. He is a Trustee of the Geffrye Museum in London, of the Frederick Parker Foundation set up to preserve the Parker Knoll Collection of Chairs, and of the Chiltern Open Air Museum of Buildings in Buckinghamshire. He is a member of the Art Workers' Guild and a Course Adviser on Furniture Restoration at West Dean College, Sussex. He lectures and writes on furniture of all types.

Design Style during the Period

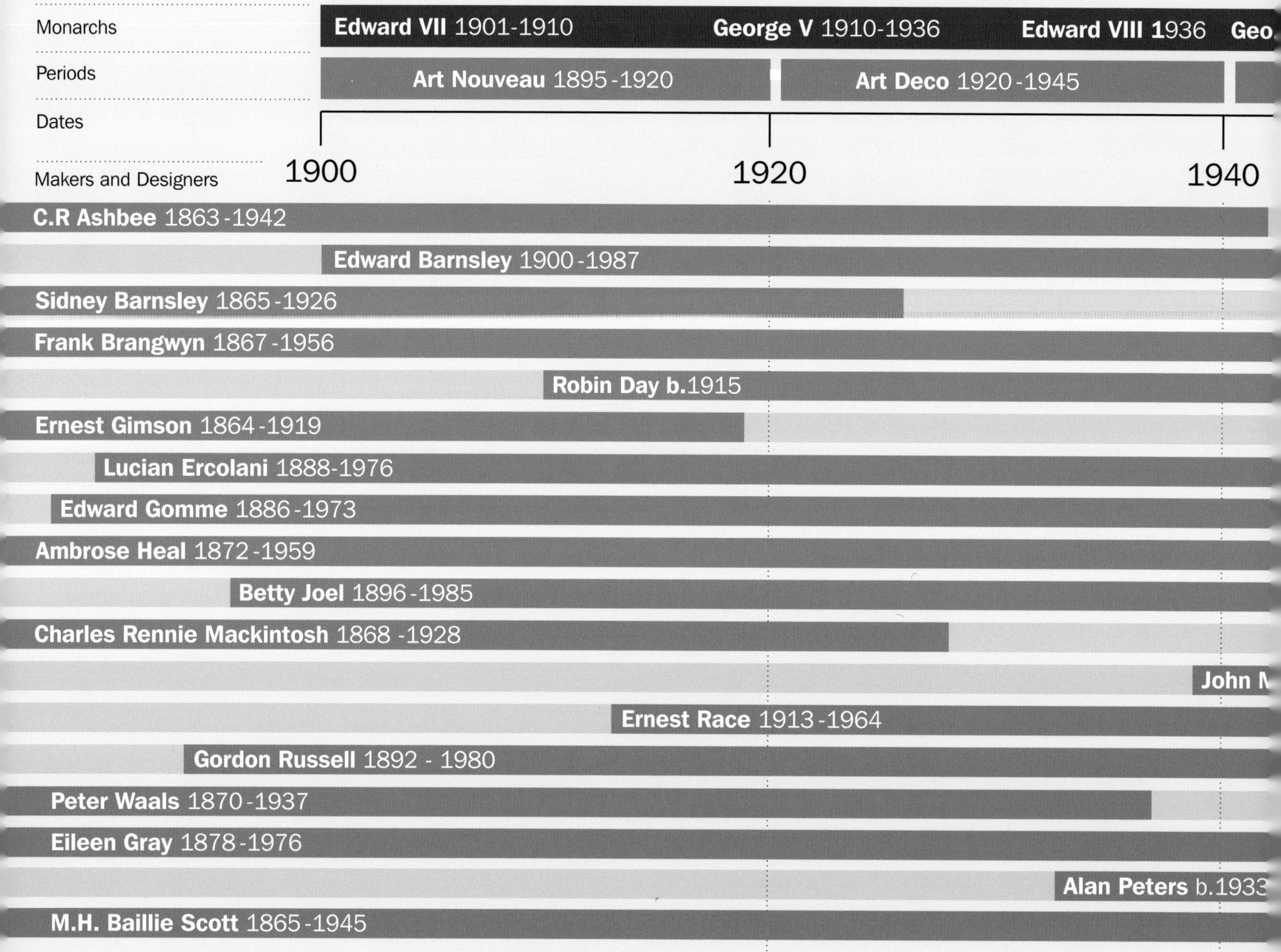

Monarchs	Edward VII 1901-1910	George V 1910-1936	Edward VIII 1936	Geo
Periods	Art Nouveau 1895-1920	Art Deco 1920-1945		
Dates				
Makers and Designers	1900	1920	1940	

C.R Ashbee 1863-1942

Edward Barnsley 1900-1987

Sidney Barnsley 1865-1926

Frank Brangwyn 1867-1956

Robin Day b.1915

Ernest Gimson 1864-1919

Lucian Ercolani 1888-1976

Edward Gomme 1886-1973

Ambrose Heal 1872-1959

Betty Joel 1896-1985

Charles Rennie Mackintosh 1868 -1928

John N

Ernest Race 1913-1964

Gordon Russell 1892 - 1980

Peter Waals 1870-1937

Eileen Gray 1878-1976

Alan Peters b.1933

M.H. Baillie Scott 1865-1945

bonised mahogany writing cabinet designed by
harles Rennie Mackintosh for Walter Blackie 1904

Kidney-shaped twin pedestal desk designed by Betty
Joel c1935

Reclining chair designed by Robin Day for Hille, teak
armrests and black enamelled tubular metal frame 1952

Birch and ebonised sideboard designed by Robert &
Dorothy Heritage for G.W. Evans Ltd 1954

1952

Elizabeth II 1952-

Modern 1945-

1960   1980   2000

1939

VI

The Twentieth Century

Craft or Mass Production?

Christopher Claxton Stevens

Standing so close to it, it is difficult to take a succinct overview of the British contribution to furniture history in the 20th Century. However, although others might have been included, the seven people focussed on here have each played an important role and are representative of the many strands of a complex picture.

The British Arts and Crafts legacy continued in only a few oases: Edward Barnsley, son of Sidney, at Froxfield, Peter van der Waals, Gimson's foreman at Chalford in Gloucestershire until his death in 1935, Arthur Romney Green at Christchurch, Dorset, Stanley Davies at Windermere, and not many others. Indeed, Morris's ideals tended to have a greater influence in other countries: Germany and Austria set up their own Arts and Crafts societies which, by emphasising honesty in design and materials, led on perhaps surprisingly to the Bauhaus and Modernism. Meanwhile in Sweden Carl Malmsten championed the romance of handwork and in the US, Gustav Stickley led the movement for simple wooden furniture.

However to the great majority of the British population, the Victorian legacy of ornament and clutter persisted. Blame for the general lack of incentive for innovative design has long revolved between what the purchasing public demanded and what retailers were prepared to stock and manufacturers to make. All too often the latter's decision making has been based purely upon financial rather than altruistic considerations and design evolution has been at best pragmatic, leaving the lead in developments to European countries and the US.

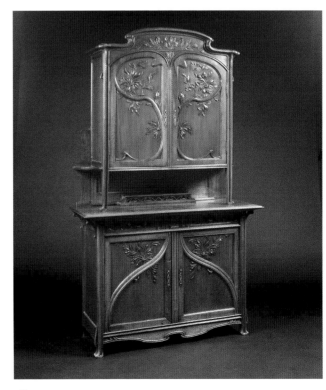

Above:
A French Art Nouveau walnut dresser,
circa 1905 Courtesy of Christie's Images

Opposite: Eltham Palace, Greenwich, London: view from the Dining Room to the Entrance Hall, 1999 reconstruction of the 1936 Art Deco house built for the Courthaulds. Courtesy of English Heritage

The frequency of international exhibitions and printed magazines encouraged the spread of new styles and the century opened with Art Nouveau, named after a Parisian shop, in full flow in France and across Europe. At its best this brought an invigorating curvilinear, organic and naturalistic mingling of Gothic, Rococo, Japanese and Islamic styles and, at its commercial worst, an excess of over-inlaid and applied ornament used for the sake of fashion. Another, less flamboyant and more rectilinear form was developed by the Vienna Secession Werkstätte (1903-32) and the German Werkbund (1907-34) and became one of the contributory factors to Art Deco. France was again the hot-bed of Art Deco, although its origins were eclectic, including the geometric shapes of Cubism, exotic features and materials from the Far East, Africa and Byzantium, archaeological discoveries in Egypt and Greece, and a revival of Louis XVI and Directoire neo-classical styles. It emerged before 1914, but developed after the First War and had its focus at the lavish 1925 Paris Exhibition of "Arts Décoratifs" from which it took its name. At a luxury level the most spectacular exponent was perhaps Jacques-Emile Ruhlmann, but again, the style led to a plethora of often badly designed hybrid versions between the Wars in Britain, which encompassed flush surfaces, geometric abstraction and a simplified Beidemeier style, including the use of light-coloured and figured "Empire" veneers. This suited the new suburban culture which sought a degree of novelty.

There was a clear overlap between Art Deco and Modernism, with its origins in the German educational institute the Bauhaus (1919-33). Its designers, of completely integrated buildings with functionalist interiors marked by tubular steel furniture, included Ludwig Mies van der Rohe in Germany and Charles-Edward Jeanneret (Le Corbusier) and Eileen Gray in France. Although other influential members, Walter Gropius and Marcel Breuer, spent some time designing in England on their way to the US, it was moulded laminated wood rather than more austere tubular steel and chrome that caught on more widely here. Jack Pritchard's Isokon (revived in recent times), Gerald Summers' Makers of Simple Furniture and Betty Joel's Token Works, were the chief exponents, but Modernism in Britain had but a brief flowering, interrupted by the upheavals of the War.

It was not until the 50's that the idea of a new, modern world really began to take root in people's minds, although a contemporary interior was rarely looked upon as a status symbol in Britain as it was in many European countries. Sir Ambrose Heal and Sir Gordon Russell sought to adapt their love of simple Arts and Crafts to greater volume furniture production, but apart from these only a handful of enlightened retailers stuck out for Modernism: Dunn's of Bromley, Bowman's of Camden Town and Gane's of Bristol. The major manufacturers such as Harris Lebus, who early in the century were the largest in Britain and by the 1950's the largest in the world, remained focussed on the mass market, whose cultural values saw the three-piece suite as a symbol of respectability and Tudorbethan as a mark of social status.

The development of Fifties Contemporary should have been aided by the Government enforced Utility Scheme which was introduced during the wartime shortages of resources to bring to the needy well-designed, simple products that were controlled in design, timber content and price. The first range was shown in 1942 but, by the time that restrictions were finally lifted in the early 50's, the term 'utility' had become a derogatory one for its institutional look, rather like council housing. Although there had previously been a few opportunities for the British public to see the latest trends in design, such as the Daily Mail Ideal Home Exhibitions (since 1908), as many as 1½ million people visited the "Britain Can Make It" exhibition at the Victoria and Albert Museum in 1946, and the 1951 Festival of Britain drew eight million in five months. Although conspicuously little was done by Government to build on this great achievement, designers such as Robin Day, Ernest Race and Robert Heritage successfully introduced new styles including modular furniture and new materials including plastics, metals, particle-board, rubber webbing and latex foam, which also kept down prices.

There were strong influences from the international scene. In America manufacture had been able to progress relatively uninterrupted by war, although Charles Eames did make use of wartime developments in plywood and fibreglass for his classic chairs, while Harry Bertoia focussed on sculptural shapes and the use of wire mesh. Italy had many craft-based manufacturers who were championed by Gio Ponti, best known for his chic "Superleggera" chair (1956) which was based on traditional principles. He worked with Piero Fornasetti, famous for his Surrealist trompe l'oeil architectural designs, while, in the 60's, Joe Columbo pioneered abstract sculptural furniture in plastics and the long career of Ettore Sottsass ended with his colourfully anti-functionalist Memphis Group in the 80's.

However the most influential area, with which British furniture had long had a close connection, was Scandinavia. Here Kaare Klint and Hans Wegner in Denmark, Karl Bruno Mathsson in Sweden and Alvar Aalto in Finland, all designed furniture that was intended for industrialisation but had both functional and traditional appeal. They worked in wood or plywood, often adapting traditional forms including British ones, such as the Windsor chair.

The parallel with Lucian Ercolani in England is an obvious one, and it was on these elegant, slender forms that Sir Terence Conran's Habitat focussed so successfully for the younger market in the 60's. Another well-known brand name based on simple units was G-Plan, launched by Gomme's in 1953, although it suffered through recession and was sold to Christie Tyler in 1961. Other important designers of organic pieces in fibre glass and plastics included Verner Panton and Arne Jacobsen in Denmark, the latter known particularly for his Egg and Swan chairs (1958) and the Finn, Eero Saarinen working in the US, who designed the Tulip chair in 1956.

The furniture industry in Britain continued to be fragmented which allowed for smaller specialist markets, although the marketing revolution which occurred in the 70's brought large superstores to cater for mass demand, such as MFI and the Swedish IKEA, the most successful retailer of low price furniture in the world. By this time a throwaway culture was developing, including the novel use of colourful moulded plastics and even paper, often sculptural rather than practical. Fashions became increasingly media-led, with a huge growth in choice and diversity, and brief fashion cycles. With the advance of the DIY market, flat-pack furniture aided mass production, while built-in furniture and lighting was space-saving and gave a simpler look for smaller homes.

The 80's glut of rather bland matt black and chrome and standardised units with little variation, led to somewhat less austere furniture and more environmental and sustainable values in the 90's. The great increase in interest in interiors and home furnishings has led to a more discriminating clientele, but quality furniture has not fared well in most people's spending patterns besides cars, electrical goods and holidays. However some of the post-War classics by designers such as Eames, Day and Ercolani have been enjoying

revivals, and since the mid-90's, there has been a surge of creativity in Britain in all areas of avant-garde design. Some designers such as Tom Dixon who found the need to venture abroad in order to find opportunities to work with industry, have returned and, with the likes of Jasper Morrison and Matthew Hilton, Britain now has perhaps more internationally famous designers working here than at any time in the 20th Century. At the same time the future is looking bleak for many larger manufacturing firms as imports, especially from the Far East, now account for well over 30% of sales, a problem which is also confronting industry in the US.

At present nearly 90% of British furniture manufacturers comprise firms with fewer than 15 employees. Technology and reduced machinery costs have helped the viability of small firms. The dichotomy between craft and industry was a nagging problem for most of the century but, with more money available, more people are now able to afford to commission unique and lasting pieces, tailored to their requirements, or to buy from small batches. Craft can achieve a complexity and quality that mass production cannot. Its scope has also widened from the solid wooden furniture of the Arts and Crafts makers. Some designer-makers today embrace other materials like metal and "found" objects (such as Ron Arad) and glass (such as Danny Lane). Many are based in London and produce sculptural pieces, more for display than function.

However, alongside John Makepeace and Alan Peters is a host of smaller, more traditional workshops round the country producing remarkable pieces. The Barnsley Workshops also continue at Froxfield as an educational trust set up in 1980. The Crafts Advisory Committee (later the Crafts Council) was established in 1948 in parallel to the Design Council, and many regional crafts guilds have sprung up since the 50's, acting as focuses for fine makers who may not be well known on the national scene, such as the late Judith Hughes in Devon. It is in niche markets such as these, and the slightly larger firms offering bespoke pieces for contract commissions, that the emphasis of the future of the British furniture industry would seem to lie.

Opposite:
A laminated birch "Short Chair", designed
by Marcel Breuer for Isokon 1935-6
Courtesy of Christie's Images

An oak "St. Ives" wardrobe with fall-front cupboard below, stamped Heal & Son,
circa 1897. Courtesy of The Millinery Works Gallery and Jefferson Smith

Biography:

Sir Ambrose Heal
(1872-1959)

*A walnut sideboard from a
labelled dining suite, c.1932*

A sweet chestnut: "Owl" cabinet, c.1904

An oak "Settle" chair, c.1899

A "Letchworth" oak dining table, c.1904

Ambrose Heal enjoyed a great advantage by being born into a family firm that had been run successfully by three generations before him. As an imaginative designer and an astute businessman with unfailing energy, he was the first to bring the legacy of the Arts and Crafts Movement into 20th Century industrial manufacture.

The firm was established in London as a feather-dressing business in 1810, moving to Tottenham Court Road in 1818 and to the present site in 1840 as Heal & Son, Mattress and Feather-bed Manufacturers. It expanded into bedroom furniture, and later into other furnishings, using innovative methods such as selling through catalogues and, by the 1860's, with room setting displays, but the bedding side remained its main staple with a factory behind the shop. The eldest of five children, Heal had no architectural training like so many other designers at the time, but he was an accomplished craftsman and

gained experience from two years' apprenticeship with Messrs. Plucknett of Warwick and six months at Graham and Biddle of Oxford Street. In 1893 he joined the family firm in the mattress shop, but he wanted to design furniture and was deeply interested in the Arts and Crafts idyll.

Continuing the firm's tradition of producing catalogues, he designed some simple oak pieces with metal mounts, to be left unvarnished, and published them in 1897, cleverly combining this with a testimonial by Gleeson White, the influential editor of *The Studio* magazine. The furniture was an instant success. It was made initially by the Guild of Handicraft before the Guild's foreman C.V. Adams went to work at Heal's and a workshop was set up in 1898. Other craftsmen, including perhaps metalworkers, came to Heal's when Charles Ashbee moved to the Cotswolds in 1902.

Left:
Sir Ambrose Heal. Portrait by Edward Halliday CBE, 1933

Heal's showed a bedroom suite at the Paris Exhibition of 1900 which won two silver medals. This had ebony and pewter panels and, for the first time, chequered inlay which was to become a hallmark of the firm. The trademark "at the sign of the Fourposter" also seems to have been devised by him about 1904. Although a majority of pieces were made in plain oak or chestnut, a few ranges were tastefully decorated, such as "Fine Feathers" (1898) with its peacocks and mottoes. He saw a suitable market in the new Garden City clientele and his designs for furniture for the "Cheap Cottage" exhibition at Letchworth in 1905, and later for Hampstead Garden Suburb, remained in production for many years. Other distinctive features, such as recessed squashed heart-shaped hand grips, recessed circular hand-holes operating door latches, discreet chip-carved edges and circular panels on quartered square doors, gave this well-proportioned furniture its own character. It could also be marketed at a price level

well below makers such as Gimson and the Guild of Handicraft. The extent that plagiarism of ideas might have taken place, a charge of which has been levied against him (certainly Gimson was wary), is unclear, but Heal was close enough to become a member of the Arts and Crafts Exhibition Society in 1906 (and showed with them from 1899) and of the Art Workers' Guild in 1910. He also bought in work from John P. White's Pyghtle Works at Bedford and rush-seated ladderback chairs from the chair-maker Phillip Clissett of Bosbury, Worcestershire. This batch-produced furniture was selling side by side with a wide range of mass-produced derivatives of 17th and 18th Century pieces, as well as the bedding side.

Heal's became a limited company in 1907 and he was made Managing Director, becoming Chairman on the death of his father in 1913. He also lost his first wife and his eldest son Cecil was killed in Belgium in 1915. However, having married again, his sons Anthony

Left:
A high-backed oak "Easy chair", inlaid with pewter and ebony, part of a bedroom suite that won two silver medals at the Paris Exhibition 1900. (The Architectural Review *described it as "a triumph of craftsmanship") Courtesy of The Millinery Works Gallery and Jefferson Smith*

and Christopher were to play important rôles in the business. In spite of wartime shortages, he persevered with the rebuilding of much of the shop to a design by his cousin Cecil Brewer of the architects Dunbar Smith & Brewer (1913-16). This still stands, sympathetically extended to the south and into Alfred Mews by Sir Edward Maufe in 1937.

Heal's interest in design went much further than furniture. The firm also sold china and glass, and in the Mansard Gallery at the top of the new building, carried on the previous idea of room settings, including a garden with a fountain and gained a reputation as one of the best venues for contemporary art and design. This was particularly useful for getting contract work from architects. He was pleased to become a founder member and treasurer of the Design and Industries Association which was set up to promote industrial design in 1915 and laid the foundation for the Council of Industrial Design and later the Design Council. As Sir Gordon Russell later wrote, "he was perhaps the only man in the retail furniture trade of that time who had a real interest in and knowledge of design". They met after the First War and became life-long friends. Anthony Heal was even sent to Russell's factory in Broadway for two years' work experience.

The firm's steadily expanding influence was helped considerably by the excellent team that Heal put together. Cecil Brewer died young, but J.F. Johnson was head of the Cabinet Department, Arthur Greenwood, who was a brilliant draughtsman, became head designer, and both Hamilton Temple-Smith, a craftsman as well as a designer, and Prudence Maufe, wife of Sir Edward, joined in 1915. She was a consultant on interior design and exhibitions and later set up Heal Fabrics with Tom Worthington. In addition, Heal involved a number of designers who were members of the DIA, both in exhibitions and the succession of eye-catching themed catalogues that were produced and mailed out to up to 35,000 people. The ingenious design ideas in these included: in 1898 a reversible garden chair in case one side is wet, in 1904 a dresser for a weekend cottage which folded closed to keep crockery clean when it was not in use, a drop-front escritoire with its lock in the carcase rather than the flap to stop the key falling out and, in the garden furniture catalogue of 1930, a wheeled lounger called a "garden coach" which could easily be moved, transporting books, rugs and cushions. Heal was also asked to design a cleverly concealed wireless cabinet for the BBC to present to King George V in 1924, in an effort to increase his interest in broadcasting. Three years later came a prestigious Royal Warrant as Makers of Bedsteads and Bedding. In the early 30's a special range of signed edition furniture was produced, although many normal production pieces had been marked with ivory discs since early in the century, and a stamped name before that.

The problems in obtaining hardwoods during the First War are said to have led to the development of painted pine furniture, sometimes with attractive effects like colour-combing. This was the start of the Embroidery and Decorating Studio which flourished very much as a female domain. Between the Wars other new finishes were tried and "weathered" oak proved popular in the 20's, using plaster of Paris on quarter-cut Japanese oak, as opposed to earlier "fumed" oak which was darkened with ammonia. More exotic woods, such as black bean and Australian maple joined the more usual oak, chestnut, walnut and cherry.

One trend that Heal did not apparently warm to at first was Art Deco and Modernism, but with the Depression of the early 30's slashing sales, he saw the commercial benefits of the new tubular steel furniture which tended to be cheaper than wooden furniture.

Above:
A sweet chestnut "Owl" cabinet, circa 1904.
Illus. in Heal's catalogue, Simple Bedroom
Furniture. *Courtesy of The Millinery Works*
Gallery and Jefferson Smith

Left:
A limed oak sofa table from the "Churchill" range, including a secret drawer, designed by Heal and P.Tilden, circa 1920 Illus. in Heal's General Catalogue, *p.39. Courtesy of The Millinery Works Gallery and Jefferson Smith*

Left:
A "Letchworth" dresser in chestnut, designed circa 1905 for the "Cheap Cottage" Exhibition at Letchworth Garden City, Hertfordshire. Made until the 1930's Courtesy of The Millinery Works Gallery and Jefferson Smith

The ranges sold included pieces designed by Mies van der Rohe and Marcel Breuer, who were both then in London. Heal himself designed pieces using oval section tube which he patented for a bed frame in 1933. The 1932 catalogue of *Economy Furniture* succeeded in pulling the firm out of the slump. It included, besides metal furniture, Russett Oak and Waxed Walnut ranges, including distinctive settees, bookcases and desks with bookshelves in the ends. At this time Anthony Heal also set up an electrical department and Prudence Maufe led an initiative to offer whole house furnishing packages for fixed prices. This idea was revived after Utility furniture in the 50's. It was a credit to the firm to see how similar some of the official Utility designs were to Heal's pre-War furniture.

After receiving a KBE in 1933 for services to improving design standards, Heal was much involved in the "Art in Industry" Exhibition at the Royal Academy in 1935. This he saw as a coming of age, but the modish Modernist exhibits, which included an early use of anodised aluminium for a table frame, were criticised for being expensive and too out of touch. In response he mounted a more pragmatic exhibition at Heal's the following year, "Contemporary Furniture by 7 Architects". These included his son Christopher, who became Design Director at the firm from 1942 until 1975.

Later in the 30's bent plywood furniture, including pieces by the Finnish designer Alvar Aalto, made by Isokon, was a focus at the shop. Heal had, ever since 1899, maintained links with Scandinavia and especially Sweden, including export sales and showing Orrefors glass. In 1939 he was elected a Royal Designer for Industry alongside names like Eric Gill and Charles Voysey.

During the Second War furniture production ceased and the workshops were turned over to war work, making beds, parachutes and life-jackets. By this time Heal was designing less and increasingly acting as a patron of young designers. The firm developed the storage system that won Robin Day and Clive Latimer their 1948 furniture prize and made A.J. Milne's perforated metal chairs for the Festival of Britain in 1951. They contributed more exhibits than any other company to the very successful "Britain Can Make It" Exhibition at the Victoria and Albert Museum in 1946, and from 1954 an annual "New Designers" exhibition was held at Tottenham Court Road. Heal remained firmly in charge, although he did spend more time on scholarly research. His six published books included *London Tradesmen's Cards of the 18th Century* (1925), *The London Goldsmiths 1200-1800* (1933) and *London Furniture Makers 1660-1840* (1953). That his roots always remained in the British tradition of honest craftsmanship is clear from the splendid 15th Century farmhouse in Buckinghamshire that he took over in 1919 and lovingly restored in the Arts and Crafts vein. This still survives in the family.

Prosperity at the firm continued under Anthony Heal's chairmanship (1953-1981), with a further extension to the building in 1962 and a flourishing fabric side, but in the depression of the 1970's it lost its identity. After Anthony had handed over to his son Oliver, the business was sold to Sir Terence Conran's Storehouse Group in 1983. Most of the firm's archives are now housed at the Victoria & Albert Museum.

Above:
An elongated octagonal limed oak desk with bookshelves and cupboard behind the kneehole, labelled, circa 1925.
Courtesy of The Millinery Works Gallery and Jefferson Smith

Above:
A Modernist walnut revolving book/coffee table, circa 1935.
Courtesy of The Millinery Works Gallery and Jefferson Smith

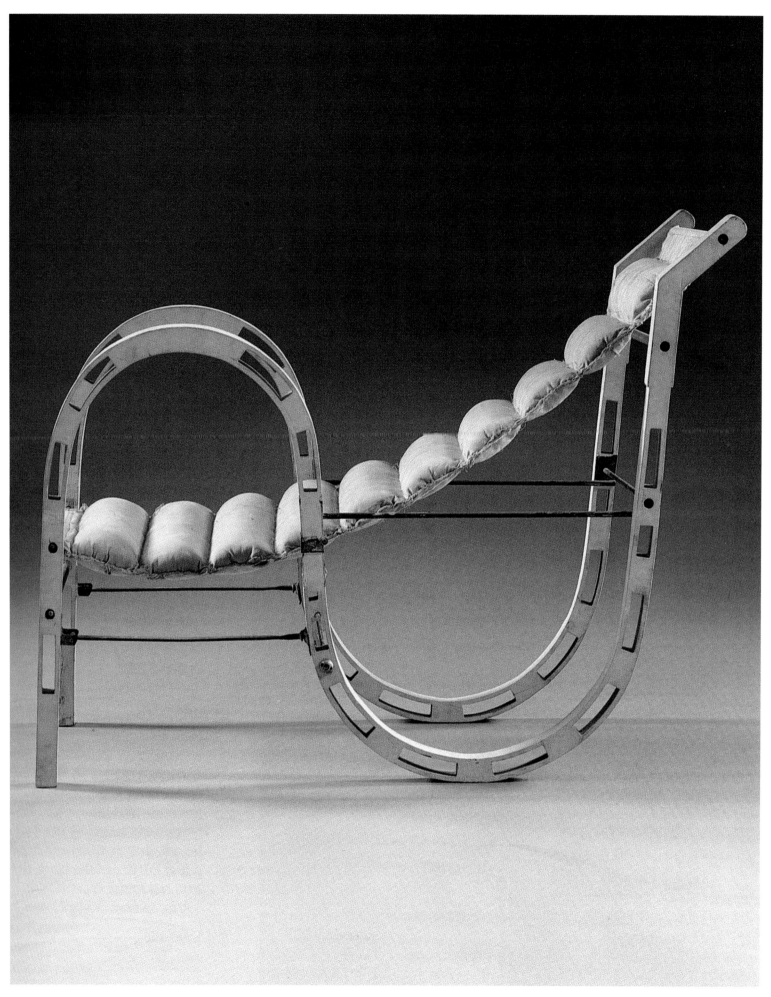

Eileen Gray
(1878-1976)

A sycamore veneered cabinet desk, c.1925

A painted wood, cork and nickel-plate extendable table, c.1926-29

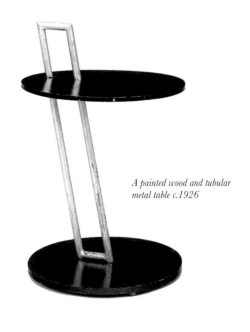

A painted wood and tubular metal table c.1926

A wood, nickel-plate and synthetic leather armchair c.1925

Opposite: *A white-painted bentwood and metal "S" folding terrace chair with padded canvas seat, c.1932-4, made for Gray's home "Tempe a Pailla" at Castellar, France Courtesy of Sotheby's*

In a book which focuses on British furniture, the inclusion of this Anglo-Irish designer, who spent most of her life in France (although she never took French citizenship), can be justified on the basis of her radical vision and achievement towards the birth of "contemporary" design, at a time when conservatism typically held sway in Britain. Although she was not alone as a female designer – Betty Joel and Sybil Colefax for example were well known in London – she had to contend with many slights and misrepresentations in a world so dominated by men.

Gray was born in County Wexford in Ireland and studied at the Slade School of Art in London before settling in Paris in 1902, where she found a wealthy society with a sophistication more attuned to her professional and social needs. Family money provided a measure of security which was essential since, for the most part, she worked outside the mainstream as a rather reclusive and shy individualist, who was obstinate and difficult to work with and at times turned out to be her own best client. However she was passionate and persevering with her ideas.

Her early interest was in lacquer, which she began to work decoratively in a fresh, abstract way several years before Jean Dunand, the most famous French lacquerist, made it popular in the 1920's. Through her Dunand met the expatriate Japanese craftsman Seizo Sugawara.

Right:
A "Transat" (Transatlantique) armchair in wood, nickel-plate and synthetic leather, made for Gray's house at Roquebrune, designed circa 1924, patented 1930
Courtesy of Sotheby's

The painstaking work on opulent lacquer tables, seating and screens was not a profitable undertaking, but nevertheless it was a figural red lacquer screen, known as "Le Destin", exhibited at the Salon des Artistes Decorateurs in 1913, that first gave her recognition in fashionable society (and was the only piece she ever signed). When it was auctioned in 1972 for a world record price for 20th Century furniture, it was the same screen that suddenly brought her back into the limelight, four years before her death.

Gray looked back upon this period of richness as the "sins of her youth". Wool carpets also took her attention and she started a small hand-weaving factory in 1907. Her designs became gradually more abstract, but they sold well. She did not generally work at pieces herself but employed a number of small workshops to realise her designs in different materials including ivory, textiles and exotic woods.

In 1919 she began to work as an interior designer taking on whole apartments, the first for the milliner Suzanne Talbot. Although in the luxurious taste of the period, she fulfilled the brief with a simplicity and practicality that marked it out from other interiors of the time. Here her exotic furnishings included a lacquer and silver-leaf canoe-shaped day-bed known as "Pirogue" and distinctive articulated lacquered block screens. Another venture was opening a gallery in Paris in 1922 which she called Jean Désert, in order to attract an élite clientèle to her furniture, carpets and lighting. It survived eight years but was not profitable. As her radical approach was becoming increasingly functionalist, she was not invited to exhibit among the heavy ornamentalism of the important "Arts Décoratifs" exhibition of 1925. Her links were closer to the austere Dutch De Stijl group and the German Bauhaus whom she admired and with whom she had considerable contact. The Dutch magazine *Wendigen (Turning Point)* devoted a whole issue to her in 1924 saying that she "occupies the centre of the modern movement. In all her tendencies, visions and expressions, she is modern".

The following year Gray's career took another turn, towards architecture, when she designed, in conjunction with the Rumanian Jean Badovici, a pioneering "house by the sea" (known as E 1027) at Roquebrune on the French Mediterranean coast where they spent their summers. She designed a good deal of furniture for this and subsequent houses in the area. Some of this furniture was built-in and totally integrated with the modernist architecture of the buildings and some was movable, in "camping" style for versatile and easy living. She hoped that many of these pieces would be prototyped for mass-production.

Above:
A later painted nickel-plated tubular metal dining chair, designed 1926-8 and a model used in most of Gray's apartments
Courtesy of Sotheby's

Above:
A painted wood and chrome-plated tubular metal occasional table, circa 1926
Courtesy of Sotheby's

At the time, her use of chromed tubular steel was right at the forefront of its international development. Indeed it is difficult to know if her first use of it came before or after Marcel Breuer's "Model B3" club chair (known as the Wassily chair since the 1960's revival), which is generally considered to be the first of the type. Flat and tubular metal framed furniture had its origins in 19th Century hygienic iron bedsteads and rocking chairs, but only in the 1920's did it come to symbolise a new world of technology which linked *avant-garde* art with industry and functionalism. Seamless tubing was used for bicycle frames, gas and water pipes and architecturally in staircases and balconies; it was strong, light-weight, less bulky than wood and its innate springiness suited it better to cantilevered forms.

In Germany and Holland tubular steel furniture was used in a most austere fashion on the basis of form following function, while in Britain there was general resistance to its acceptance, at least domestically, until the 1930's although a visible early use was the fitting-out of Broadcasting House, Langham Place, London (1928-32) by PEL (Practical Equipment Ltd). Gray, for whom furniture had to be practical and comfortable as well as aesthetically pleasing, tended to offset the coldness and severity of steel by combining it with the use of exotic woods, leather, animal skins and other organic materials.

She also employed cork sheets for similar aesthetic reasons, as well as the practical one of stopping the clatter of china on table-tops and trolleys. The shapes of her furniture were often rounded and she liked elements that rotated, including pivoting drawers and metamorphic furniture with adjustable heights such as a writing table that turned into a low coffee table or a chair that became steps.

Other pieces included screens made from industrial perforated aluminium sheets, a bedside table that fitted over the side of a bed, bar stools, and an S-chair (c.1932) of laminated wood perforated with rectangular slots which folded for storage. She liked to introduce an element of wit or irony into her work, such as the "Bibendum" chair (1925-6) which resembled three stacked leather tyres on a chromium support and rather looked forward to the inflatables of the 1960's, or the "Non-conformist" armchair (1926-8) of continuous metal tubing with a single armrest. Her interest in lighting encompassed built-in concealed lights with rotating discs to create different moods, as well as flexible anglepoise lamps and ingenious "Satellite" mirrors with integral lights and the versatility to look at one's back.

In the mid-1930's Gray devised a new range of furniture, making use of thinner tubular steel and frames with legs like hairpins, reminiscent of the "Eiffel Tower" bases used by Charles and Ray Eames in the late

Above:
A painted wood, aluminium and cork mirrored dressing-cabinet with swivel drawers, circa 1929
Courtesy of Sotheby's

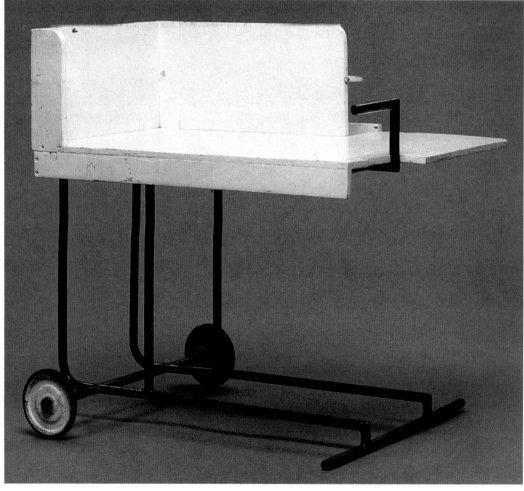

Above:
A painted wood and tubular metal wheeled trolley, circa 1929
Courtesy of Sotheby's

1940's. Indeed she never ceased designing architectural projects and experimenting with new materials but, from this time on, with increasing ill-health, she became more solitary in her Paris apartment until at last in her 90's, recognition of her true talent came and she saw her designs beginning to be produced cheaply enough for a larger public to be able to afford them. This was begun by Zeev Aram and Ecart International in the mid-1970's and it pleased her greatly.

In 1972 she was made a Royal Designer for Industry in England (one of seventy by that date), and the following year was elected an Honorary Fellow of the Royal Institute of Architects of Ireland, while several exhibitions of her work were held, notably one which contained a good deal of furniture at the Victoria and Albert Museum and the Scottish Arts Council Gallery in 1979. By this time, however, she had died. Although most of her comparatively small output is now dispersed (a lacquer screen and some chairs are in the Victoria and Albert Museum), her status in France was such that a "Transat" armchair from her house at Roquebrune was pre-empted as an item of national and historic importance for the Musée d'Art Moderne in Paris in 1991.

Above:
A sycamore veneered cabinet desk in two parts,
with swivel drawers and chrome-plated handles,
made for Gray's rue Bonaparte apartment,
circa 1925. Courtesy of Sotheby's

Above:
A painted wood and cork extendable table
on nickel-plated and later painted metal base,
circa 1926-9. Courtesy of Sotheby's

Biography:

Lucian Ercolani
(1888-1976)

*Detail of a Saville range
sideboard, 1986*

*A Latimer Windsor
armchair c.1986*

A stained wood fireside chair, c.1930

*A Saville range ash, two-drawer
side table, 1986*

*A Renaissance range three-seat settee
with slatted ash frame, 1993*

Opposite: *Windsor range Stacking chairs in elm and beech, widely used in schools, designed 1957*

Luciano Randolfo Ercolani was born in St. Angelo in Vado, Tuscany and came to England with his parents Abdon and Benedetta when he was ten. Although he came from a humble background and was not naturalised until 1923, he went on, through sheer hard work and determination, to build up one of the most successful furniture manufacturing businesses in Britain, Ercol Furniture.

He had an unsettled childhood, born to a father who was a woodworker and particularly skilled in making ebony picture frames, but who underwent a militant Protestant conversion through the Salvation Army, which in time necessitated the family's emigration to England. Acutely aware of their poverty, Ercolani left school at fourteen and was soon working in the Salvation Army joinery department, while he also went to evening classes in drawing and design at Shoreditch Technical Institute (later London Metropolitan University). Here he specialised in furniture and passed his City and Guilds examinations first class.

By 1908 he had become a freelance designer and artist and before long the quality of his work was noticed by Harry Parker of Frederick Parker & Sons (later Parker Knoll), one of the major manufacturers in High Wycombe, Buckinghamshire, which at that time led the world in high class furniture manufacture. He moved to Wycombe to design for Parker and also became an instructor in advanced furniture design evening classes at the local Technical Institute. One of his pupils, who became a friend, was Ted Gomme, grandson of the founder of another of the Wycombe dynasties (later producing G-Plan furniture). He moved to this firm as a designer and works manager in 1913.

In contrast to Parker's, which made fine reproduction furniture for the wealthy few, he preferred the greater elegance and simplicity of Gomme's style and the idea of working for a wider market. During the First World War Ercolani designed a bomb sling base which was made in bulk by Gomme's and he managed to escape call-up. He also at this time married Eva Brett whom he had met some years before.

Above:
Barry (d.1992), Lucian B. and Lucian R. Ercolani

Above:
A Chinoiserie bedroom suite, typical of pre-War fancy models, circa 1930

Opposite:
A Chairmaker's double-bow Windsor chair in elm and beech, designed 1962
Courtesy of the Frederick Parker Collection

After the War he astutely realised how the market for furniture had changed along with the balance of economic power, and he saw the potential in the age of suburbia for inexpensive but well-made and attractive products. His great break-through came in 1920 when, fired by his untiring enthusiasm, he managed to get a business syndicate to agree to back his grand plan for a factory on a narrow 12-acre site above the railway line in Wycombe. He planned that it would grow in sections as money became available and Furniture Industries Ltd began production the same year with twelve men using second-hand machinery and with an overdraft at the bank. He insisted on being Managing Director and even got his fellow directors to vote him £1000 to buy himself shares that he could not otherwise afford.

He proved himself to have a flair for business and turnover rose year by year. It must be said that between the Wars he was not generally happy about the designs of the furniture that was produced, most of which were reworkings of existing ideas: leather suites, "Jacobean" tables, fireside chairs and the like. Yet in a market where plagiarism and competition were rife, he had to keep churning out "new" designs to keep afloat, trying nothing too *avant-garde* as he found retailers had an antipathy to it. Unlike the more limited market for which firms such as Gordon Russell were manufacturing, Ercolani had chosen to make for the mass public who, he admitted, did not know much about good taste and preferred "knobs and novelty". This was a fact of life, as was the fact that his furniture was largely machine-made, but he never cut corners on materials and his craftsmen gave it the best possible hand-finish. His great attention to detail saw to that.

Above:
An Old Colonial buffet in traditional stained solid oak, designed from 1937

Right:
Carved elm Master's and Wardens' chairs, made for the Worshipful Company of Furniture Makers 1972

Opposite Right:
A Saville range ash two-drawer side table, designed by Don Pedel and Mike Pengelly, 1986

The early 30's was a time of worldwide economic slump. Indeed 1932 saw Furniture Industries' first loss in profits which required all Ercolani's talents for inventiveness and dedicated salesmanship to pull through. He did however manage to take over Walter Skull & Sons Ltd, another of Wycombe's high class manufacturers who were on the point of collapse. He turned their fortunes around with remarkable speed by simplifying production and cutting costs. He also diversified into contract work such as fitting out Council Chambers, and in seeking an identity for the firm's products he adopted a lion motif as a trademark and the name Ercol in 1928, although the Company of that name was not registered until 1958.

Ercolani had always had an interest in simple, well-proportioned early furniture, which was apparently further inspired by seeing early Pilgrim furniture at the Metropolitan Museum in New York. He returned to it in 1937 when he brought out the Old Colonial range of solid oak furniture and publicised it in typically romantic vein with a booklet, *Furniture with a Human Story*. He once said "how very mistaken are those people who seek for modernity at all costs". Made later also in beech and elm, the range continues in production. It was his first attempt at a new style, showing his respect for the past and the use of solid wood, whereas almost all his earlier furniture had been of plywood and veneers.

Always devoted to his family, Ercolani welcomed his two sons into the Company, Lucian in 1934 who trained in the Drawing Office and later took over in the Works, and Barry a few years later, who went into the sales and marketing side. They each had distinguished careers in the RAF during the Second War and returned to carry on afterwards. Meanwhile Ercolani worked hard on Government contracts, making munitions boxes, pulley blocks and millions of beech tent pegs. For the latter he devised a method of using locally grown trees and smaller sections of timber, which had normally been rejected for furniture-making, thus conserving resources and saving money in a way that other firms were not equipped for.

Towards the end of the War he took on Utility Furniture, in particular a Windsor chair (Model 4A) for which he built a new, more efficient assembly line. He was always keen to adapt machines to designs, rather than the other way round. The chairs were constructed as simply as possible from fourteen component parts, although it took a year of experiment to transfer the nuances of what had been done by hand and pole lathe to machinery. He managed to supply them for the 10/6 (52½p) each offered by the Board of Trade. Many in the furniture industry considered that it was disgraceful that years after the War had ended, people were not allowed to buy anything better than Utility furniture. Yet the simplicity of Utility pleased Ercolani and he built on what he had learned from it when he was able to return to normal production, including wartime advances in chemical glues, latex cushions, rubberised cotton webbing and high tension springs.

From this he developed the Windsor range, eventually of over thirty pieces including tables and cabinet pieces. The "simple" kitchen chair eventually took 80 separate operations to make, designed with an eye to "the geometry of comfort", based on the proportions of the human body. He continued to use almost entirely solid timber, particularly elm,

the traditional wood of the Windsor chair seat, which needed particularly careful stabilising by drying in kilns and so had been avoided by manufacturers. Left with its natural surface, its wild figure and red-brown colour made a pleasing contrast to pale beech. Some of the range was shown at the "Britain Can Make It" Exhibition in 1946 and at the Festival of Britain in 1951. Ercolani felt that at last he had reconciled the designer, the craftsman and the businessman and succeeded in his quest for "fitness of purpose" and a distinctive image.

He caught the consumer demand which blossomed in the 1950s, especially among the young, when orders soared way beyond supply. This led to further extensions of the factory until it was half a mile from one end to the other, the timber arriving from the mills at Amersham at one end and finished products being despatched from the other. By 1967 the turnover reached £3m making it one of the largest furniture manufacturers in the country, having tripled in some twelve years. Ercolani's success was recognised by an OBE in 1964. At its peak the workforce reached nearly 1000. He always greatly valued his staff and the Ercol Brass Band, loyalty medals and watches and the Annual Outing became great traditions in the firm.

In 1975, the year before he died, he published an autobiography which he called *A Furniture Maker*. Part of the purpose of the book was to drive home his conviction that success in life is possible through hard work, ambition and a creative mind. Ercolani has been called many things – mercurial, perfectionist, impatient, melancholy, confident, radical – to name but a few, but his greatest legacy was perhaps the achievement of his aim to produce well-made, well-designed furniture for the High Street that was affordable by most people. He always thought of himself first and foremost as a designer and he remained involved until his death. His last pieces were a Master's and two Wardens' chairs for the Worshipful Company of Furniture Makers (of which he had been Master in 1957) in 1972 in true Arts and Crafts tradition.

Like many self-made businessmen, Ercolani wanted to keep the firm in the family as a private company. As such it still remains Britain's leading manufacturer of solid wood furniture with his grandson Edward Tadros as Chairman since 1992 and granddaughter Lucia still active. The Old Colonial and Windsor ranges continue to be made, but design has developed under Don Pedel from the 60's, Mike Pengelly, his right-hand man, from the 70's and Floris van den Broecke from the 90's. The "Old Man", as he was affectionately known, would no doubt be thrilled by the magnificent new state-of-the-art factory that opened at Princes Risborough in 2002 with the most modern manufacturing technology, making domestic and contract furniture.

Right:
A Windsor range Butterfly dining chair, beech with walnut veneer, designed 1958

Below:
Gina reclining chair with solid ash
showwood frame, removable upholstery,
and gas strut mechanism, designed 2004

Biography:

Sir Gordon Russell (1892-1980)

An oak dining table, 1925

An English walnut armchair, c.1924

A bog oak, burr elm and laburnum cabinet, 1925

A mahogany and rosewood sideboard, c.1950

Opposite: *A chest commissioned by the Prime Minister Lloyd George in 1930, veneered in holly from a tree in his garden, on to Honduras mahogany with cedar of Lebanon drawer linings and rustless iron handles. Courtesy of the Gordon Russell Trust*

Although Russell was twenty years younger than Ambrose Heal, the two men shared a great deal in common in trying to tread a path between the Arts and Crafts traditions and Modernism without losing traditional values, but at the same time making their furniture accessible to as wide a public as possible. Besides an autobiography, *Designer's Trade*, published in 1968, a number of books have been published on Russell (much more than on Heal) but several intriguing questions remain about his life.

Unlike Heal, Russell was not born into a successful London manufacturing family. He, and his two younger brothers, Don (1894-1970) and Dick (1904-1983), grew up in the Cotswolds. Their parents, Sydney and Elizabeth, moved to Broadway in Worcestershire in 1904 to set up a country house hotel at the early 16th Century Lygon Arms, which would attract a wealthy English and American clientele. Russell left school aged 15 with no training, but in time took over the running of the restoration workshop and small antiques business that his father had set up in outbuildings. His father, whom he called the "Guvnor", was a stern man, but always supportive and perhaps passed on to him some of his calligraphic and drawing skills, his aesthetic judgement and his obsession with quality. At a time when the Cotswolds had become the centre for Arts and Crafts activity of all kinds, he was fascinated by manual skills and remained so throughout his life, showing particular talent in areas such as stonemasonry and lettering, although he seems never to have made a piece of furniture. The four years he spent with the Worcestershire Regiment during the First War may have influenced his respect for the "common man". His army record book called him "a great influence among men" and showed that his aspirations were already clear in that he gave his occupation as a designer of furniture.

Returning after the War, a farmhouse down the road was bought as a showroom and Russell set about expanding the business, being joined by Dick when he left school. In order to make furniture as well as restore antiques, the workshop needed new skills and craftsmen. To find new contacts and help for this, Russell joined the Design and Industries Association. One person of assistance was Percy Wells of Shoreditch Technical Institute in London, who sent him some cabinet-makers, including W.H. "Curly" Russell (no relative), who stayed with the firm, later as Chief Designer, until 1968. They also established their own metal workshop to ensure quality fittings.

Beginning with bedroom furniture in unpolished oak, Gordon Russell designed prolifically throughout the 20's. It was fortunate that at first there was some backing with income from the successful hotel, but, through publicising the firm by showing at a series of exhibitions, at Cheltenham (1922), the Victoria and Albert Museum, alongside Heal's (1923), the British Empire Exhibition at Wembley (1924) and the Paris International Exhibition (1925), its reputation soon spread to the international stage. At Paris they won two silver medals and a gold for a superbly-made cabinet, very much in Gimson taste.

The workforce grew from 30 in 1924 to 120 in 1928 and the following year the company's name was changed to Gordon Russell Ltd to mark the achievement. They also rented a shop in Wigmore Street in London, selling glass (which he designed) and textiles as well as furniture. The enormous energy required in engineering this expansion was helped by the "great source of support" of Elizabeth Denning (known as Toni). Russell married her in 1921 and they had four children. A house was built for them at Kingcombe near Chipping Camden in 1925, and this was to become increasingly a focus of his craft skills and interest in landscape gardening throughout his life. Although sometimes shy and reserved, at 6ft 3ins tall, he was powerful at manual labour.

In the mid-1920's other important developments were occurring. In 1923 Russell privately published a pamphlet entitled *Honesty and the Crafts – a Plea for a Broader Outlook*, in which he railed against reproductions and fakes of old pieces and made a manifesto for modern design. There followed the first signs of experimentation with modern geometric simplicity using flush veneered doors. *The Studio* magazine in 1927 called his designs "virile and convincing" and "modern in conception". By 1928 he was using stainless steel together with wood. At the same time machines began to appear in the workshop as the firm increased batch production to keep down costs and entered the contract market, providing furniture for schools and colleges.

He had no fear of machinery provided that it was controlled. He saw machine craft as merely an extension of handcraft, both requiring skill. This, it is said, was much to the consternation of the Art Workers' Guild which he had joined in 1926. It was this attitude that caused him to lose patience with the narrow-minded views of the Arts and Crafts Movement. Just before the First War, in the wake of Charles Ashbee, he and his father seem to have tried to set up an Arts and Crafts workshop in Chipping Campden, three and a half miles away, but the venture never succeeded. Whilst he always remained an Arts and Crafts man at heart and believed that the work of the past should never be ignored, he was also convinced that new problems had to be solved in new ways. To reinforce this, in 1929 the company's trademark was changed from a cottage and tree to a circular saw.

Opposite:
A typical Gordon Russell label from an elm "Stow" writing table, designed 1924. Courtesy of The Millinery Works Gallery

Left:
A print cabinet in bog oak, burr elm and laburnum "oysters", designed 1925. Courtesy of the Gordon Russell Trust

Another surprising change was that, having pretty well monopolised design at the firm since the First War, he suddenly stopped completely when he seemed to be at the height of his powers in 1930 and concentrated on managing the business instead. The main reason for this seems to have been his encouragement of his brother Dick. He had supported Dick's studies at the Architectural Association in order to introduce an architectural perspective to the firm's work and when Dick returned in 1929 he, and a number of his fellow graduates including his future wife, the carpet designer Marian Pepler, were committed to Modernism and machine production. Russell saw the danger that Modernism could be sterile and lose the human touch that he valued so much. His own interest in supervising the craftsmen who worked to his designs is illustrated by the idiosyncratic practice adopted from at least 1923, of affixing labels to pieces with details about them including the makers' names. However he was typically supportive of Dick as Chief Designer and took a close interest in his work without criticism.

As with many other firms, the early 30's brought them to the verge of bankruptcy, but the situation was saved by a timely relationship with the Irish radio engineer Frank Murphy, for whom they designed a series of modern radio cabinets. These set a fashion, merging them in rather than stressing them as individual items of furniture. Murphy's slogan was "making wireless simple" and it led to work for other radio manufacturers including Bush, Pye and Ekco. The need to concentrate on such mass-production at a lower price level and at the same time to function with engineering precision, led to a factory being built at Park Royal in West London which operated from 1935 to 1941 with a workforce of up to 800. At the same time a larger shop in Wigmore Street was opened in 1935 and became a symbol of English Modernism with a stock that was over 95% English made. Nikolaus Pevsner, later the noted architectural writer, was chief buyer here for four years, the choice being characteristic of Russell's desire to encourage young talent. In 1933 Gordon Russell became Managing Director of the firm, taking over from his father who died in 1938. In the latter year he established a "Good Furnishing Group" of like-minded retailers, but the initiative, like many others, was cut short by the War.

Above:
A "Stow" oak chest of drawers with grey bog-oak handles, circa 1920, Courtesy of the Gordon Russell Trust

Above:
An oak dining table with twin octagonal end supports, circa 1925, Courtesy of The Millinery Works Gallery and Jefferson Smith

For not entirely clear reasons, as the economic climate and timber supply worsened in 1940, Russell was forced by the banks to give up control of the company, and although he later became Chairman at the age of 78 after the death of his brother Don, he never again held an executive position there. This did however free him to carry on his crusade for modern design in the national and international arenas. In the same year he was elected a Royal Designer for Industry (Dick followed in 1944), and in 1942 invited to join the Utility Furniture Advisory Committee where he became Chairman of the Design Panel. He saw the State control embodied in Utility as a way to educate the public in good modern design. When the Council of Industrial Design was established in 1944 he was a founder member, and Director from 1947 until 1959. In this capacity he played leading roles in the "Britain Can Make it" exhibition (1946) and the Festival of Britain (1951). In his autobiography he looked back on the frustrations of dealing with bureaucracy and changes in government, for example when so many of the positive achievements of the Festival were not capitalised upon, likening his life to "trying to... push a tank uphill". Nevertheless he launched *Design* magazine in 1949 and opened the Design Centre at 28 Haymarket in 1956, which became a model for many other countries. Russell wanted the public to be the focus for new design, although later the direction of the Design Council, as it became, was changed to industry. He was knighted in 1955.

Below:
An English walnut side chair, designed 1924, Courtesy of the Gordon Russell Trust

Below Left:
An oak cabinet on chest of drawers with grey bog-oak handles, circa 1924, Courtesy of the Gordon Russell Trust

Opposite:

An English walnut cabinet inlaid with ebony, yew and boxwood, which won a gold medal at the 1925 Paris International Exhibition. Courtesy of the Gordon Russell Trust

Below:

A sideboard in mahogany with doors of Bombay rosewood veneered on to birch ply and cut through for the contrasting pattern, designed 1950 by David Booth for Gordon Russell Ltd, still adhering to Government Utility restrictions on materials but with the design restrictions relaxed. Courtesy of The Country Seat

He continued his public service energetically as a lecturer and writer, seeing education as a core need and concentrating on the Royal College of Art to train new industrial designers. He even travelled to India to help with the establishment of design schools. At home he set up a consultancy at Kingcombe in 1960 to offer advice to large industrial firms, which included the Bank of England and British Rail. Suddenly in 1977 he designed some pieces of furniture again for his own use, combining hand and machine techniques in traditional style. It was just as if he had never stopped nearly fifty years before. He died of motor neurone disease shortly after receiving an Honorary Doctorate from the RCA in 1980. This self-taught "peculiarly English genius", as Sir Terence Conran has called him, with his extraordinary determination to pursue his vision whatever the cost, will be remembered as an unrivalled international ambassador for British design.

The family firm flourished through the 50's but began to suffer in the 60's like many small independent businesses among larger competitors. In the early 70's it left the retail market for office contract and international work, finally breaking away from Russell's aim to make "decent furniture for ordinary people". But its reputation continues, even after its acquisition by Giroflex and then by Steelcase Strafor in 1989, and Gordon Russell Ltd has been reborn in Worcester since the Millenium. Both the Lygon Arms and Kingcombe are also back in private hands, while the Gordon Russell Trust, which preserves over sixty pieces of furniture, drawings and other archive material, is shortly to open a Centre at Broadway.

Polypropylene chairs, single chair (1963), armchair (1967) on a variety of bases. The original colours were charcoal and flame red.

Biography:

Robin Day
(b. 1915)

Director's desk in rosewood, leather and stainless steel, designed for Hille 1962

Royal Festival Hall occasional table in mahogany and steel rod, designed 1951

Royal Festival Hall lounge chair in moulded plywood and steel rod, designed 1951

Axis seating in die-cast aluminium, designed 1966

Lucian R. Ercolani wrote in his autobiography that "a designer worth his salt is really a very humble man." This description seems singularly appropriate of Robin Day who, for some 70 years has played an unassuming, but important role in innovative design for furniture and in several other fields, including developing what is probably the world's best-selling chair.

He was born in High Wycombe and, although his family had no connection with the local industry, it had its influence on him. He showed a natural gift for drawing and won a scholarship to High Wycombe School of Art (later Buckinghamshire Chilterns University College), where the emphasis was on technical drawing and practical cabinet-making. Soon after being offered a design job by Lucian Ercolani, he moved to London to take up a Royal Exhibition Scholarship at the Royal College of Art, intending to become a freelance designer. He found the RCA sadly hidebound by art and craft, but amongst the furniture he designed for his Diploma Show in 1937 was a Macassar ebony sideboard with burr ash doors which was chosen for exhibition at Burlington House (the Royal Academy) the following year.

His fourth year scholarship was marred by the outbreak of War and he turned to designing and teaching. In 1940 he met Lucienne Conradi and from the start they were kindred spirits, both committed to establishing a new clean-lined, uncompromisingly modern style. They married in 1942 and, although they generally practised separately, she mainly in textiles and ceramics, their work was often complementary and they have consistently been a great support for each other.

After the War, Day taught three-dimensional and furniture design at the School of Architecture at the Regent Street Polytechnic (later the University of Westminster). His talent in graphics brought a number of commissions for poster designs for the Central Office of Information, as well as exhibition stands for firms such as ICI and Ekco. Aided by Ambrose Heal, he collaborated with Clive Latimer on an entry for an international competition for low-cost adaptable furniture for small homes, run by the Museum of Modern Art in New York in 1948, in which they won the storage section for a range of bent plywood units suspended on tubular aluminium frames. This gained high-profile recognition and brought other important commissions, and crucially, an invitation in 1949 from Ray Hille

Right:
*Hillestak chairs, moulded plywood
seats and beech frames, the first
low-cost chair designed for Hille,
1950 (modified 1956)*

to join the manufacturers S. Hille & Co., where, with her daughter Rosamind and son-in-law Leslie Julius, she was committed to modern design and modern materials. Day had a huge influence over the firm until the 1970's, but chose to remain Design Consultant, so that he might take on projects elsewhere.

He saw that, as wartime restrictions gradually diminished, they could benefit from the growing feeling of optimism towards a bright new world and the surge of modern design that followed it. He considered that progressive design contributed to the quality of people's lives. His early designs for Hille proved rather too novel for the British trade, but American buyers were enthusiastic where new trends were already taking place. His Hillestak chair (1950) with a moulded plywood seat and back which Charles Eames and Alvar Aalto had pioneered in the US, was a great commercial success, domestically and publicly over two decades. He added dining furniture, a desk and storage units to make a flexible group which broke away from the notion of the traditional suite.

1951 was an important year for Day, when his friendship with the London County Council architect Peter Moro led to the challenge of designing the seating for the concert hall, orchestra, restaurant and public areas of the Royal Festival Hall, the first modern public building in London since the War. For the folding auditorium seats he used glass fibre padding, steel tubing and pressed steel – techniques from the motor industry – and elsewhere moulded plywood, the lounge and restaurant chairs with stylish flat arms integral with the backs.

This model was subsequently made for production by Hille. The complex curvature was made possible by urea formaldehyde adhesive that had been developed for Mosquito aircraft during the War. He was also very active in working for the Festival of Britain, for which he designed three interiors for the Homes and Gardens Pavilion, including a glass-shelved room divider held in place with brass rods and tension cables. In the same year he and Lucienne were invited, after the UK itself had officially declined, to put on a display at the Milan Triennale, the first of many exhibitions in which they were involved. They both won gold medals and their international reputations were much enhanced.

As well as the domestic market, Day focussed Hille's production on furnishing contracts for the post-War construction of offices, airports, universities and other commercial buildings. These included the new London Airport Terminal (1953) and Gatwick Terminal (1958). Several ranges of office furniture were produced at different price levels, usually on variously finished square tubular steel legs, desks with linoleum tops, and the best pieces with fine rosewood veneers, leather and black vitrolite glass doors. He liked to incorporate a mixture of metal for strength and lightness, rubber for comfort and efficiency and wood for touch and appearance. Styles were generally simple and rectangular to complement the architecture of the period.

He also pioneered the introduction of standardised unit furniture into Britain, which George Nelson was developing in the US, first for storage and later seating, beginning with the Hilleplan range in 1952. With the Form Group of modular seating (1960), intended for the home, he broke away from traditional upholstery in favour of easily replaceable rubber webbing with metal clips. With its mix-and-match covers and optional backs and flat surfaces, it was a great success and won a Design Centre Award in 1961.

Versatility in form and variety in finish were always a key to wide appeal and commercial success and both Days were committed to making their work affordable to as many people as possible. One feature of his design has been an expression of structure and materials, exposing metal framing and comb joints in timber, thereby harking back to the honesty of structure practised by the Arts & Crafts manufacturers. Also, believing space to be the ultimate luxury, his cabinets and easy seating were raised from the floor, allowing visually free-flowing space in the room.

Other Design Centre awards included a convertible bed-settee and a television set for Pye, both among the first awarded in 1957. The latter led the way in emphasising the functionality of an electronic instrument and a number of other such designs followed. In 1959 he was appointed a Royal Designer for Industry and was joined in this three years later by Lucienne – the only married couple to share the honour.

Always keen to experiment with new materials and techniques, the chance came to do so with the thermoplastic polypropylene which had been invented by the Italian Guilio Natta in 1954. Day realised that

Left:
Axis seating, a die-cast aluminium frame of knock-down construction with table-top assembly bolted between, designed 1966

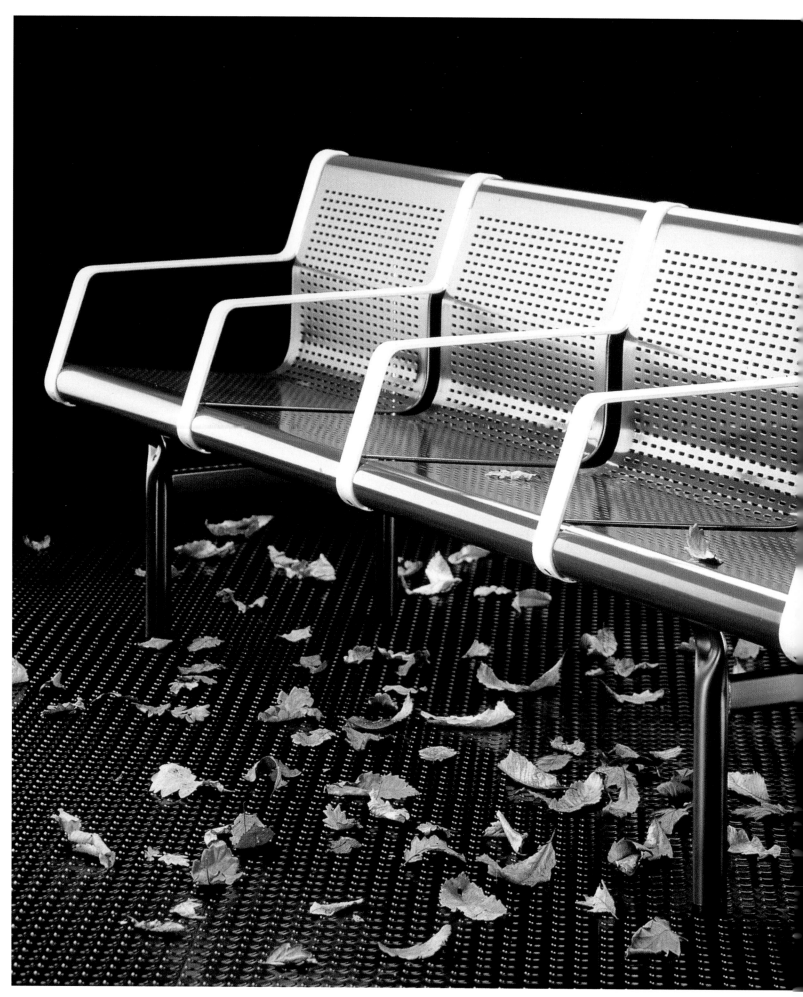

this light-weight, strong, comfortable, scratch-proof, heat-resistant and very durable material would lend itself to injection moulding, a quick and cheap process once expensive high-grade steel moulds had been made. The polypropylene stacking chair was born in 1963 and is still in production over forty years later with tens of millions made worldwide. A host of variations have evolved over the years, including Series E, multi-sized school chairs with rectangular lifting holes in the backs, and Polo with its series of graduated holes making it suitable for indoor and outdoor use.

From the mid-60's Hille concentrated more on the contract market with seating continuing to dominate Day's work. The Axis chair (1966) with its knock-down star-shaped frame was his first design in die-cast aluminium, a material which was also being used by Eames. The seats could be used singly or in linked groups. As the firm grew internationally during the 70's, new designers such as Fred Scott were employed and Day had less overall control, until after the exhibition held at the Victoria & Albert Museum in 1981, "Hille – 75 years of British Furniture", the Hille family sold their controlling interest to Ergonom in 1983. Day's own work was increasingly focussed on auditorium and stadium seating and contract models such as his all-metal Toro seating (1990), with its distinctive curl-over on the beam supports at the top and the bottom.

There were a few occasions when both Days were invited to work together, such as during the 60's and early 70's designing aircraft interiors for British Overseas Airways Company (BOAC), and the new Churchill College, Cambridge (c.1964), when the oiled teak dining furniture was made by Heal's, and for the John Lewis Partnership, where they were design consultants from 1962 until 1987, giving the growing firm, including Waitrose, a corporate identity and working for other specific projects. In 1969 Day was also appointed Seating Design Consultant for the huge concrete complex of the Barbican Arts Centre, a project which ran over twelve years. As previously, some of the designs became product ranges for Hille.

Among the numerous awards he has received have been an OBE for services to design and export in 1983 (Lucienne had to wait until 2004 for hers), a Senior Fellowship at the Royal College of Art (1991) and an Honorary Fellowship of the Royal Institute of British Architects (1997). The end of the 20th Century saw a revival of interest in the post-War period and in the Days' work, marked by the landmark exhibition at the Barbican Art Gallery "Robin & Lucienne Day – Pioneers of Contemporary Design", curated by Lesley Jackson in 2001. Since then he has worked with Habitat and now, at 90, is designing for the Italian manufacturer Magis. As he predicted in 1968, "I tend to think I will keep working for ever", and the astonishingly productive career of Britain's most distinguished post-War designer looks set to run a while yet.

Left:
Toro seating, beam-mounted, hard-wearing all-metal, including pressed sheet steel, designed 1990 and widely used throughout the London Underground System.

Alan Peters
(b. 1933)

*Library steps in walnut,
aluminium and carpet, 1972*

*A pyramid revolving bookcase
in ebony and sycamore, 1990*

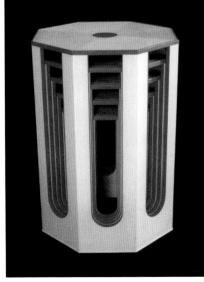

*A nest of five octagonal tables in ash
with red dyed veneer edging, 1988*

*A "mushroom" table in walnut
and sycamore, 1992*

Opposite: *One of a pair of fan-shaped side tables in Indian rosewood and Indian satinwood, made in 1989 for Lloyds TSB
Group plc and presented to the Fitzwilliam Museum, Cambridge, in honour of Sir Nicholas Goodison in 2000
Courtesy of the Fitzwilliam Museum*

"My furniture is rooted in the British Arts and Crafts Movement and I still share and am inspired by many of its ideals. I aim for a delicate balance between truth to materials, honest construction and the needs of today."

Described thus in his own words, Alan Peters has shown himself to have achieved these objectives as one of the most consistently successful furniture makers working today.

He was born in Petersfield, Hampshire, only three miles from the Barnsley Workshops. Both his father and grandfather had been precision engineers and toolmakers and he was hooked on wood at an early age. At fourteen he was supplying local shops with toys and aeroplanes that he had made. At sixteen, just after the War, he began a formal five-year apprenticeship with Edward Barnsley who then employed about ten craftsmen, but with no electricity or powered tools. These came in the mid-50's, although designs did become a little more delicate and refined after the War. Here Peters learnt his idealism and his sensitivity for wood.

In 1957 he entered Shoreditch Training College in London for a two-year teacher training course, followed by a scholarship to the Central School of Arts & Crafts to study interior design. Teaching has always remained a valued experience for him, for example at Portsmouth College of Art and Design in the 1960's, Parnham College in the 70's and 80's, Letterfrack College, Galway in the 90's, and on many foreign

Above:

A serving table in wenge and yew, designed in 1985 for Practical Woodworking Magazine and Evo-stik Ltd and now in the Cheltenham Museum & Art Gallery

tours, particularly to Summer Schools at the Centre for Furniture Craftsmanship in Maine. However he really wanted his own workshop, which he finally set up in 1962 with an order book of six months' work but no capital.

He soon moved to Grayshott on the Surrey/Hampshire border and married his ever-supportive wife Laura. At the time a majority of what furniture makers there were, made a living from producing reproductions of antiques or doing restoration work. He made a decision to do neither and instead eked out furniture commissions with high quality joinery work and designed for an industrial firm, offering better work and greater attention to detail than his competitors. He also produced batch ranges such as cheeseboards, bookends, lamps, low tables and stools, when he could sell them. His furniture was attracting attention however and by 1970 he had become fairly self-sufficient in following the ideals and principles that he holds so dear.

After ten years at Grayshott the family moved to a larger and idyllic 16th Century farmhouse at Kentisbeare in Devon, remote but with good rail and road connections. Here he was able to operate a separate machine shop to keep his workshop quieter and cleaner. Just as Barnsley, Heal and Russell eventually succumbed to the need for machinery to make work commercial, so Peters accepted it, provided a balance was maintained between the over-use of machines that could

starve creative work, and the temptation to spend too long on handwork that could lead to too much technical perfection and loss of spontaneity. Knowing where to stop is an important discipline.

In the early 70's developments in industry clearly had their influence on his use of aluminium frames for tables etc., preferring its softness to stainless steel or chrome. He also experimented with inlaying metals into wood. Indeed it was to research this further that he gained a bursary from the Craft Advisory Committee (later the Crafts Council) to travel to Japan in 1975. While he was there, however, he found that it was the architecture, traditions, the use of woods and joinery techniques that most interested him. This trip, and the Winston Churchill Travelling Fellowship that was awarded in 1980 to visit South Korea, Taiwan and Hong Kong, had a profound influence on his designs and techniques. Since his return he has used little decoration on his furniture and relied very largely on solid timber.

These visits also very much reinforced his feelings about the logical, honest and straightforward use of materials, construction and techniques. In this he sees himself as differing from John Makepeace and the more "art-conscious" makers. His penchant for bowl-tables was a result of Korea, while his three-plank stools with concave seats began directly after his return from Japan. His later travels had direct influences too: he credits the inspiration of a visit to Morocco for his pierced octagonal tables, while Rumania (1993) was the source of a

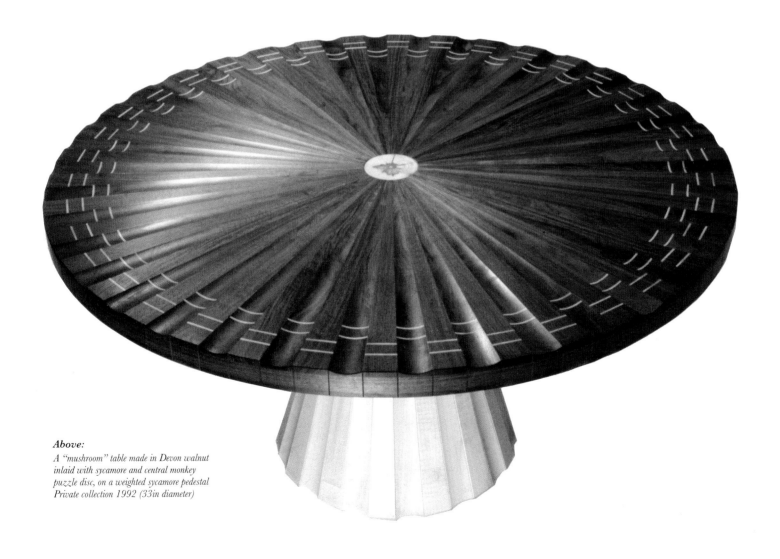

Above:
A "mushroom" table made in Devon walnut
inlaid with sycamore and central monkey
puzzle disc, on a weighted sycamore pedestal
Private collection 1992 (33in diameter)

wooden-hinged clothes chest that was part of the One Tree project, in which 74 craftsmen and women made furniture and objects from every scrap of a single oak tree (2001-2). In 1984 a lecture tour to New Zealand, Hawaii, Australia and Tasmania influenced him in the use of decorative fluted surfaces.

Apart from whole pieces, certain key themes recur which help to give Peters' work a personal stamp: for example the contrast between textured surfaces made by hand tools and the smoothness of machine planing; Italian veneer sandwiches in bright red and green; dovetails and plugs of contrasting timber; decorative laminations and end-grain blocks, fan shapes and the repeated arch and inverted arch motif.

Where possible Peters uses locally felled timber, much from the Duchy of Cornwall estates, which he seasons himself for five years or more. Experience has led him to allow for the movement of wood in modern heating, in constructional design and by favouring PVA glue for its slight elasticity. Sometimes he uses more decorative imported woods, generally in veneer with generous solid facings to protect them.

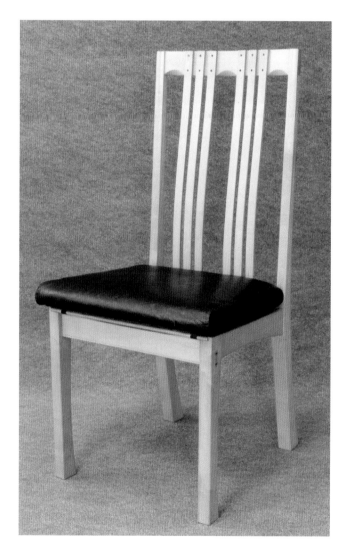

Above:

A dining chair in sycamore with leathered seat, originally a one off commission for the Crafts Council's collection in 1978 and subsequently a standard design

Left:

A pyramid revolving bookcase in Indian ebony and rippled sycamore, designed 1990

On occasion particularly good Rio rosewood might be recycled or drawer-linings made of very stable old mahogany with cedar of Lebanon bottoms. As for finishing, he has long sought a surface which resists marking and improves rather than deteriorates with age. He prefers natural finishes such as oil, but tough colourless lacquer, nowadays always water-based, is used on veneers and light woods to retard darkening.

As time has passed he has seen more clearly the distinction between the Design Council and the Crafts Council, between industrial design using the latest technology and man-made materials, and the situation of the designer-craftsman making bespoke furniture for a discerning public who wants quality and individuality. There is also a danger of design becoming an academic subject divorced from the workbench, while the designer-craftsman exercises complete control from start to finish and can respond to design ideas that might arise during the course of manufacture.

Something like 90% of Peters' work has come through direct commissions, even for successive generations of the same family. There are pieces in numerous public and private collections, sometimes, as in the case of museum public seating at Bristol and Glasgow, the result of limited competitions. Not all his commissions have stood the test of time, however. For example the furnishings of the Swiss Catholic Mission Chapel at Westminster (1977) were subsequently dismantled, but saved from destruction at the eleventh hour. There is a similar story with some of the work for his most prolific client, Sir Nicholas Goodison. Since their first meeting in 1983, Peters has not only made a good deal of furniture and fittings for Sir Nicholas's home, but also during his successive chairmanships of the Stock Exchange and the Trustee Savings Bank in London. The refitting of the chairman's Office and Boardroom at the former (1986-8) was largely repeated at the latter (1988-9), using mainly walnut rather than rosewood and ebony as previously, but adding a splendid 21-foot oval boardroom table on three pedestals in 1993-4. Because of its "user-friendly" shape, this apparently improved the quality of meetings. Much of these ensembles were later split up, with some pieces, such as the pair of fan tables, going to the Fitzwilliam Museum, Cambridge.

Peters believes firmly in the apprenticeship system. He has always been keen to offer workshop training opportunities and to share his

Above:
A curved writing table in Devon walnut and satin aluminium with leathered top, made for the British Embassy in Pretoria, South Africa 1972

Right:
A side table in Macassar ebony and ripple sycamore, exhibited at the Queen's Silver Jubilee Exhibition 1977

Below:
A storage cabinet in solid Devon walnut with handles of bog oak from the Somerset levels, Private commission 1994

experience, and among his craftsmen, who have numbered up to eight at various times, have been Jane Cleal, and Michael Fortune from Toronto. To the same end, in 1984, he published his book *Cabinetmaking, the Professional Approach* (Stobart & Sons Ltd) which sets out in a very practical way, advice on the problems of becoming a professional furniture maker and designer. He also revised Ernest Joyce's manual *The Technique of Furniture Making* (Batsford) in 1987.

He has been indefatigable in showing work at exhibitions, but perhaps the most memorable was held to mark his first thirty years, "Thirty Pieces for Thirty Years", at Bedales School near Petersfield in 1992. He has also received many awards, including an OBE in 1990 for services to furniture design, and in 2002, along with John Makepeace, he was given a prestigious Award of Distinction by the American Furniture Society. The dedication of his 1984 book was to Bert Upton, the retired foreman at Barnsley's, "still actively making because he cannot stop". The same conceit might be used of Peters: having moved to smaller premises at Minehead in 2002 and set up a fine new workshop, this revered elder statesman with his quiet integrity still has, in spite of illness, ambitious plans for the future.

Above:
A fluted bowl table in laminated Devon ash, 1983, showing the contrast between the gouged fruit bowl and smooth top surface.

Above:
A dining table in solid Indian Sisso rosewood and sycamore, the top with delicate reed moulding. Private commission 1989

The Mitre Chair (1977), the frame a tour-de-force in ebony, laminated and kerfed to overcome the unyielding nature of the wood, the seat and back woven with nickel silver wire in a traditional cane pattern

Biography:

John Makepeace
(b. 1939)

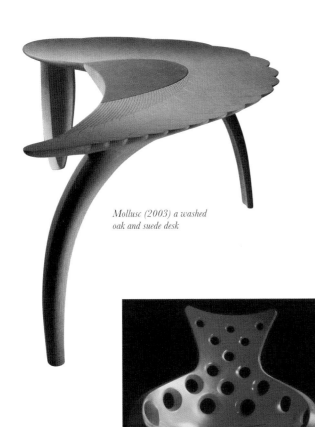

Mollusc (2003) a washed
oak and suede desk

Millenium (1989), armchair
in laminated holly

"Throne" (1991) chair in carved
lime and burnished lacquer

"Knot" (1997) armchair
in burr elm and oak

John Makepeace is perhaps the most influential British designer-maker of the last quarter of the 20th Century. His broad vision has brought a new relevance to craft in the age of technology and has influenced an entire generation of furniture makers both in Britain and internationally by, as he puts it, "extending the boundaries of function, structure and expression beyond those ordinarily associated with furniture."

His career has embraced a variety of different facets. Forsaking his family background in industry, and the advice of Edward Barnsley that there was no future in craft furniture making, his fascination for wood led him to apprenticeship with Keith Cooper, a designer-maker in Dorset, where he learned basic technical skills. In 1959-61 he went to teach craft and design in Birmingham and also set up his own workshop making pieces to order. At an unusually early age he was accepted for membership of the Craft Centre in London and the Red Rose Guild in Manchester. He went on to establish workshops on country estates, first at Hodnell Manor and then at Farnborough Barn, near Banbury, employing up to six people. Here his work developed towards the softer, rounded organic shapes for which he is best known and with which only handcraft can cope, rather than the more hard-edged rectilinear ones of the industrialised Modern Movement.

He made a series of volume retail accessories in the mid-1960's, the Ionic Range, and glass-topped tables that were sold in flat-pack form by Heal's, but the fate of an industrial-looking range of simple melamine-topped tables and chairs showed that he could not sell furniture that was more expensive to produce than its appearance suggested. For a while he worked on special commissions for private clients side by side with batch production of retail lines, exploiting machine techniques in order to remain competitive on price. However, when he reached the point where the latter required a considerable injection of investment to achieve greater commercial volume, he made the decision to concentrate on quality rather than growth. In 1968 he took the astute step of appointing a business school graduate to manage his workshop in order to bring commercial experience to bear on his labour-intensive craft production. He also began contract work on complete interiors, cooperating with leading architects, although he found that furnishings in such projects tended to suffer when budgets and deadlines were tight.

In the early 1970's Makepeace saw his profile enhanced by a string of museum commissions, for Birmingham City Art Gallery (a folding screen), Cardiff City Museum (a chest of drawers), The Fitzwilliam, Cambridge (a cabinet for contemporary sculpture), Leeds City Art Gallery (a display cabinet) and The Victoria and Albert Museum (a pivoting birch ply cabinet on stainless steel column). In 1972 he became a founder member of the Crafts Council, set up by the Government to promote higher standards for designer-craftsmen in Britain, at a time when much of the manufacturing industry was derivative and repetitive. Some of his experiments in materials, structure and form became ambitious ones, including the 1975 commission from Liberty & Co for a 10 feet diameter table to commemorate their centenary. But his single-minded determination led him to relish each successive challenge of devising innovative forms and new uses of materials.

Two of the major challenges of Makepeace's life have been the move to Parnham near Beaminster in Dorset in 1976 and the launch of the School for Craftsmen in Wood there the following year (its name was changed to Parnham College in 1991). The acquisition of this magnificent 16th Century Grade I house with a professional design studio and workshop side by side with, but separate from, a financially independent college, forming a self-supporting creative community, showed great vision and courage. The house and gardens, which were opened to the public and received up to 18,000 visitors a year, were a perfect way to show how successfully fine contemporary furniture can look in grand traditional surroundings and this helped to broaden the audience as he attracted an international reputation.

The College, which took eleven students a year for a two-year course under the guidance of the Principal, Robert Ingham, was without doubt the best of its kind in the country during its 23 years of existence. It created a distinctive design movement and spawned numerous well-known names, including David Linley, Nicholas Pryke, Rupert Senior and Rod Wales. Makepeace tried to instil into the course the three essentials that he saw from his own career: creative design, technical skills and business management. Commercial realism, essential for self-sufficiency, has tended to be lacking on courses elsewhere.

By managing to run his own workshop with up to ten assistants, many of whom he took on straight from school, he has since the mid-1970's spent less time at the work bench himself, enabling him to have more time for travel and consultancy and developing his design theories. He believes, for example, in three broad divisions in furniture design: that tables effectively raise the floor to place on

objects for celebration (food, drink, books etc.), cabinets are for storing objects of value which need protection, and chairs reflect the needs of the human body. These distinct functions require quite different structural solutions.

In an average year some two-thirds of production would be made to commission and of this perhaps two-thirds again would be for private individuals rather than companies or museums. Each project would be entrusted to one person who would grow in stature from that responsibility and achievement. He sees his own rôle as similar to that of the composer and conductor of a piece of music, regularly reviewing progress during manufacture. He has always had a fascination for precision engineering and "high tech" and has worked in collaboration with engineers and craftsmen in media other than wood. This multi-disciplinary understanding has allowed him to develop the use of machines as a stimulus to creativity, rather than a restraint to hand skills; his work remains undoubtedly craft-based. He was awarded an OBE in 1988 for his services to furniture design.

Increasingly he has shown concern for the environment. In the 1990's he brought the natural world more than ever into his work with large scale motifs such as boulders, vines, sheep's fleeces, shells and feathers. Although in his early work he often made use of tropical hardwoods, British ones are now the focus – holly, sycamore, cherry,

Above:
Trine (1998), a chair laminated
in yew and bog oak

Above:
Petal II (1992), a pair of armchairs in
laminated and carved ripple sycamore

yew, ash and oak – where sufficient unusual figuring or surface effects by carving, liming or scorching can be achieved to create dramatic results. Generally these timbers are not available in large enough quantities to interest major manufacturers. Indeed it is a fact that in the 1990's Britain imported some 90% of its timber and timber products requirements.

The other major environmental initiative that Makepeace has undertaken, was the foundation of Hooke Park College – 330 acres of mixed forest four miles from Parnham, purchased by the Parnham Trust in 1983. Here he set about creating a second school, unlike the first not concerned with the luxury of high-value furniture, but based on research into the sustainable use of discarded forest thinnings (up to 8 inches in diameter). Here the links between construction techniques of furniture and architecture could be investigated further. Indeed, the results of an international research programme led by the Trust were demonstrated by a series of innovative buildings each using materials harvested from Hooke Park. Many of the technologies have been adopted for other environmental projects and furniture making in the UK and as far afield as Japan, where the forest industry shares

similar problems. A good deal was accomplished including the initial courses which have led to the setting up of businesses such as Trannon, Gaze Burville, Simon Pirie and i tre.

Now that the Trust had its own purpose-built campus with ideal facilities, it was decided to combine both programmes at Hooke Park. At that stage Makepeace was pleased to hand over to the new director, although it was subsequently decided to cease the Trust's operations and to pass Hooke Park to the Architectural Association as a base for its practical modules. This chapter in Makepeace's life closed with the sale of the big house in 2001. He and his wife Jennie have since set up a new studio in Beaminster, ready to tackle new challenges.

Undoubtedly Makepeace has been at the forefront of the craft revival that has been gathering momentum in Britain since the 1970's, led in a parallel manner by Wendell Castle in the US. By deliberately moving away from industrialisation and by challenging convention, he has moved craft to a new relevance in the age of technology and shown that, with a fusion of technical and artistic imagination, furniture can be raised to a level with the finest of fine art and sculpture, without losing sight of function and fitness for purpose.

Right:
An East Indian satinwood and green lacquer Collector's Cabinet (1982), with velvet-lined drawers and ivory knobs, based on oriental precedents

Far Right:
Eighteen (1996), a cabinet of eighteen drawers in burr elm and cherry

Right:
Desert Sand (2000), a chest of ten drawers in sculpted ripple ash, the drawers lined in chestnut and cedar

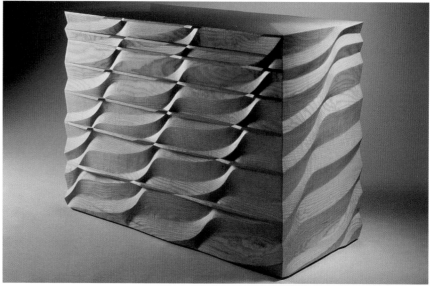

Above:
*Ginkgo (1979) one of a batch of low
tables in kingwood and bird's eye maple,
based on the leaf of the Chinese ginkgo tree*

Further Reading

The Thames & Hudson Dictionary of 20th Century
Design and Designers - G. Julier (1993)

Twentieth-Century Furniture Design
- Sembach, Leuthäuser & Gössel (Taschen)

Twentieth-Century Furniture: Materials,
Manufacture and Markets - Clive D. Edwards
(Manchester University Press 1994)

Furniture for the 21st Century
- ed. Betty Norbury (Viking Studio 2000)

A History of Heals - Susanna Gooden
(Lund Humphries 1984)

Eileen Gray, Architect/Designer
- Peter Adam (Abrams 2000)

A Furniture Maker - Lucian R. Ercolani
(Ernest Benn 1975)

Designer's Trade, An Autobiography
- Gordon Russell (George Allen & Unwin 1968)

Robin & Lucienne Day, Pioneers of Contemporary
Design - Lesley Jackson (Mitchell Beazley 2001)

Cabinetmaking, The Professional Approach
- Alan Peters (Stobart 1984)

Makepeace, A Spirit of Adventure in Craft & Design
- Jeremy Myerson (Conran Octopus 1995)

Index

Exhibitions